A Directory of Goods, Services & More

THE NEW JEWISH YELLOW PAGES

A Directory of Goods, Services & More

THE NEW JEWISH YELLOW PAGES

by Mae Shafter Rockland

SBS PUBLISHING INC. / New York

SBS Publishing Inc.
14 West Forest Avenue
Englewood, N.J. 07631

ISBN 0-89961-016-1

Library of Congress Catalog no.: 80-52177

Typographic design by Stanley S. Drate

Cover design by Hermann Strohbach

PHOTO CREDITS:
Cover—Puppets, Rivka Weil; Havdalah set by Joan Mesznik, photo Kenneth Bernstein; Seltzer bottles, *Gimme Seltzer*; Roberta Kaplan, photo Otto M. Berk; Purim Megillah, Daniel Blumberg, Lion applique, Mae Rockland; Necklace, Daniel Blumberg; Rooster hallah, photo Kenneth Bernstein.

Title page, Mae Rockland; p.1, Joan Benjamin-Farren; p.95, Richard Speedy; p.159, Richard Sobol; p.187, Fabrangen Fiddlers; p.227, Dr. Victor Youcha.

Printed in Israel by Peli Printing Works Ltd.

9 8 7 6 5 4 3 2 1

In memory of my parents,
Bella and Joe Shafter,
who loved every spark
of the multi-faceted Yiddishe soul
and taught me to value
every honest expression

CONTENTS

PLAYING *187*

OBSERVING *227*

ACKNOWLEDGMENTS

This book began as a simple revision of *The Jewish Yellow Pages* which was published in 1976. My intention was just to update the addresses and add a few new people. But as the new material began to pour in it soon became apparent that there was more than enough to make a completely new book. I am very grateful to my publisher, Nissan Balaban, who was as enthusiastic as I about documenting the flowering cultural life of Jewish-America, and to Seymour Barofsky who brought us together. I very much appreciate David Olivestone's editorial skills which have saved the reader from pain and me from embarassment.

Without the cooperation of hundreds of people across the country who filled out questionaires, wrote letters, sent pictures, slides, and samples, this book could never have happened. *THANK YOU EVERYONE, EVERYWHERE!*

And then there were those who helped in many special capacities, so special thanks to: Rabbi Albert Axelrad, Idi Benjamin, Hillary Danziger, Michael Ehrenthal, Julie Frank, Sarah Furoh, Rabbi Everett Gendler, Rabbi Aryeh Kaplan, Billy Mencow, Renee Miller, Bernie Pucker, Joe Riley, Brenda Tracy, Rabbi Frank Waldorf.

And for those three special souls who live with me: Tevya the cat, who showed remarkable restraint by not using the piles of accumulated information and samples as *his* litter—my daughter, Keren, who is patient and astute beyond her years—and my husband, Myron Tupa, whose impeccable taste, human insights, and general good will were more helpful than even he knows—to them a great big kiss and a home cooked meal.

PREFACE

"Were it not for the crazies the world would not subsist"

Maimonides

A friend of mine and the young woman he lives with—who were both brought up in religious Jewish homes—have put aside all of the ritual celebrations and observances, and yet they are slowly, consciously, and aesthetically building a Jewish nest in which to live. At the beginning they did nothing special for the Sabbath and it drifted by like any other day. Then they found that by Wednesday they were concerned as to whether they had Shabbat wine in the house, Thursday they were checking the candle supply, and Friday morning's visit to the bakery for a golden braided hallah was a spiritual journey. They are not quite to the point of making blessings over the wine, candles, and bread, but they are planning a wedding under a handmade wedding canopy. Some of my readers will be appalled by this story and others intrigued. For me these friends embody the quest of American Jews to define and "own" their Jewishness.

There are many prophets of doom via assimilation and intermarriage. They count in numbers that which must be reckoned by a more mystical system of measurement. I feel that we have turned the corner on assimilation. As Jerzy Kozinski's character Chauncey Gardner might say, "The fragile plant of European Judaism, transplanted in America's rich soil, has suffered some transplant-shock and lost some leaves, but the roots have begun to adapt themselves to their new environment and nutrients, and new blossoms and leaves are forming". New and exciting growth is taking place and while some of it may not "look Jewish" by some standards, the efforts are sincere, authentic, and very often beautiful. *The New Jewish Yellow Pages* is a celebration of what in my eyes is the best and most interesting of what is available in the Jewish-American cultural smorgasbord as we enter the demanding 1980's.

We have all had the fantasy of having a party and introducing our favorite people one to another; to stand by and watch wonderful interactions take place. There are talented and creative people all over the country working in one area of Jewish culture or another. They often feel isolated; even those living in the midst of large urban concentrations of coreligionists have expressed this. I want this book to introduce people to people. I want potters, metalsmiths, filmmakers, calligraphers, musicians, and actors, who are just beginning to grapple with

Jewish thematic material, to learn from those in our community who are steeped in learning and tradition, and I hope our scholars and sages will be inspired by the work in pursuit of holiness and truth by our artists. I would like teachers to look beyond the *Learning* chapter of this book and see, for example, what Danny Siegel is doing and integrate some of his philosophies of charity into the classroom. When my son Jeffrey, a ballet dancer, writes that he wishes there were a "Latkah Suite" to dance in as well as a "Nutcracker Suite", I hope composers and choreographers are listening.

I have had an addiction to Jewish culture since my Yiddish-speaking childhood. When my own children were born I worried about how to transmit the intensity of my feelings about the beauty and specialness of Jewish life to them. The vehicle became the Sabbath and holidays and filling our home with Jewish books, music, and artifacts, many of which I made or commissioned. As my own work in graphics and textiles became more involved with Jewish themes, friends and acquaintances increasingly asked me where to buy holiday items and antiques, what Jewish camp to send their children to, and where to find a calligrapher to write a wedding contract. The fact that I love to give advice and to play *shadchan* (matchmaker) resulted in the publication of *The Jewish Yellow Pages* in 1976. Since then I have been inundated with enthusiastic letters from people all over the country who either wanted to be in a future issue—or who knew someone who *must* be included—or who were so inspired by the book that they have turned their creative, professional, or business efforts towards making or merchandising Judaica. Then came the letters from people in the first book who were moving or changing their style or product. It soon became obvious that what was needed was *The New Jewish Yellow Pages,* and after a very intense year of researching and writing, here it is.

Some people think "The Jewish Yellow Pages" is an institution. Let me tell you, it's only me. With very occasional part-time secretarial and filing help, I have been alone with this project. When I was afraid that I was going to be swallowed by a mound of resumes, slides, and brochures, when I thought that I couldn't stand another trip to the post office or another interview, the phone would ring and a southern drawl or midwestern twang would tell me how wonderful it was to be in touch with Jewish life "back East"—they must have noticed my Bronx accent—or a letter would come like this one from a Lubavitch scribe in Brooklyn saying:

> Please accept my best wishes and Blessings that G-D should grant you utmost success in being a vehicle to bring only *good* and "nutrient packed" *wholesome kosher* articles to our People Israel and *you* will have a share in all the mitzvos which are done through your sincere efforts in The New Jewish Yellow Pages. I will sign with the Axiom of our Great Rabbis: "G-D does not place an obstacle in one's path *(or a challenge)* greater than she/he can master."

And so, moved and inspired, I would return to the task of compiling and evaluating the mounds of accumulated material, looking for that which is indeed "nutrient packed".

I have tried to be representative of Jewish cultural life all over the country and to provide something for everyone. While it cannot be denied that the greatest amount of Jewish cultural activity takes place where the greatest number of Jews live, it is a mistake to assume that all there is of any interest exists only on the East Coast or in big cities like Chicago and Los Angeles. Judaism has a centuries-old record of portability and adaptability and in the smaller or more outlying communities the intensity of expression is often greater than in areas with a large Jewish population. It is my hope that this book will serve both those of us who live far from the large concentrations of Yiddishkeit and also those of us living where Jewishness is taken for granted. Because our experiences as Jews vary in this vast country and Jewish-American geographic regionalism does exist, there is much that we can learn from one another. For the most part I have tried to treat the people and organizations in these pages objectively, but I must admit that I cannot totally resist promoting my own favorites from time to time. I have focused on the personalities of certain people as much as on their products in order to show the reader a cross-section of the variety of Jewish-American lifestyles and many of the photographs were also chosen with this in mind. The beauty and strength of Judaism lies as much in its diversity and flexibility as in its adherence to a continuous tradition.

"God's gift to us is a world that is new every morning, and we should believe that we are reborn each day."

The Baal Shem Tov

Note: The ▲ symbol appearing throughout the book indicates that the individual or group is available for lectures or programs.

CREATING

"Artisans maintain the fabric of the world, and in the handiwork of their craft is their prayer."

Ben Sira 38:34

There have been artists and craftspeople in my family for generations. In the *shtetlach* of Eastern Europe they were potters, (cousins who lived on the clay banks of the river making Seder and other holiday platters along with everyday dishes), signpainters (Uncle Avraham who also painted portraits and embellished the interior of many Polish wooden synagogues with fantastic floral and animal forms and gilded Hebrew letters), carpenters (my great-grandfather and great-uncles who built synagogues and churches), and seamstresses (my grandmother and *her* mother who sewed the trousseaus of the village brides and embroidered many a Shabbat tablecloth and Passover pillow cover). Their works were lost along with them in the Holocaust; ephemeral folk art, ephemeral folk.

And in this country too, our family has its share of artists. Here we are architects, stage designers, graphic artists, interior decorators. Only two of us work with Jewish themes—myself and my ninety year-old Great Uncle Layzer who, after many fruitful years as a carpenter, both in Poland and America, has returned to the craft he learned as a boy, that of papercutting. His dining room table is his "factory" and there he turns out treasured greeting cards for family and friends.

For a while, when I first plunged into Jewish themes twelve years ago and made the commitment to myself to integrate my Jewish and artistic halves, I thought I was alone. I knew about a few *great* artists and craftspeople, such as Marc Chagall, Ben Shahn, Ludwig Wolpert, and Moshe Zabari, but it seemed that all of the other Jewish artists I knew were not interested in Jewish subject matter. But, as I searched, I began to meet other people like myself who were involved with Jewish expression, often almost "secretly" alongside their "regular" work. Many Jewish artists feel that they work in isolation. They are cut off from their fellow Jews because they are artists and from their fellow artists because their work is Jewish. Wanting to put artists and craftspeople in touch with one another and with the patrons who, by buying and commissioning work would bring more of it into being, prompted me to put together the first edition of this book in 1976. Since then the sheer number of artists and craftspeople working with thematically Jewish material has grown remarkably, and I am convinced that there are even more people "out there" whom I haven't yet found or who haven't found me. If you are an "undiscovered" craftsperson (or if you know of one) please write to me at 106 Francis St., Brookline, Mass. 02146. Artists and craftspeople working with Jewish themes and anybody interested in encouraging Jewish-American expression in the visual arts should consider affiliation with the National Council on Art in Jewish Life, 15 E. 84th St. New York, N.Y. 10028, a nonprofit organization which, through exhibitions, publications, seminars, and referrals, provides a liaison between the public and the artist.

In this section of the book you will meet artists and craftspeople from all over the country who work in a broad variety of styles and media. When one buys a work of art one really buys a piece of the life of its creator. One of the thrills of shopping at craft fairs is meeting artists in the flesh, so I have tried to provide a glimpse into the thoughts and lifestyles of as many of the artists and craftspeople as possible by letting them speak for themselves. A good proportion of them are eager and willing to demonstrate and lecture about their work and related subjects, many are available for craft fairs in their geographic areas, and many welcome visits to their studios (write or call first). It is exciting to be a Jewish-American artist at the beginning of this new decade. The last ten years have seen so much growth, I am looking forward to what the 80's will bring.

A NOTE ON COMMISSIONING ARTWORK

"The purpose of every person, and of all creation, is to make a dwelling-place for the Creator in this world."

Tanya, by Rabbi Shneur Zalman of Lubavitch

It has been very gratifying these last few years watching the growth towards maturity of Jewish-American crafts. (I even think I am beginning to spot characteristic differences between a Jewish West Coast style and an Eastern Seaboard look; it's a little too early to tell if such differences really exist or if I am making them up.) An active and overlooked participant in this phenomenal development has been the *buyer*. For everytime something is bought it creates the need for more and provides the artist with food for body and spirit to go on producing. So, "Thank you, clients and patrons!" Sometimes commissioning a work is a nervewracking business for the client as well as the artist. I've heard (and participated in) some hair-raising horror stories. The culprit most often at the bottom of dissatisfaction between artist and client is poor communication. The fault lies on both sides and can be avoided by carefully working out all details in advance. Things like dates of delivery, color, size, material, and price are the obvious considerations. Ticklish problems also include: who pays for long-distance phone calls, how many preliminary sketches for how much of a consulting fee; shopping for price when quality varies considerably; asking for brochures with no intention of buying; not returning slides and photographs; materials increasing in price after a fee has been decided on; not liking the finished object; not delivering or paying on time; and so on. The key to avoiding as many problems as possible is to anticipate them. Before any commission is begun a letter of agreement or contract spelling out everything you can think of should be worked out. Since the artist will be making many such agreements and the client probably very few, most of the responsibility for coming up with a sensible agreement falls on the artist. Each artist should decide under what conditions he/she works best and draw up a simple statement or contract, allowing for individual variations, which can be presented to prospective clients.

Hopefully, none of this will frighten away prospective patrons of the arts. Most of the artists in these pages are open to commissions and have long experience in working out the details. Most of them also have finished work ready for immediate sale.

Art for Architecture

Temple Mt. Sinai, El Paso Texas; Sydney Eisensdat, Architect; Jean-Jacques Duval, glass. *(See Creating: Glass and Enamel.)*

The Jewish people have never had one particular architectural style. Wherever we have found ourselves, we have built our synagogues according to the prevailing architectural fashions of the time and place. In this country we have built "colonial" synagogues and buildings which are examples of every revival and vogue from Greek through Gothic, Islamic, and Victorian. Most recently, our synagogues are as "contemporary" as the places of worship of any other faith. It is not enough, however, to build glorious edifices; we must think not only of the cost to the congregation, but of the cost to the environment. For this reason, before we turn to the talented interior designers and specialists in ritual objects and art for public places whose work you will find in these pages, I would

like to draw your attention to the interview with Everett Gendler excerpted from the May, 1980 issue of *Genesis 2*. I know that talking about using alternative energy sources is easier than doing it, but I would like to think that if our nation's religious institutions set something of an example, then perhaps all the "Eternal Lights" will continue to glow into the future.

The artists and firms mentioned in this chapter will undertake work on almost any aspect of a building's interior; also look at the listings for various specialties, such as *Glass*, *Metal*, and *Textiles*, for artists working specifically in those media, whose work can also enhance a building on a major scale.

Building a solar consciousness

(reprinted by permission from *Genesis 2*)

For the past year and a half, Temple Emanuel in Lowell has been using a Ner Tamid *(Eternal Light) powered by solar energy. Rabbi Everett Gendler of Temple Emanuel, who first conceived of the idea for a solar paneled eternal light has long been an advocate of energy conservation and of honoring the Biblical mandate to respect and preserve the earth's natural resources.*

Interviewed by Cherie Brown,
Public Affairs Editor

genesis 2: What made you decide to install a solar *Ner Tamid*?

Rabbi Gendler: Ah! It happened about a year ago last autumn when there was a particularly beautiful day, and I could feel the shortening of the daylight. At the same time, I was especially aware of the power and strength of the sun. I was musing at the Temple. Every once in a while I think about Psalm 19 with its celebration of the sun. I begin thinking about the sun as a symbol of the Divine, so inferior to, yet derivative from the great Source. A mutation of that, the *Ner Tamid,* is what symbolically stands above the ark.

I was thinking, my God, here's this reality of enormous Power and energy which for our eternal lights is mediated by such questionable sources of power, either rapidly disappearing fossil fuels— coal or oil or the really lethal and dangerous to the future of human existence—nuclear power.

It suddenly struck me so forcibly that such sources of power for the *Ner Tamid* were incredibly inferior to the beautiful solar collector which is the olive tree and the olive oil. I managed to resist the temptation to say: "Abolish all electrified eternal lights and return to olive oil," which was my first thought.

I had heard about photo-voltaics. Symbolically, at the spiritual level, how beautiful it would be if the light above the Torah directly derived from the

sun. Also, I was thinking, my God, what a contribution to all of our awareness of the energy question at a practical, societal level.

genesis 2: Can you add anything else that Jewish tradition has to say about energy and natural resources?

R. Gendler: There are several propositions that guide my approach to this kind of question. One is a verse from Isaiah 45:18:

. . . the Lord Who created the heavens
(He is God!)
Who formed the earth and made it
(He established it),
He did not create it a chaos,
He formed it to be inhabited!

Proposition number one is that this planet was created as a kind of life experiment and we're part of it. Everything we do has to be measured against maintaining the inhabitability of the planet. One of my favorite Midrashim, "Your World" is from a collection by Nachum Glatzer, *Hammer on the Rock.* It says:

In the hour when the Holy One,
blessed be He,
created the first man,
He took him and let him pass before all the
trees of the garden of Eden, and said to him:
See My works, how fine and excellent they
are!
Now all that I have created, for you have I
created.
Think upon this, and do not corrupt and
desolate
My world:
for if you corrupt it, there is no one to set it
right after you.

The second point is that the earth was created to be inhabited, and we are primarily responsible for

Rabbi Everett Gendler on the roof of Temple Emanuel in Lowell, Massachusetts, which now has silicon solar panels generating power for its Eternal Light. Inset shows the light inside the sanctuary. (photo: Arthur Pollock/The Lowell Sun)

maintaining it as a hospitable place for other creatures and for us. Any energy that's proposed has to conform to these requirements. It has to operate in a way that doesn't threaten either the possibility of future life continuing on this planet or else assume that somebody else will pick up the pieces and clean up the mess after us. In so far as any source threatens the basis of human life, to that extent it seems to me it's invalid and has to be ruled out.

American Draftsmen's Council
29 W. 53rd St. • New York, N.Y. 10020

The council maintains a list of artists willing to accept commissions for ceremonial Judaica for home and synagogue.

Architects Advisory Panel
Union of American Hebrew Congregations
838 Fifth Ave. • New York, N.Y. 10021

UAHC makes available a three-page listing of accredited synagogue artists and craftspeople. It also has a synagogue architectural design consulting service. The Architects Advisory Panel is a voluntary association of more than forty architectural firms all of which, having constructed synagogues, are dedicated to the advancement of synagogue architecture. Members of the Advisory Panel are available for consultations with building committees and synagogues, but in no way replace the individually commissioned architect. There is a contribution fee of $50, which goes towards the maintenance of UAHC's architectural library. This contribution is requested only once regardless of the number of requests for consultations made by a congregation.

Sampson Seymour Engoren
11 Holmes Place • Lynbrook, N.Y. 11563

Sampson Seymour Engoren designs, fabricates, and installs lecterns, arks, Torah holders, lead glass windows, sanctuary doors, memorial plaques, and just about anything else a synagogue needs. His brochure shows several interesting multi-leveled, carpeted bimah designs.

Edward Goldman
50 Elm St. • Framingham, Mass. 01701

Painting is Edward Goldman's favorite art form, and during W.W. II his war scenes in France won him an appointment as Battalion Artist. He is, however, also at home in other media including metal sculpture and metal collage. He designs and makes welded sculpture and metal collages for synagogues and religious collections.

Betty Goldstein
35 Benedict Rd. • Scarsdale, N.Y. 10583

Betty Goldstein is a temple interior designer. She provides a complete design service, including sculpture, lecterns, Torah covers, arks, stained-glass windows, memorials, menorot, and tapestries.

Harry Green
4735 Mercier • Kansas City, Mo. 64112

Harry Green grew up in Lexington, Kentucky, the son of Russian-Jewish immigrants. He served in the Marine Corps as a photographer from 1945-47 and 1950-52. During Israel's War of Independence in 1948 he fought with the Irgun. It is a treat to listen to him talk about the work he loves, not only because of the lyrical cadences of his southern accent (call me a provincial north-eastener!), but because of the strength and honesty of his ideas. He is committed to exploring and redefining thousands of years of Jewish symbols and history. He writes; "I try to make the viewer want to reach out and touch, to feel, to be fascinated, to take him away from where he is for the moment, to recapture the feeling of wonder and awe that's in him."

Harry Green's bas reliefs are simultaneously timeless and contemporary in feeling. He has

HARRY GREEN, "Lion of Judah", mizrah, 15" × 16".

taken the underused and often abused medium of sand casting and raised it to the level of profound personal expression. The results are visually decorative (in the best sense of the word), powerful statements. He specializes in wall sculptures—from minuscule to a whole wall—and also does three-dimensional portrait busts and presentation pieces. He works in bronze and ceramics as well as casting in hydrocal. He will be happy to send his gorgeous, well-illustrated brochure to potential clients and to discuss specific projects, special themes, symbols, and logos.

Mr. Green also teaches Jewish Art and Culture at the Hyman Brand Jewish Academy in Kansas City. He is available to lecture on Jewish Art and to demonstrate the sandcast process with which he creates much of his fascinating and appealing Judaica. (See *Creating: Ceramics; Observing: Life Cycle* and *Holidays and Ceremonies* for more examples of Harry Green's work.)

Hugh Mesibov
377 Saddle River Rd. • Monsey, N.Y. 10952

Hugh Mesibov is a printmaker, painter, and muralist. He began to paint murals under the Works Projects Administration (W.P.A.) in the 1930's and one of the pieces he did then can be seen in the Hubbord, Ohio, Post Office. He recently exhibited a collection of drawings, watercolors, and etchings based on themes from the Book of Job at the House of Living Judaism in New York City. These pieces were done in preparation for his mural, "The Book of Job," at Temple Beth El in Spring Valley, N.Y. Mr. Mesibov is interested in doing murals for public buildings and religious institutions. Inquiries are invited; slides are available on request.

Emanuel Milstein
R.D. 1 Box 81C • Marlboro, N.J. 07746

Sculptor and architect Emanuel Milstein writes: "Houses of worship, traditionally shelters for the spirit of man, have always been patrons of the arts. The architect for a house of worship need not have to justify a spiritual approach to his work . . . nor need he justify his desire to incorporate works of art within his concept, or, in fact, to make a unified work of art of his entire effort." Milstein's commitment to the scale and form of architecture and

EMANUEL MILSTEIN, ark for the Sephardic Temple, Cedarhurst, N.Y.

his understanding of spatial relationships make his "art work" for architecture an integral part of the building for which his works are commissioned. All of the artifacts, stained-glass, and architectural sculptures designed by Milstein are fabricated in his own studio, but are done with such sensitivity to the light and space of the buildings for which they are destined that they seem to grow organically from the structure itself. He accepts commissions for individual ritual objects, stained-glass, and sculpture as well as total synagogue interiors. He has a well-illustrated brochure and a set of slides available to prospective clients. (See *Creating: Glass and Enamel; Learning: Holocaust.*)

Scopia
18350 Chesterfield Airport Rd.
Chesterfield, Mo. 63017

Saunders Schultz and William Severson began working together over twenty years ago in order to direct their combined talents and expertise toward the challenge presented by architectural sculpture. At Scopia, their studio-workshop, they

SCOPIA, Synagogue B'nai El, St. Louis Mo.

work alongside a number of skilled craftspeople. The ample (five acres) physical facilities allow them to undertake sculptural challenges of monumental size and to work in diverse materials. Severson and Schultz have designed and executed work in forty states. In accepting commissions they enter a very close relationship with their clients and the architectural team involved. They have prepared an unillustrated six-page description of their philosophy, services, and background.

Shamir Studio
**Office: 609 Kappock St.
Riverdale, N.Y. 10463
Workshop: 307 W. 38th St.
New York, N.Y. 10018**

Ami Shamir is a versatile Israeli artist-designer who has been living and working in the United States since 1968. He designs and executes one-of-a-kind murals for public institutions, mainly synagogues. He employs a stylized and dramatic vocabulary of symbols and motifs including amuletic hands, suns, menorot, architectural details, Magen Davids, eyes, Hebrew letters, and natural forms. He works in glass, concrete, wood,

metals, stone, marble, and textiles. His works are created on a commission basis only and he will oversee the installation of the finished project. An illustrated brochure is available. (See also *Creating: Glass and Enamel, Textiles* and *Learning: Holocaust.*)

AMI SHAMIR, "Justice you should pursue," relief sculpture in molded concrete, 20' × 12', for Cardozo School of Law, Yeshiva University, N.Y.

Charles J. Stanley
P.O. Box 1132, Peter Stuyvesant Sta.
New York, N.Y. 10009

Charles Stanley is a very talented painter and a recent *Baal Teshuvah* (returnee to Orthodoxy). After an impressive amount of secular work, he is now painting Jewish themes. His forceful and folkloric murals already grace the walls of several New York Jewish buildings. He will very definitely accept commissions for more thematically Jewish murals and will travel outside the N.Y. city area. Prices are negotiable. (See also *Creating: Pictures*.)

CHARLES J. STANLEY, "Burning Bush," detail of a mural painted directly on cement blocks.

Frederick Terna
115 E. 89th St. • New York, N.Y. 10028

Terna is a design consultant on synagogue art and decor. (See *Creating: Pictures*.)

Erna Weill
886 Alpine Dr. • Teaneck, N.J. 07666

Erna Weil sculpts in stone, concrete, and terracotta as well as in bronze. She has sculpted portraits of Elie Wiesel, Abraham Heschel, and Martin Buber and will accept portrait commissions and requests for architectural sculpture and ceremonial objects.

Efrem Weitzman
334 W. 86th St. • New York, N.Y. 10024

Every piece of artwork done by Efrem Weitzman is custom-designed to fit a specific location; color, form, and materials are integrated with those of the room it is placed in. Mr. Weitzman designs, fabricates, and installs artworks for synagogue interiors in a variety of media, including stained-glass, mosaic, and tapestry.

EFREM WEITZMAN

Sanford Werfel Studios
133 Avenel St. • Avenel, N.J. 07001

Sanford Werfel offers a full range of synagogue design services and furnishings. He will accept mail orders and has color brochures of a variety of different tree of life donor walls.

Ludwig Wolpert, Director
Tobe Pascher Workshop
The Jewish Museum
1109 Fifth Ave. • New York, N.Y. 10028

The renowned silversmith Ludwig Wolpert has designed many major pieces for synagogues all over the country. Just as he is available for the creation of small commissioned ceremonial objects, he will undertake large architectural commissions for institutions and synagogues. (See *Creating: Metal.*)

Albert Wood and Five Sons, Inc.
One Pleasant Ave.
Port Washington, N.Y. 11050

Founded in 1932, this family business has had more than forty years of experience in creating handsome interiors for business and religious buildings. There really are five sons, and at least one grandson also carries on the family tradition. In accepting commissions for interior design the firm works in collaboration with the building architects. A well-illustrated brochure with photographs in color as well as black and white is available.

Joseph Young
1434 S. Spaulding Ave.
Los Angeles, Calif. 90019

In the past fifteen years, Joseph Young has originated more than twenty major liturgical art programs for Jewish institutions of prayer, learning, and assembly. He creates profound new symbolic meanings in a host of permanent art media. Working closely with the building architect, his firm designs, executes, and installs everything from arks and bimah furniture to murals and sculpture. He works in mosaic, stained-glass, metal, wood, and tapestry design. Most of his work has been on the West Coast but he is open to commissions from all over the country. He will coordinate, design, and install original works of art especially created for the particular commission; murals, sculpture, etc. He welcomes mail inquiries and has a brochure and other background material available.

JOSEPH YOUNG, Working line drawing for stained-glass window for Beth Knesset Bamidbar in Lancaster, Calif. The window measures 6'2" wide and 11' high. It will be installed over the ark. This project is Mr. Young's 21st major synagogue commission. The drawing is reproduced with special permission of the artist and is protected by his copyright.

Calligraphy

JAY GREENSPAN at work (photo: © Bill Aron, see Creating: Pictures).

When my childhood friends and I looked for bits of wood and old newspapers with which to make fires so we could roast our potatoes ("Mickies") in the empty Bronx lots where we played, we would never use the Yiddish papers— not even the Communist *Freiheit*—for we knew that the Hebrew letters themselves were somehow holy. There are so many beautiful stories about the *alef-bet* and even about the individual letters. It is said, for example, that when Moses arrived in Heaven, he found God weaving crowns for the letters of the *alef-bet,* for the Universe had been created through them.

It is not surprising, then, to find that many artists and craftspeople employ Hebrew letters for symbolic, meaningful, and decorative effects. The traditional master of the Hebrew letter has always been the *sofer* (scribe) who is completely familiar with Halakhic detail and follows very careful procedures insuring that his documents are ritually kosher. According to strict interpretation of Halakhah, only a male scribe can write a Torah scroll, tefillin, a mezuzah, or a bill of divorce *(get)*. Women, however, can do the ketubah (wedding contract). And it is in this area that female calligraphic artists all over the country are making a significant contribution to an ancient, authentically Jewish art form. Like their colleagues, they also design and make everything from bookplates to presentation certificates and mizrahim (ornaments for the eastern wall). There are so many more dedicated calligraphers than there were just a few short years ago. It is indeed gratifying to see an American revival of our most hallowed craft.

Shel Bassel
305 Palmwood Drive
Trotwood, Ohio 45426

Shel Bassel is a terrific designer who manages to incorporate traditional forms into modern design and color schemes. Black and white photographs simply do not do his work justice. Shel is a trained scribe (sofer sta'm) and can write, fix, and sell Torah scrolls, tefillin, and mezuzot. He is available for speaking engagements on sofrut as well as calligraphy. His calligraphic work is mainly ketubot, which are individually commissioned, but he also does invitations, quotations, testimonials, etc. He has recently begun to print a series of his work. The first lithograph is a traditional ketubah text (8" × 10"), printed in black on a sheet of 100% cotton fiber Nph paper, with blanks for the names and other pertinent information. It is accompanied by instructions for filling in the text. The extra-wide margin is for an optional border which can be painted, drawn, or papercut. He is available to fill in the text and/or do a border, or the purchaser can do his/her own. Future reproductions will include a ketubah with a full-color border and a mizrah. These will be limited edition lithographs. He has a brochure and does accept mail orders and welcomes inquiries.

Cynthia Pearlman Benjamin
25 Thatcher St. #4 • Brookline, Mass. 02146

Because I like her work so much, when I celebrated my marriage to Myron Tupa in 1979, we asked Cindy to do our marriage contract. We wanted a special document, mostly in English, defining our relationship and our commitment to my children. We also asked for lined space where all 32 of the people present at the wedding could sign their names; and we wanted tulips, jonquils and angels. All this had to be done in colors and shapes which would "live" happily in the space we had selected for it between two stained-glass windows. Quite an order—and Cindy came through beautifully. All of her work is by commission and she will "happily explore your ideas and gather information through the mail and/or on the telephone." A portfolio is viewable on request. (See Cindy's bookplate design in *Learning: Books*)

SHEL BASSEL, ketubah for Debbie and Ethan Schuman.

CINDY BENJAMIN at work. (photo: Michael Goldberg)

CINDY BENJAMIN, ketubah.

Rose Ann Chasman
6147 North Richmond • Chicago, Ill. 60659

Ruth Ann Chasman works in a variety of media, taking inspiration from old amulets, samplers, herbals, and manuscripts. She enjoys researching Judaica, folklore, and art history, and she will undertake any calligraphic project. Her current price for an individually commissioned ketubah is $200—more for goatskin or vellum. She takes great care to use permanent materials, after seeing someone else's ketubah which had *run* when it became wet during framing. Her work could be held under the faucet and come· out safely. She gives demonstrations on the art of the ketubah and has prepared a slide program on Ben Shahn. She charges $50 for these programs. Ms. Chasman is a multi-talented woman; look for more about her work in *Creating; Pictures, Playing: Travel,* and *Buying: Cards, Gifts and Collectibles.*

ROSE ANN CHASMAN, 150th Psalm, 18″ × 24″. (photo: William and Myer Co., Chicago)

Yehudah Clapman
719 Montgomery St.
Brooklyn, N.Y. 11213

Rabbi Clapman is a Lubavitcher *sofer* who specializes in writing the parchments for mezuzot and tefillin. He also repairs damaged Torah scrolls

CINDY BENJAMIN, ketubah.

and manufactures the leather containers for tefillin. In addition to his work as a scribe, he has a small business called Judaic Heritage (see *Buying: Gifts*) which endeavors to bring unique Jewish objects to the public.

Mr. Clapman has designed an interesting program (which he tailors to fit any age group from six to adult) about the traditional scribal arts. He feels that "if more people would find out what a mezuzah (or tefillin) are really all about, the battle against fraudulent items would be won." If you are interested send for his flyer.

Peggy H. Davis
4421 4th Ave. So.
Minneapolis, Minn. 55409

Peggy Davis is a delightful young woman who works in pen and ink, tempera and collage. She will undertake commissions in Hebrew and English for the full range of calligraphic projects. She has also designed a printed ketubah which is available from Degi Designs (see *Buying: Cards, Gifts and Collectibles*).

Lipot Friedman
1311 43rd Street • Brooklyn, N.Y. 11219

Lipot Friedman writes: "I am a soifer from Chust. I fix Sefer Torahs, sell and examine tefillin and mezuzahs. I am doing it for fifty years; starting in Chust and then Hungary, Williamsburgh, and the lower east side of Manhattan. For information call: (212) 438-6044."

Kadish Gaibel
Herzog 55, Jerusalem, Israel
In USA: c/o Josarah Enterprise
422 N. Wells • Chicago, Ill. 60610

Kadish Gaibel is the adviser to the department of ceramics at the Bezalel Academy of Art on the subject of Hebrew letters. He invites commissions, charges about $200 for a hand-done ketubah, and also has a selection of silkscreened ketubot in limited editions of 100 for $10 each. His English is excellent, so don't be afraid to write him for more details. His brochure is available from either address.

Isa Goldfarb
137 Norwood Ave.
Newtonville, Mass. 02160

I met Isa Goldfarb when she registered for a batik workshop I was teaching at Brandeis University. I was immediately impressed with her superb design sense and exquisite use of color, and I was not surprised to learn that she is a professional calligrapher. Isa feels that her involvement in holistic healing is reflected in all of her work—in her choice of symbols, designs, and colors. She works very closely with the couples for whom she makes ketubot. Her prices for ketubot and other illuminated manuscripts begin at $250. She has a brochure and will also mail slides to prospective clients.

ISA GOLDFARB, ketubah.

Nancy Greenberg
7045 SW 110th Terrace • Miami, Fla. 33156

Nancy Greenberg is an elegant watercolorist whose ketubot incorporate such diverse motifs as portraits of the couple, historical, and biblical scenes. Each is created in response to the needs of the client through photographs, sketches, and

NANCY GREENBERG, ketubah with true likeness of newly-married couple.

slides. The price varies according to the size and complexity of the design. She has a well-illustrated and informative brochure.

Jay Greenspan
P.O. Box 914 • New York, N.Y. 10025

Jay Greenspan's calligraphic designs are precise and clean. The borders on his ketubot that I like the best have a simple folkloric quality often consisting of stylized arrangements of flowers, pomegranates, birds, or other natural forms. He specializes in megillot as well as ketubot and will also accept commissions for invitation and bookplate designs. He also does presentation certificates, diplomas, and scrolls as well as mezuzot. He has a brochure and will send sample photographs on request.

Renana Gross
8320 Ridge Road • Cincinnati, Ohio 45236

Renana Gross will undertake calligraphic projects from birth announcements and greeting cards to ketubot with elaborate papercut borders. Prices are open to discussion and range from $25 to $250.

RENANA GROSS, ketubah for Leslie Grant and Bill Schwab with equalitarian texts and papercut border.

Nissim Hizme
89 Canal St. • New York, N.Y. 10002

Hizme designs the master copy for Hebrew wedding and bar mitzvah invitations. He does artwork with Hebraic motifs for book jackets, ketubot, and organization journals. (See also *Creating: Metal.*)

Reeva Kimble
2352 Van Ness • Eugene, Oreg. 97430

Reeva Kimble uses calligraphy in Hebrew and/or English to produce camera-ready art for printing (invitations, address labels) or for display (poems, naming certificates). All items can be ordered in a variety of colors, papers, and choice of alphabet.

Jonathan Kremer
124 Oxford St. #5
Cambridge, Mass. 02140

Words such as meticulous, elegant, careful, and exquisite come to mind in describing Jonathan Kremer's work. Since creating his first marriage

JONATHAN KREMER, ketubah.

contract in 1972, Jonathan has written and decorated more than 100 ketubot for couples throughout the United States, Canada, and Israel. He has also executed numerous testimonials, scrolls, invitations, and other unique calligraphic works for individuals and organizations. I was so pleased with the lettering he did for some party invitations that I asked him to design and make the ketubah for my son David's wedding. He has an attractive, well-illustrated brochure which is available on request. As well as domestic and personal pieces, Jonathan is very interested in doing large projects of decorative lettering, murals, and architectural lettering for synagogue interiors and exteriors. (See also: *Buying: Gifts and Greeting cards*)

Sally Akiva Mandel
545 108th N.E. #6
Bellvue, Wash. 98005

Sally Mandel is a 19 year-old student working her way through school. She does original ketubot, invitations, bookplates, and graphic designs for buttons, T-shirts, letterheads, and posters. She is available for craft fairs and lectures, and will travel in pursuit of jobs. She also does oil paintings.

JONATHAN KREMER, ink and watercolor on paper, 15" × 15", based on Hosea 2:21; collection of Dr. and Mrs. L. Berman.

SALLY MANDEL, ketubah, 18" × 24", available as a serigraph print for $15.00 or painted in oil on parchment for $500.00.

Cara Goldberg Marks
388 Kenridge Rd.
Lawrence, N.Y. 11559

Multi-talented Cara Marks is a commercial illustrator and designer as well as a fine calligrapher. She has designed everything from coins and packages to giftware and of course ketubot. While most of her commissions recently have been for commercial products of one sort or another—most, by the way, with Judaic themes—she does accept a number of private commissions each year. Each piece she creates is distinctive and truly custom-made to the client's specification. In addition to ketubot, she has done Torah portions, monograms, mizrahim, wedding contracts, proverbs, and poetry. "Just let them ask", she says. Corresponding with her is a treat because her stationery is so gorgeous, as is her brochure. For those readers who would like to know more about the calligrapher's craft, Cara has just finished a book on the subject to be published in the fall of 1980 (*Handbook of Hebrew Calligraphy*, SBS Publishing, Inc.)

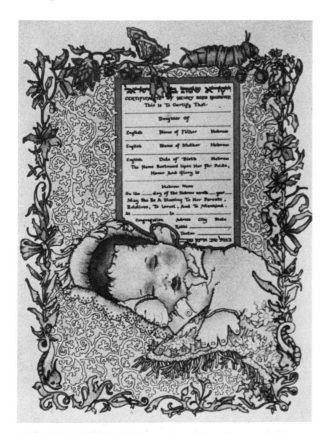

CARA GOLDBERG MARKS, naming of daughter certificate, watercolor, pen and ink.

Joan Mesznik
441 West End Ave., 15-C
New York, N.Y. 10024

Simplicity and elegance characterize the work of Joan Mesznik. She specializes in ketubot but also makes very handsome wall decorations of poetic inscriptions. Joan will happily send you her lovely brochure. She loves to travel to craft fairs and to give lectures, bringing slides and actual pieces with her. She is as lyrical with words as with images. She writes: "My life is totally devoted to my art. When I work on calligraphy I feel I am in direct contact with God. It is my form of praying . . . When I finish a piece and believe it to be without blemish, and feel that I have achieved the total perfection that I strive for . . . I lift my head and sing praise to God that I have been given the talent and the patience to do what I was born to do, and then I am totally mentally, emotionally, and physically exhausted. As if I have given birth to each and every new piece. What I do for today is different from what I did yesterday. And what I shall do tomorrow will be different from what I did today." Learn more about this remarkable woman in *Creating: Ceramics*.

JOAN MESZNIK, The 100th Piece! Artist's collection.

JOAN MESZNIK, ketubah for Mr. and Mrs. Osher Sebrow, Brooklyn, N.Y.

David Moss
1235 Peralta • Berkeley, Calif. 94706

The ketubot of David Moss are so special that one must say that not only is he a link in a chain of 2300 years of ketubah makers but that his own vision

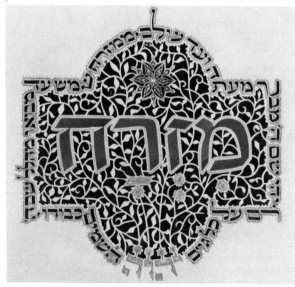

DAVID MOSS, mizrah, 17" × 17", ink gouches, gold leaf on paper(cut). Courtesy Moriah Gallery, N.Y.

and abilities may very well define the form this ancient Aramaic text takes into the future. Unlike most scribal products—tefillin, mezuzot, or Torah scrolls—there are no restrictions as to embellishment, materials, or lettering for the making of a legally valid ketubah. Moss becomes genuinely involved in emphasizing the taste, vocations, or favorite religious symbols of the couple whose wedding document he is making. The resultant ketubot cover the spectrum from intricate medieval-style manuscripts replete with gold-leaf illumination, to ketubot in wood, ceramic, cut paper, and collage. As well as for ketubot, he accepts commissions for birth and bar mitzvah certificates, mizrah plaques, amulets, mezuzot, and designs for needlepoint. (See also *Creating: Pictures*.)

Naomi Nadata
39 Stevens Place • Lawrence, N.Y. 11559

Sharon Savitsky
20 Park Ave.
Newton, Mass. 02158

Naomi Nadata and Sharon Savitsky live miles apart and probably have never met, yet they have much in common. They both combine Orthodox, Shomer Shabbat lifestyles with the demands of family and careers as calligraphic artists. While they will both undertake the full scope of calligraphic work from invitations to poetry, they specialize in ketubot. Their styles, however, differ markedly, even as they each have a certain folkloric quality. Write or call for brochures.

Fred Spinowitz
5 Overlook Road
New Rochelle, N.Y. 10804

Yeshiva and Pratt Institute trained, Fred Spinowitz does intaglio prints (etchings and embossings), as well as illuminated ketubot on parchment. Prices begin at $300 which includes a consultation and original sketch. Glossy brochure with four photographs available.

Betsy Platkin Teutsch
251 W. 101st St. • New York, N.Y. 10025

While Betsy Teutsch designs bar mitzvah and wedding invitations for commercial reproduction,

BETSY PLATKIN TEUTSCH, Purim bat mitzvah invitation.

SHOSHANNA WALKER, illuminated ketubah.

sells greeting cards of her own design, and will accept commissions for assorted English/Hebrew calligraphic documents, this talented young rebbetzin says that her specialty is the ketubah. She has done ketubot in rectangles, circles, ovals, in geometrics with representational and nonrepresentational artwork. Her natural style gravitates toward the use of bright, vivid colors and flowing, lively shapes. She uses 100% rag-content paper for her ketubot, which generally measure about 24″ × 18″. At the present time she charges $300 and needs at least eight weeks notice; more if it's a June wedding. If possible, she likes to meet with the bride and groom personally, but will accept mail-order commissions. She has also made anniversary ketubot commissioned by a couple's children for their twenty-fifth or thirty-fifth anniversary. Betsy has an informative and interesting pamphlet about ''Creating Your Ketubah,'' which is replete with suggestions for quotations and symbols, and ideas for where to look for more. There is also a form to fill out with all the information the artist will need. She requires a five dollar deposit (refundable) for a set of slides.

Shoshanna Walker
691 Empire Avenue
Far Rockaway, N.Y. 11691

Most people don't bother to list their high schools on their vita. But those of us who went to the High School of Music and Art in New York City continue to include it in our resumes, no matter what other credits we may list. So it is with landsman-like pride that I write about Shoshanna Walker who, after graduating from Music and Art went on to the Parsons School of Design and has exhibited her work twenty times in the last four years. When given complete designing freedom by her clients, Shoshanna Walker usually bases her work on Persian and Mid-Eastern styles of decoration. She uses this type of elaborate ornamentation for large Kabbalistic paintings, which though meant for synagogue use can also be commissioned by individuals. Since her designs and sizes are not standardized, her prices are negotiable. As well as ketubot, invitations, certificates, and scrolls, she makes ornate mizrahim and calligraphic ''amulets.'' For those in her immediate area she gives private calligraphy lessons. She has a gorgeous brochure available on request.

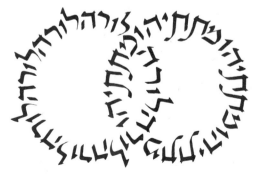

TERRI BAREL EISENBERG, wedding notecard design.

JOAN MESZNIK, ketubah for Chazzan and Mrs. Sherwood Goffin, N.Y.

MORE CALLIGRAPHERS

The following calligraphers will all design and execute hand-lettered ketubot, invitations, and other special projects, often in a mixture of Hebrew and English if so requested. Like the calligraphers listed earlier, their prices and styles vary. I therefore suggest you call or write the one closest to your home to see if your needs can be met. Many of them have color photos of previous commissions that they will send to prospective clients.

Charles H. Baum
72 Calhoun Avenue
Trumbull, Conn. 06611

Sharon Binder
Beth Tzedec Congregation
1700 Bathurst St.
Toronto, Ontario M5P 3K3

Frances Zak Cohen
Hill Crescent-Belle Terre
Port Jefferson, N.Y. 11777

Terri Barel Eisenberg
1555 Beacon St. #8
Brookline, Mass. 02146

A. N. Goldstein
c/o J.C.C. of Greater Minneapolis
4330 Cedar Lake Road So.
Minneapolis, Minn. 55416

Renanah Halpern
6801 University Drive, Apt. 2W
University City, Mo. 63130

Marcia Kaunfer
50 Sargent Ave.
Providence, R.I. 02906

Rabbi Stuart Kelman
1140 S. Alfred St.
Los Angeles, Calif. 90035

Daryl Rothman Kuperstock
1002 Crane
Evanston, Ill. 60204

Eve Moscowitz Pardo
58 Wiggins St.
Princeton, N.J. 08540

Norman Sapoznik
2333 East 22nd St.
Brooklyn, N.Y. 11229

Danny Steiner
149 Sixth Avenue
Brooklyn, N.Y. 11217

Debra Walk
127 North Laffayette Ave.
Ventnor, N.J. 08406

Lili Wronker
144-44 Village Road
Jamaica, N.Y. 11435

JONATHAN KREMER, calligraphic design for Psalm 34.

Ceramics

Behold, like clay in the hand of the potter, so are you in My hand, O House of Israel.

Jeremiah 18:6

JOAN MESZNIK at work in·her pottery studio-shop, "Vessels."
(photo: David Landau)

"The image of the hand and clay are used often in biblical writings to symbolize both power and the process of creating. The Hebrew word 'Yetzirah' has the dual meaning of 'creation' and 'pottery,' signifying the basic connection understood between the creation of the universe out of the void, and the potter's art of forming beautiful objects out of inanimate clay." So writes Minneapolis potter Lynn Rosen. At one time or another, almost all of us have experienced the magical fascination of playing and working with clay. To take mud, shape it, pass it through the mystery of fire, and have something useful and hopefully beautiful emerge, is a thrill that even the most experienced ceramist rarely outgrows. I am delighted to find that there is an ever-growing number of ceramists producing handmade objects for Jewish use that combine a contemporary feeling for clay with traditional functions and meanings.

Fern Amper
375 Riverside Dr., 7F
New York, N.Y. 10025
or 65-50 Wetherole St.
Rego Park, N.Y. 11374

Fern Amper learned her trade as an apprentice to a Greek production potter on one of the smaller Greek islands. This experience has given her a very "down to earth" approach to ceramics. Her objects are simple, pleasing statements of utility and craft. She has a "line" of artifacts for Jewish home use, which she will mail (add postage and $1 handling charge per item). She will be happy to discuss commissions for other items such as Seder plates, synagogue ornaments, or larger versions of the things she already makes: Kiddush goblets, large, $15, small, $10; Havdalah sets including a spice box, candlestick, and wine cup on a tray, $15–20; candlesticks, $15; and a handwashing *bekher* with the blessing carved on it, $6–8. Fern has a handsome, well-illustrated brochure of her wares. It has an order form explaining quantity discounts and is available free on request.

FERN AMPER, buffet set for sugar, honey, and milk, $20 plus postage and handling. (photo: Eli Schaap)

Nathan Bushwick
901 Madison Ave. • Scranton, Pa. 18510

Nathan Bushwick has a complete line of ceramic Judaica. Write for his price list which includes wine bottles as well as Kiddush cups, Seder and Havdalah plates.

Jonathan Craig
1 Swallow Lane • Hauppauge, N.Y. 11787

Jonathan Craig calls his ceramics Judaic "metaceremonials." This is what he writes:

Ritual objects not only enhance one's performance of mitzvot (sacred deeds), they inspire and make more intimate man's relationship with the concept that God is contained in the existence of man. This happens when the ceremonial object, such as the Kiddush cup, is combined with the religious act, the sanctification of wine, resulting in the contemplation of object and act separately. . . . Since ritual objects are required to fulfill mitzvot, they have special significance and therein, become symbols themselves . . . so that the user's thought passes from performance to concept. . . . The object is no longer limited to being a means to an end but includes being an end in itself. Its function is stimulation. Value is found in giving esthetic expression to Judaism as experience.

The work of this talented ceramic sculptor/potter is as powerful and poetic as his statement. His interpretations of ceremonial artifacts in white, black, and brown clays indeed "open the door to contemplation." He accepts commissions for both functional and nonfunctional Judaica, including one-of-a-kind objects for synagogue and homes as well as large (6') indoor or outdoor architectural works.

Susan Duhan Felix
1437 Addison St. • Berkeley, Calif. 94702

Susan Felix has been potting since 1958. Her dramatic stoneware and porcelain work has been shown and sold in museums and galleries all across the country, including the Museum of Contemporary Crafts, the Jewish Museum, and America House in New York; and the Oakland Museum and the San Francisco Art Festival in California. She has been teaching ceramics at the Art Co-op in Berkeley since 1968. She makes handbuilt Hanukkah lamps, spice boxes, Sabbath plates, and Kiddush cups. Commissions to make Torah breastplates and spice boxes have come from the Judah L. Magnes Museum in Berkeley, and the Hillel at the University of California has asked her to make a communal Kiddush cup. She would "be happy to try almost anything on com-

SUSAN DUHAN FELIX, handbuilt stoneware menorah-form Hanukkah lamp. (photo: Sandy Solmon)

EDITH FISHEL, three stoneware spice boxes with luster glaze.

mission,'' and she does accept mail orders. Because of the elegance and simplicity of her textured clay forms, Susan Felix's work has a timeless quality about it. Her Hanukkah lamps, for example, while elegantly contemporary have a starkness and strength suggestive of the Maccabean revolt.

Edith Fishel
1192 Park Ave. • New York, N.Y. 10028

The delightful porcelain and stoneware ''street'' hanukkiot of Edith Fishel were on display 'at the Jewish Museum in November 1975 and were sold in their gift shop. They are available by mail directly from Ms. Fishel on special order. They can stand or be hung on a wall; several together make a charming street scene. It might be nice to commission one for each of your children. Again, using the house motif, Ms. Fishel makes porcelain mezuzot, which, because of their attention to detail and ornament are reminiscent of traditional silver mezuzot. I've struck up quite a correspondence with Edith and several of her pieces grace my own collection of contemporary Judaica. Her

most recent efforts include a series of exquisitely charming porcelain Havdalah spice containers. She writes that she has ''no catalog . . . prefer doing one-of-a-kind things. I have enjoyed doing commissions and would be delighted to take more. I will answer any letters, but do not mass produce anything.'' Since *The New York Times* featured her work, along with that of Renee Vishinsky and Joan Mesznik, in its ''Home Beat'' section in December 1979, I don't think she will have any trouble finding homes for her unique art objects.

Sarah Fuhro
20 Elm Street • Brookline, Mass. 02146

Sarah Fuhro is a graphic artist and painter who makes intriguing stoneware tiles illustrating stories from the Bible. The tiles vary in size from about 8″ × 12″ to 10″ × 14″. The background color of the clay is a light yellow ochre. The incised lines are filled with metal oxides so that the drawings stand out clearly. Some of the picture surface is painted with earth tone oxides and slips in shades of blue, brown, green, and black. Sarah likes drawing in the clay because ''the surface adds something of its own to the image; it also seems to connect to the period that these stories come from. Clay lasts a long time without deteriorating, just as these stories have. The colors of the clay and

SARAH FUHRO, stoneware tile, David the shepherd playing for King Saul.

LESLIE GATTMAN, porcelain platters, $20; Kiddush cups, 7", $7; mezuzah with woodscrews, 3½" × 1", $4.00; minimum order $100; 3% packing charge.

oxides seem like desert colors and I try to make the illustrations as close as possible to the way I heard these stories before I could read." Each tile is set in a ready-to-hang bracket which can be removed easily if another method of display is preferred. The tiles vary in price from $25–$100; most are about $50. Sarah will send slides ($5.00 deposit) to prospective clients and would be willing to illustrate particular stories or to expand the concept of these drawings so they could be used in a large public space.

Leslie Gattmann
9261 E. Zayante Rd. • Felton, Calif. 95018

Leslie Gattman's work is refreshing and extremely usable. Her full-color brochure describes it as "ovenproof, dishwasher safe, and finished in nontoxic glazes." She has been a serious potter for four years, two at the University of California and two in business. She began making Judaica because she wanted to integrate her "Jewishness" with her ceramic work. She lived in Israel for a year and a half and became enamored with Hebrew calligraphy which she uses exuberantly to decorate her wares. Her Kiddush cup is lovely in the hand; it is simultaneously folkloric and elegant.

Kathy Goos
11 Peters St. • Cambridge, Mass. 02139
or: 720 Massachusetts Ave. #8
Cambridge, Mass. 02139

Whether she is working with handbuilt or wheel-thrown forms—or a combination of the two—this extremely talented potter consistently produces

KATHY GOOS, stoneware Hanukkah lamp, $40 plus shipping.

ware with a clean, elegant, almost Scandinavian line. Most of her glazes are thinned to allow the manganese flecked clay body to show through. Her glazes are applied by dipping but nevertheless show a sure painter's eye. Her platters, for instance, seem to contain elemental landscapes, and her use of blues and purples must be seen to be believed. She has certain standard items, such as the Hanukkah lamp shown here, an extraordinary Havdalah set, and a simple yahrzeit candle holder. She will also accept special commissions for tableware, as well as for ceremonial objects.

Harry Green
4735 Mercier • Kansas City, Mo. 64112

Even though Harry Green's sculpture is primarily described in the *Art for Architecture* section, it is not beyond the means of the individual collector. Many of his pieces are made in limited editions of about 100 and begin in price at about $60. I particularly covet the lion head mizrah shown in *Art for Architecture*; it is 15″ × 16″ and costs $105. Mr. Green likes to be visited in his studio by out-of-towners interested in Jewish art because he feels "isolated . . . not only as an artist but geographically." So, if you are planning a trip his way, write or call and make a date. *(See Creating: Art for Architecture and Observing: Life Cycle and Holidays and Ceremonies)*

Elee Koplow
c/o Clay Dragon Studios
26 Otis St. • Cambridge, Mass. 02141

A painter and ceramic artist, Elee Kaplow has been making art objects since childhood. At first, her Jewish work, which was inspired by memories of her mother blessing Shabbat candles and by family celebrations, was done almost "in secret" and it was her secular work which took precedence. But after a seven-month stay in Jerusalem, she began seeking ways to interpret her love of Jewish life in a contemporary manner. The resultant works are absolutely captivating. Her sculptured figures, which are made with a clay armature over which thin slabs are draped to resemble clothes, are ordinary people with their endearing qualities and foibles out in the open. Some of the work is in colored clays with bright and muted glazes; other pieces are white, highly-glazed porcelain. Her prices range from $75–$800 and she is open to commissions. Right now she is working, along with another ceramist at Clay Dragon Studios, on 600 large tiles for a playground in Cambridge. Several neighborhood children are working on the tiles along with her. This type of community-artist interaction would be a very worthwhile direction for Jewish centers and synagogues to consider.

HARRY GREEN working on a commissioned bust of the Biblical Ruth.

ELEE KOPLOW, "The Mayor" (12″ tall), and "The Mayor's Wife" (10″ tall), stoneware.

ELEE KOPLOW, "Rabbi", 20" tall, porcelain.

Eve Lurie
2736 Forest Ave. • Berkeley, Calif. 94705

Eve Lurie specializes in wheel-thrown porcelain and stoneware dinnerware, Seder plates, and Hanukkah lamps. The colors she favors are tones of brown and blue. Her prices range from $6 for a mug to $35 for a Seder plate. Prices do not include shipping, which is paid for by the customer. Minimum order for wholesale is $100. Orders will be delivered within six weeks of receipt of the order.

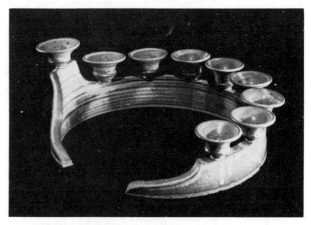

EVE LURIE, wheel-thrown stoneware Hanukkah lamp, $35. (photo: Ed Kirwan)

Joan S. Mesznik
VESSELS
254 West 81 St.
New York, N.Y. 10024 (212-799-8085)

Joan Mesznik, whose portrait begins this chapter, is as incredibly capable in calligraphy as she is in ceramics. She has a wide range of Judaica available; some of the more popular items are Kiddush cups, Havdalah sets, Hanukkah lamps and Seder plates. The items are priced from $12–$65 and she accepts mail orders. Send an SASE for her brochure. In June 1977 she opened her store, Vessels, which has a small showroom in the front and a studio where visitors will always find Joan at work in the back.

Joan is a very special person. While the photographs in the book speak eloquently of her work, I would like to let her tell you a little about herself. We are very good friends and I hope that she will forgive me for making public snatches of her letters to me. I feel that what she has to say could be important for others also.

WORK: "The shop which I opened, VESSELS, is really taking off nicely. I have quit my social work job (Nov. 1978 after 12 years), and am now working in Hebrew calligraphy and Jewish ceremonial objects out of clay full-time. I have never felt so good about a decision. Of course, working free-lance is scary as I do not know where the money is coming from on a day-to-day basis. But somehow I know that this is my spot in life and will persist in this as long as I am able. The people who come into the shop and purchase things are mostly under 40. I have come to terms with the silver-crystal crowd and now have a better understanding of them and their way of life.

I work about 16–18 hours a day and yet it is not like work at all. It is just expressing myself in the most wonderful way possible, through my Judaism and through my art. And I do hope that someday I shall be able to say that I helped bridge the gap between Art and Judaism and that others will remember me for this effort. This is most important to me. To help others become aware of what lies within their very midst, within the heart of Judaism. As you can see, I am a bit of a romantic. Every artist is."

JEWISH ART: "I am so proud to be a part of the new renaissance of Jewish Art. Sometimes I feel like hitting my head against the wall but the rewards are much more than the rejections. I have kept a very exact account of what has been going on in the past 5 years and I see that the interest has grown greatly. I find that dealing with Jews exclusively is sometimes very frustrating. They want the best, the biggest, and the cheapest. A tough crowd to do business with. But it keeps me on my toes and the quality must be of the best at all times."

QUALITY: "I always find it strange that I may do 99 wonderful pieces, and the 100th piece may not be up to par. And it is that 100th piece that people hear about. So, I constantly try to avoid that 100th piece! But, once in a while it does crop up. If someone is not happy with the piece, which does happen from time to time (fortunately, not too often) I keep the piece, with no obligation to the purchaser. I never take a deposit, and Mae, I have *never* had a bad check! I must be sure that the purchaser is 100% happy with the piece before I will give it to him/her."

Is it any wonder that I think Joan Mesznik is wonderful?

JOAN MESZNIK, stoneware etrog container available in choice of 4 glazes and different knobs. Author's collection.

JOAN MESZNIK, Havdalah set ($65). Author's Collection. (photo: Kenneth Bernstein)

CHAVA WOLPERT RICHARD, Seder plate, 12", porcelain. The plates are made to Ms. Richard's specifications and are available from her studio in the Tobe Pascher Workshop. (See *Creating: Enamel.*) (photo: Chava Wolpert)

Mudflat Pottery
Ken Rosenfeld and Lois Hirshberg
25 First St. • Cambridge, Mass. 02141

The Boston area has a number of cooperative ceramic studios, and Mudflat is one of the most interesting. It is there that Ken Rosenfeld and Lois Hirshberg make their distinctive ceramic Judaica. Lois studied for a year in Jerusalem at the Bezalel

MUDFLAT POTTERY: KEN ROSENFELD, oil-burning Hanukkah lamp. The wicks are held in place by small handcarved clay "stones". (photo: Walter Silver)

Academy of Arts and Design. Her work is functional and sculptural and she has recently started to make delightful doll-sized Hannukah lamps. She has a price list available ($5–$60) and accepts commissions.

Ken became interested in Judaic festival crafts after entering a fair held in the Jewish Community Center in Marblehead. This encouraged him to explore his Jewish heritage from a new and exciting perspective. He is always looking for new things to make and new ways of making them. He recently spent a morning in my study poring over books on ceremonial art. After much discussion, he came up with several powerful interpretations of Yahrzeit lamps, which are dramatic enough for synagogue use but which can also be used at home since they accomodate a standard memorial candle. He is a master of subtle glazing. Write for an updated price list.

Leon I. Nigrosh
11 Chatanika Avenue
Worcester, Mass. 01602

The domestic ceremonial objects of Leon Nigrosh are elegant, careful, and sophisticated. Each piece is one-of-a-kind, handmade in porcelain, and decorated in one or more semiprecious metallic luster glazes. His prices depend on the size and complexity of the piece, as well as the glazes used,

LEON I. NIGROSH, Elijah's cup and plate, wheel-thrown porcelain with metallic and gold luster glaze, 9" tall. (photo: John L. Russell)

but they range from $30–$165 and up. He invites commissions and dealer inquiries. There is no charge for his descriptive list but an SASE is helpful.

Lynn Rosen
Yetzirah Pottery
1904 W. 49th St.
Minneapolis, Minn. 55409

Pottery by Lynn Rosen has a sturdy, playful quality which is very appealing. She often collaborates with Barbara Davis who embellishes the pottery with fine brushwork. They offer a variety of clay colors and glazes and welcome orders combining other possible variations. Prices range from $15 for Kiddush cups to $100 for decorated Seder platters. Inquiries are invited from individuals and dealers. Brochure is available free of charge. Lynn is available for craft fairs and lectures in the Midwest— elsewhere if her way is paid.

ARMAND SZAINER, ceramic synagogue menorah, approximately 3' high. (photo: Bill Finney)

LYNN ROSEN, oil-burning Hanukkah lamp, 9" wide, 7" tall. (photo: J. Ben Rosen)

Armand Szainer
308 Sagamore St. • Manchester, N.H. 03104

Armand Szainer was born into a traditional Jewish-Polish family in 1914. His father was a Torah scribe and taught *cheder*. In 1918 the family moved to Germany, where Armand was raised and educated. In 1933 he fled to Paris where he worked as a display designer. When the war broke out, he was granted French citizenship and was called into the army. He was taken prisoner in 1940 and shipped to Germany, where he worked in a forced-labor camp as a lumberjack, until he was liberated in 1945. His brother died in Auschwitz and all his Polish relatives perished. After the war Armand went back to Paris, took up his art studies again and then worked as a stage designer for the Yiddish Art Theatre in Paris and Brussels. With his wife Sylvia, a dermatologist, he emigrated to the United States in 1951 and settled in Manchester, New Hampshire. In June 1980 he retired from his teaching position at Notre Dame College where he taught design, drawing, and painting, and plans to spend a lot more time in his studio painting and sculpting. He writes that besides menorahs he has some ideas for Seder plates, wall plaques, spice boxes, etc. He is interested in commissioned work and would submit sketches to the prospective client.

Schaefer Studios
9125 St. Marks Pl. • Fairfax, Va. 22030

Rita Schaefer is half of this husband-and-wife craft team; she does ceramics and he silversmithing (see *Creating: Metal*). She has several production items for which she will accept mail orders. I particularly like her natural clay mizrah plaque which, because of its two "domes" and stonelike texture, is suggestive of Jerusalem. It is available in two sizes: 5″ × 8″ and 8″ × 10″. Her stoneware Sabbath candlesticks are unusual in that they are formed like a bottle with two or three necks. Each opening holds a candle and the body of the bottle form has the candlelighting blessing carved into it. It is approximately 12″ high. She also makes a series of pleasantly shaped goblets with Shalom or L'chaim in Hebrew carved in the base. She will accept commissions for other objects. Interesting illustrated brochure available.

Hal Silverman
62 Somerstown Rd. • Ossining, N.Y. 10562

Hal Silverman makes free-form sculptural oil- or candle-burning menorot. His work is unglazed but because it is fired to stoneware temperatures becomes vitreous and the oxides in the clay itself give subtle earth-tone color variations to the surface. Since he works as a ceramist only part time, he has no inventory. He rarely makes the same piece twice. Exceptions to this, however, were the very handsome oil-burning Hanukkah lamps he made for the Jewish Museum. He will accept commissions for the oil-burning lamp but says he can't usually promise quick delivery unless he happens to have one already made.

HAL SILVERMAN, stoneware, oil-burning "Wall" Hanukkah lamp. (photo: Karen Silverman)

Renee Vichinsky
446 12th St. • Brooklyn, N.Y. 11215

The ceremonial objects made by Renee Vichinsky include Hanukkah lamps and Sabbath candleholders assembled from wheel-thrown parts, plates for Passover, wine goblets, washing vessels, and Havdalah spice containers. Her work is highly fired stoneware. She has a variety of lead-free glazes in matte and glossy colors. A round Hanukkah lamp in a matte green glaze ranges in price from $20 (8″ diameter) to $30. An 8″ high menorah-form candlestick for two candles costs about $15. She will accept mail orders with a deposit and is happy to negotiate commissions.

RENEE VICHINSKY, menorah-form Hanukkah lamp.

Rebecca Lynn Wachtel
807 Haines • Champaign, Illinois 61820

The pleasure Rebecca Lynn Wachtel takes in her work is evident in the unpretentiousness of her designs and in the sheer number of different things she makes. For Shabbat there are candlesticks, hallah plates, Kiddush cups, Havdalah sets; for Hanukkah: lamps for candles or oil and dreidels; for Pesah: Seder plates, matzah plates, wine decanters and goblets, Elijah's cup, pitcher-and-bowl sets for washing; for Sukkot: etrog containers; for counting the Omer: Sefirat ha-Omer boards. She also makes Yahrzeit candleholders for the High Holidays and other memorial days, mezuzah containers, and personalized door plaques (name in English and Shalom in Hebrew). Her prices range from $12 (a mezuzah container) to $250, depending on the work involved. She accepts commissions.

REBECCA LYNN WACHTEL, hanging stoneware Hanukkah lamp with mirror, 15". (photo: Alex Sorkin)

REBECCA LYNN WACHTEL: handpainted etrog holder, 9" high. (photo: Alex Sorkin)

Glass and Enamel

HERA MODEL MAKERS, 300 sq. ft. stained-glass mural for Temple Israel, New Rochelle, N.Y. Dedicated to the themes of God's Creation, the Children of Israel, and The Torah. Artist Ami Shamir.

Nowhere in writing about the art objects in this book is it more frustrating to be bound by mere words and black and white images than in attempting to describe the qualities of glass and enamel. Fortunately, in recent years, glass (stained, antique, clear, and faceted) has once again become a popular medium for the artist as well as the hobbyist. So your imagination can fill in the colors and shimmering light which makes us gasp with delight when viewing an exquisite piece of glass craftsmanship. I'm happy to present in these pages artists and artisans who are revitalizing this traditional craft and using their skills to enhance the Jewish home and the synagogue. A number of artists who are listed under different specialties also work directly in stained-glass or do designs for glass workshops to execute. You will also find several craftspeople in this section who work with other forms of glass (such as enamel) to create unique Judaica.

FRANN S. ADDISON, oil-burning Hanukkah lamp, beveled glass and brass. Author's collection.

Frann S. Addison
33 Lunt St. • N. Quincy, Mass. 02171

Frann Addison is primarily a metalsmith, yet her ability to skillfully combine glass with works in silver, brass, pewter, and white metal warrants her

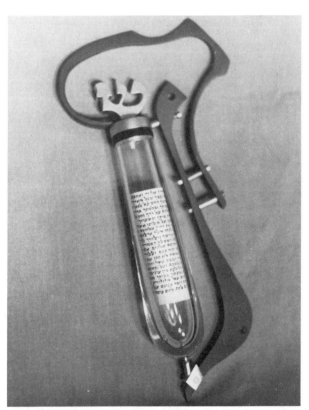

FRANN S. ADDISON, mezuzah, 24K goldplated brass, titanium, and handblown glass.

inclusion here. Of great appeal to her is the fact that the Jewish religion is largely centered around the family and the home; that each family member is in some way a participant in the religious ritual. For this reason she has put a great deal of thought and effort into the design and creation of domestic ceremonial pieces. I am particularly enamored of her beveled glass and brass oil-burning Hanukkah lamp. See *Creating: Metal* for more of Frann's work.

Ingeborg Bookstaber
100 Old Pascack Rd.
Pearl River, N.Y. 10965

Cloisonné enameling is the specialty of Berlin-born Ingeborg Bookstaber. Copper overlaid with silver and gold foil form the base for her decorative pieces. Fine silver wires define the essential areas of the design, which is then filled in with jewel-like enamel. Her pieces are either free-standing or wall-hanging; many are mounted in sculpted walnut stands. She writes that she is "mostly absorbed in my own expressions; however, when there is clear communication with the client and when the challenge lends itself to this unique art form, I occasionally accept commissions".

INGEBORG BOOKSTABER, "Pomegranate Tree", fine silver wire with transparent colors on silver foil. Enamel piece is 6" in diameter, mounted in a round walnut frame. (photo: Dennis Bookstaber)

INGEBORG BOOKSTABER, "Adam and Eve", fine silver wires with subtle opalescent enamels, approximately 7" × 8", mounted on free-standing sculpture walnut. (photo: Dennis Bookstaber)

Renate Fisher Chernoff
9417 Copenhaver Drive
Potomac, Md. 20854

Renate Chernoff considers herself to be an enamelist first and a weaver as a close second. Because enamels must be beautifully set, she is familiar with many metal techniques such as casting, forging, raising, stonesetting, etc., and has used them separately in the manufacture of ceremonial artifacts. She has worked in silver alone and in silver set with enamel: mezuzot, ceremonial wedding rings, buckles for Torah belts, pointers, Torah breastplates, Kiddush cups, and Torah finials (*rimmonim*). Sometimes Ms. Chernoff sets the enamels in wood for mezuzot, pointers, and wall ornaments. She accepts commissions for any of the above items as well as for tallitot, Torah mantles, and tapestries.

RENATE F. CHERNOFF, mezuzah, 6" × 1¼", cloisonné enamel on fine silver, mounted in walnut on sterling silver. (photo David E. Richer)

Jean-Jacques Duval
Box 351 • Pawling, N.Y. 12564

Jean-Jacques Duval has executed over 250 commissions in stained-glass, tapestries, and mosaics for synagogues and other public buildings all over the country. He works in both stained and faceted glass and will send a set of 35 mm colored slides on request. He is also the author of *Working With Stained Glass*, published by T. Y. Crowell. (Also see opening photo in *Art for Architecture* for another example of Duval's work.)

NANCY GOLDEN, etrog box, 6½"w × 4"h × 4½"d.

JEAN-JACQUES DUVAL, B'nai Jacob, Woodbridge, Conn.

Nancy A. Golden
14 Clements Rd. • Newton, Mass. 02158

Using the painstaking Tiffany method of foil and solder, Nancy Golden creates intricately designed stained-glass panels and windows which incorpo-

NANCY GOLDEN, Hanukkah lamp, 10"w × 13"h × 4"d.

rate realistic interpretations of traditional symbols. She has recently completed a set of ten windows for Beth Pinchas, the Hasidic Center in Brookline, Mass. Each of the 16" × 24" windows is made up of at least 150 small pieces of glass. She will custom-make panels in various sizes (from 5" × 8" to just about any size desired), she has several designs reading Shalom and Chai, and will do designs using family names (she suggests a tree of life). For synagogues she will make ark doors as well as windows and illuminated panels. As well as synagogue pieces, Mrs. Golden has a number of designs for domestic ritual articles. She is also interested in portraiture and will accept commissions. Write for her brochure.

Hera Model Makers
Stained Glass Workshops
307 W. 38th Street • New York, N.Y. 10018

Hera Model Makers produces superbly crafted stained-glass windows and murals in leaded antique imported glass, or contemporary faceted slab glass. They work with handpainted designs as well as etched and enameled surfaces. The workshop services all aspects of a project, beginning with the rendering of a colored sketch and through all phases of fabrication and installation. One of the stained-glass works shown on these pages, designed by Ami Shamir, was produced in the Hera workshops. For consultations, brochure, and price quotations, write or call.

Harriet Hyams
210 Van Buren Ave. • Teaneck, N.J. 07666

Harriet Hyams designs contemporary stained-glass for residences and public buildings. She also makes mirrors and will accept commissions.

HARRIET HYAMS, Justice Window in Temple Beth-El, Jersey City, N.J. (photo: Charles Shimel)

Scott and Christy Kendrick
320 Hammond St. • Bangor, Me. 04401

Scott and Christy are a self-taught husband-and-wife-team. They got started five years ago by the desire to make a lampshade to give as a wedding gift. Lamps have been their primary interest and specialty since then. Don't be put off by their informal hobbyist beginnings; the work of this remarkable couple is destined to be sought after and praised by *afficionados* of the craft. When I walked into their studio in the summer of 1979, I was awestruck by the delicacy and complexity of their designs and workmanship. Their lamps are very much in the Tiffany tradition, not only because they manipulate art nouveau motifs with ease, but because of their use of subtle colors and lines and their exquisite taste. Prompted by my desire to include them in this volume, they recently completed a Ner Tamid for the Beth Israel synagogue in Bangor. Christy had never worked with Jewish thematic material before but they researched and came up with a lamp which would be comfortable anywhere. The lead glass shade is constructed of handstenciled and etched ruby flashed glass panels depicting the Burning Bush. They always use the highest quality materials and if they are unsatisfied with a cut line or a color choice they tear the piece apart and start again. All of their pieces are one-of-a-kind or limited editions. They prefer to create special pieces for particular people, places, or groups. I am hoping that by introducing their work to the readers of this book they will get to embellish many more synagogues with their artistry.

Margaret November
6030 N. 22nd Rd. • Arlington, Va. 22205

Margaret November makes clear glass plates, which have bright-colored abstracted menorah forms kiln-fired onto them. The plates range in price and size from $7.50 for a 7¼" diameter plate (shown here) to $20 for a 12½" dinner-size plate with either a blue or patina-green abstracted menorah. It is an attractive idea, and the plates are useful for various holidays. It would be nice to fill them with homemade goodies as Purim *mishlo' ah manot* gifts. Ms. November also has several other designs, all available for the cost of the plate plus $1 for shipping and handling. Write her for more details.

Chava Wolpert Richard
The Tobe Pascher Workshop
The Jewish Museum
1109 Fifth Ave. • New York, N.Y. 10028

Chava Richard is one of three artists-in-residence at the Tobe Pascher Workshop at the Jewish Museum in New York City. She is a talented designer and has created a number of objects that appear elsewhere in these pages. Her one-of-a-kind enamel pieces are very special; it seems an ideal medium for her talent as a graphic designer to be transmuted through her skill as a jeweler and metalsmith into objects of stunning beauty. Her elegantly worked and brilliantly colored enameled *rimmonim* and Torah scroll breastplates would enhance many a synagogue. She accepts commissions.

William Saltzman
5140 Lyndale Ave. S.
Minneapolis, Minn. 55419

Bill Saltzman is as well-known in the Midwest for his secular commissions (Mayo Clinic) as for the stained-glass he has done for synagogues. He works in other media as well as glass and welcomes inquiries from all over the country.

Eva Schonfield
2412 Briarwood Rd.
Baltimore, Md. 21209

Every glass object by Eva Schonfield is executed freehand with no form or mold, using the ancient process of "lampworking," in which the glass is softened in a white-hot flame and then shaped with simple hand tools. She emphasizes usefulness and durability as much as beauty. Her material is borosilicate, the same crystal used for laboratory vessels, and her designs can be safely cleaned by pouring boiling water over them and drying with a soft cloth. The objects are available in four different colors as well as clear glass. Her elegant designs, which appear fragile, are quite strong; should one of her pieces break, it can be fused either by the artist or any professional glass blower. She makes an interesting Hanukkah lamp which combines the warmth of a rosewood base with clear glass candleholders and a unique Sabbath candlestick. The Jewish Museum in New York sells her free-form mezuzot, which come boxed and complete with screws. These are available from the artist as well. Ms. Schonfield will consider commissions if she is given latitude to carry out her own ideas freely.

EVA SCHONFIELD, handformed glass and rosewood Hanukkah lamp.

AMI SHAMIR, children's chapel at Vancouver Talmud Torah. The ark, on a stylized ladder representing "Jacobs Dream", is silhouetted against a composition of the "spheres", done in antique lead glass in brilliant greens and blues.

Ami Shamir
Shamir Studio Art and Design, Inc.
307 West 38th St. • New York, N.Y. 10018

Ami Shamir, whose work was also discussed in *Art for Architecture*, has designed some spectacular glass window walls. Two of these are shown in this chapter.

Marian Slepian
5 Overlook Drive
Bridgewater, N.Y. 08807

Marian Slepian turned from oil painting to enameling as her exclusive medium when she realized that the vivid brilliance and luminousity of color she loves are achievable only with these fused glass powders. The enamel techniques she most often employs are cloisonné and limoge.

Step-by-step illustrations of her working methods are in *The Container Book*, by Thelma Newman, Crown publishers. She makes one-of-a-kind enamel paintings based on Biblical and Judaic themes. These are raised, mounted on lucite, and framed in aluminum unless otherwise requested. They range in price from $400–$2000. Ms. Slepian is also interested in doing murals, which are priced according to size and complexity. She will also undertake small, personalized enamels for Bar and Bat Mitzvahs, Weddings, and anniversaries.

MARIAN SLEPIAN, cloisonné enamel.

MARIAN SLEPIAN at work with one of her 3 enameling kilns.

Mark Stine
Transparent Dreams
1350 Cook St. • Denver, Colo. 80206

Mark Stine is as familiar with the copper-foil technique of working with stained-glass as with lead, and he uses both extensively. The choice between the two depends upon the particular project. Before beginning a design, he explains to his client why one will lend itself better to the work at hand than the other. He will consider all commissions, and if the project is too big to be shipped he will consider moving temporarily to the site of the job and working on it there. His craftsmanship is meticulous, and he makes every effort to keep his prices low.

MARK STINE, framed stained-glass hanging piece.

Metal

FRANN ADDISON at her anvil forging a part for a ceremonial piece. (photo: Andrew Addison)

Ever since Bezalel created the first menorah of pure beaten gold, according to God's specific directions, for the desert tabernacle of the wandering Hebrews fresh out of Egypt, metal ceremonial objects and ornaments have graced our places of worship. Since the destruction of the second Temple in 70 C.E., the home table has become our altar and the ceremonies which often have the most meaning for us take place there. So, throughout the ages, domestic ritual articles of precious and humble metals have been made.

With today's escalating gold and silver prices it is not surprising to find that many craftspeople (to their client's relief) are working in less costly metals. The value, then, is where it should be: in the artistry. In this section you will find artists making everything from tiny pieces of jewelry to monumental sculptural works, working in a variety of styles and techniques which is truly impressive. Mass produced metal ritual items can be found in the *Observing* section; jewelry in the *Buying* section.

Frann Addison
100 Cypress St. • Watertown, Mass. 02172

Prophesying the future is always a risky business, but I feel very strongly that it is only a matter of time until this remarkable young woman receives the recognition her work merits. Frann Addison is, in a sense, the artistic "grandchild" of the Grand Old Man of contemporary Judaica, Ludwig Wolpert. She cites him and his disciple, Bernard Bernstein, as her two major sources of inspiration. Their influence is obvious in some of her work, but she has such a personal way of interpreting the functions of the ritual Judaica she creates that the pieces are uniquely hers. She works independently in her own studio, creating her commissioned ceremonial pieces for private individuals as well as for institutions. She will accept commissions to duplicate pieces she has already created, such as the ones shown in these pages, and to design new objects for customers with specific desires. When accepting commissions for new pieces she does several sketches for the proposed work for which there is a charge based on the complexity of the design. She is available for quality juried craft fairs and presents a 45 minute slide show and lecture on the history and development of the ceremonial objects most commonly used by the Jewish family. Contact her for further information and prices. (See also *Glass and Enamel* and *How To* sections.)

FRANN ADDISON, 2-tiered Seder plate (bottom tier holds matzah), nickel silver and Plexiglas.

Gunther Aron
The Old School House • Lamy, N.M. 87540

Working in steel, silver, bronze, and copper, Gunther Aron creates graceful and unique contemporary Jewish ceremonial objects. Particularly noteworthy are his many elegant, textured Hanukkah lamps (approximately 5' tall). He accepts commissions and is well worth contacting. Gunther says that he loves to be visited in his studio. He is just 16 miles from Sante Fe, so if you are in the area or traveling his way, call and come by.

GUNTHER ARON, Hanukkah lamp which can be enjoyed as sculpture all year long.

Suzanne Benton
22 Donnelly Dr. • Ridgefield, Conn. 06877

If Suzanne Benton's ritual masks of Biblical women were made to be used only as decorative freestanding or wall ornaments that would (to borrow

SUZANNE BENTON, "Mothers of Israel," limited edition bronze wall sculpture created under the sponsorship of the Judah Magnus Museum, 17" × 18½" × 3", $1200.

JANET BERG, silver ceremonial wedding ring. Hebrew inscription on the band says: "I will betroth thee unto me." Under opening roof inside house is the word *Mazal;* about 2" high.

from the Pesah song "Dayenu") be sufficient. But Ms. Benton's work goes further. She uses these incredibly powerful and sensitive welded-metal interpretations of our matriarchs in ritual performances of ancient tales focusing on the women as central characters. Her masks and presentation of "Sarah and Hagar," for example, provide a new approach to our understanding of the Genesis story usually known as that of Abraham and Isaac. She will accept commissions for masks based on any Biblical character of the client's choice. It is, of course, preferable to visit her studio, but she will mail a very intriguing brochure that includes photographs of a dozen different masks, as well as a detailed biographical resume. She is also available for ritual performances, lifestory workshops, exhibitions, and processions. (See *Learning: Programs* for photograph of "Hagar's Mask.")

Janet Berg
c/o Bezalel Art Academy
Metal Arts Dept.
Ado Hanavi St.
Jerusalem, Israel
or:
3741 Midvale Ave. • Oakland, Calif. 94602

Janet Berg made aliyah to Israel last year. She is now lecturing at the Bezalel Academy and making beautiful intricate jewelry. Shown here is a ceremonial wedding ring with lift-top roof, but more practical for "everyday" are the name and/or quotation rings she makes in a variety of styles and scripts. These range in price from $10 up; the average quotation ring is $100–$200. Her craftsmanship is meticulous, she studied filigree work at the workbench of some of the best Yemenite jewelers, and her designs incorporate both traditional and contemporary motifs. If you are in Israel, contact her through the Bezalel Academy; in this country you can write to her at her parent's address in California.

Bernard Bernstein
Department of Industrial Education
City College of New York
138 St. and Convent Ave.
New York, N.Y. 10031

The work of Bernard Bernstein reflects his study with Ludwig Wolpert, the director of the Tobe Pascher Workshop at the Jewish Museum in New York. Dr. Bernstein's Ph.D. dissertation in creative arts included the design and construction of Jewish ceremonial objects as well as a historical study of them. At present, he teaches design and

BERNARD BERNSTEIN, Aquarius pendant from his patented zodiac series.

DANIEL BLUMBERG, silver Kiddush cup with blessing in Hebrew and Hebrew Braille . (See also: *Observing, Charity.*)

jewelry making at CCNY and designs and makes ceremonial objects for the Jewish home and synagogue. If not already engaged in a commission he will accept a new one, "if a client is willing to wait and does not impose a deadline." His work in gold and silver includes jewelry designs which are made in quantity and available by mail. The zodiac signs have been used frequently in Jewish art and Bernie has designed a line of very abstract zodiac pendants in silver and gold. Prices range from $25 to $33 for the pendants, including chain, in silver; prices for gold jewelry available on request.

Daniel Blumberg
333 W. Girard Ave.
Philadelphia, Pa. 19123

I always like to think that if I live long enough I will get to do everything I want to. Daniel Blumberg encourages me in this belief. At age seventy, all the skills he has for so many years developed and put into his profession of dentistry have now artistically flowered into unique pieces of ceremonial Judaica. From reading the material he sent me I get the impression that at this point dentistry is his "hobby" and the making of ceremonial objects and jewelry his vocation. He works in gold, silver, enamels, ivory, and rare woods and utilizes many unusual techniques. He accepts commissions for one-of-a-kind objects, including: candlesticks, Havdalah sets, Seder plates, mezuzot, etc. For Dr. Blumberg, artistry goes hand-in-hand with the art of healing. A recent new dimension in his work is a range of objects to used by the blind which are embellished with Hebrew Braille.

Judith Brown
Winter Address: 68 Jane St.
New York, N.Y. 10014
Summer Address: Reading, Vermont 05062

Judith Brown's work in metal ranges from delicate jewelry in silver and vermeil to architectural sculpture in welded brass, copper, and steel. She has several attractive catalogs of her jewelry and sculpture as well as a biographical brochure which contains an impressive list of commissions and awards, and she accepts mail orders and commissions. Ms. Brown has done a limited edition necklace of Noah's Ark, which is six inches long and two inches wide. It comes with a stand for mounting when not being worn. Her approach to ceremonial Judaica is unique and the results are breathtaking. Photos available on request.

JUDITH BROWN, Hanukkah Lamp, steel, 2' wide × 1½' high, $1,000.

Maxwell M. Chayat
RD 1 Box 88 • Monticello, N.Y. 12701

Maxwell Chayat has executed commissions for ritual objects for synagogues and university chapels across the country. He works in bronze, brass, and silver and makes objects which range in size from a small religious pendant to an outdoor sculpture. He accepts commissions and mail orders.

MAXWELL M. CHAYAT, Torah Crown.

Ted Egri
Taos, New Mexico 87571

Ted Egri, who works on commission for synagogues and private residences in a wide variety of materials, has recently completed a striking series of sculptures on the holidays. Shabbat, Rosh Hashanah, Yom Kippur, Sukkot, Passover, and Hanukkah have been poetically abstracted and cast in bronze. These sculptures are available in unnumbered editions and range in price from $500–$1300. Write to Egri for his brochure which is illustrated with excellent photographs of the six pieces.

Annette Fettman
1317 N. 57th St. • Omaha, Nebr. 68132

Annette Fettman makes Hanukkah lamps, mezuzot, and spice boxes in cast aluminum and bronze. Each piece is individually designed, cast, and finished with a patina. Mezuzot start at about $12 (without the handwritten scroll) and Hanukkah lamps begin at $30. As well as these functional objects, she is also working on a series about the Ten Commandments. Photos are available on request. She is interested in the Holocaust and Jews at prayer as subjects for future work. Commissions without deadlines are invited.

Hana Geber
168 W. 225th St. • Bronx, N.Y. 10463

Hana Geber specializes in creating Jewish ceremonial art and figurative sculptures in silver and

HANA GEBER, Kiddush cup, silver bronze, 4" high, $200.

HANA GEBER, Sabbath candleholder with spice box, silver bronze, 8½" tall $700. (photo: Walter Geber)

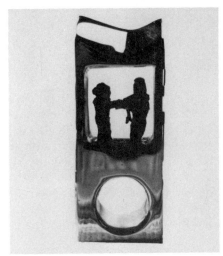

ELLEN GREENFIELD, contemporary cast silver ceremonial wedding ring, 3¾" high × 1½" wide × 1" deep. (photo: Edward Greenfield)

bronze. There is a certain dreamlike quality about Ms. Geber's approach to Jewish thematic material that I find very appealing. Many of her pieces are one-of-a-kind and quite expensive ($2000 price range) but she has made limited editions of some of her castings and they are equally beautiful and less costly. She accepts commissions from private collectors as well as from communal institutions. A descriptive brochure with four representative illustrations of her work is available upon request.

Ellen Greenfield
22 Canterbury Lane
Roslyn Heights, N.Y. 11577

Ellen Greenfield makes small editions of miniature sculptures on Biblical and Judaic themes. She also makes ceremonial pieces and will design custom sculptures based on a Bar/Bat Mitzvah haftorah or for weddings, births, anniversaries, and birthdays. Ellen also does some of her sculptures in stone. She will send photographs of available pieces to prospective clients since her brochure is general in nature. (See also *Playing: Toys*)

Nissim Hizme Hebrew Jewelry, Inc.
89 Canal St. • New York, N.Y. 10002

Because Hizme is a calligrapher as well as a jeweler, his jewelry designs incorporating Hebrew letters are very special. He has a dozen basic styles for Hebrew inscription gold wedding rings and will custom-make other designs as well. He also makes tie bars, cuff links, belt buckles, tallit clips, and pendants—all with the client's Hebrew name imaginatively used to create shapes of birds, animals, plants, or abstract designs. His firm also makes brass plaques for organization presentations. Write for a price list and photo of basic wedding ring styles. (See also *Creating: Calligraphy.*)

Harold L. Kerr
Box 110 • Bayfield, Wis. 54814

Harold Kerr designs and makes decorative sculptures in all metals. He is equally comfortable working on a small scale and on massive garden pieces. His work appears in many public and synagogue collections. A brochure is available, and Mr. Kerr will accept mail orders and commissions.

Carol S. Kestler
1311 E. Duke Drive • Tucson, Ariz. 85719

Carol Kestler's Jewish ritual art comes out of a very committed and intense Judaism in which daily practice and ritual are very important. It is a very personal expression and, like her jewelry, utilizes highly developed surfaces (reticulated, fused, chased, etc). She often mixes metals, copper, brass, silver, and gold for color and meaning. She does both cast bronze sculpture and handwrought pieces. She is personally very interested in fire and light as symbols and loves to work with these; therefore some of her favorite projects are memorial lamps and lighting devices for Shabbat and festivals. Her work combines very natural (one is tempted to say ''primitive'') forms and motifs with excellent craftmanship and sophisticated designs.

DAVID KLASS, Hanukkah Menorah Tree with Lions, copper and brass, 17" wide × 13" high, for oil or candles.

CAROL S. KESTLER, rimmonim (Torah scroll adornments), silver, copper, brass, and bronze, raised, chased, formed, and reticulated with cast bells. Approx. 10½" × 5". (photo: Carol Kestler; lab: Flint Anderson)

David Klass
136 W. 24th St. • New York, N.Y. 10011

Copper and brass are the basic materials that David Klass uses in his sculptural ceremonial objects. Sometimes an iron core is added for strength. Each piece involves the processes of cutting, welding, hammering, and grinding, and when complete it is given a special antique patina. His brochure and price list show ten different Hanukkah lamp designs ranging in price from $100–$200, two

versions of Tree of Life wall sculptures made in any size to order, an electrified menorah, an electrified Shabbat candelabra, and two mezuzot. He also has many one-of-a-kind pieces in his studio.

Kurt J. Matzdorf
19 Apple Rd. • P.O. Box 293
New Paltz, N.Y. 12561

Kurt Matzdorf's work is an effective combination of the contemporary penchant for simplicity with an almost baroque use of materials. The total effect is striking and elegant. He designs and handcrafts the following items for home use: sterling silver Hanukkah lamps, Kiddush cups, spice boxes, Sabbath candlesticks, Seder servers, megillah covers, and etrog boxes. For the synagogue, he makes sterling silver Torah crowns, rimmonim, breastplates, pointers, Kiddush cups, memorial and honorial book covers, as well as bronze menorot, eternal lights, ark door decorations, lobby sculpture, Hanukkah lamps, and memorial walls. Mr. Matzdorf often uses enamels, goldplating, and semiprecious stones to further embellish a particular piece. He accepts mail orders and commissions and will send photos and slides of his work to interested individuals and organizations.

KURT J. MATZDORF at his workbench with several ceremonial pieces.

his cut-and-welded sculptural pieces. He produces a wide variety of ceremonial and religious objects, including Sabbath candelabra, Hanukkah lamps for home and synagogue, mezuzot, Yahrzeit lamp holders, eternal lights, and ark doors, as well as sculpture based on biblical themes or Hebrew phrases. He suitably engraves award and presentation pieces if required. Prices start at $15 for a freestanding sculpture approximately 10" high. Two-light Sabbath candelabra range in price from $20 to $100, depending on size and complexity. Wall sculptures are $25 and up. Mr. Miller will mail work throughout the country and overseas and will accept commissions based on any biblical quotation or theme. Special requests and details as to price, size, and material can be arranged by mail. He will be happy to send you a well-illustrated brochure upon receipt of a stamped, self-addressed, business-sized envelope.

Stanley Miller
R.D. 1. Box 242 • Pittstown, N.J. 08867

Although he works in brass, bronze, and aluminum, Stanley Miller primarily uses steel for

STANLEY MILLER, "Shalom", 12" high, $25. There is no extra charge for a fifteen word (maximum) inscription if it is to be used as an award piece. A word base is available for an additional $3.

Katya Miller-Wallin
5829 Colby St. • Oakland, Calif. 94618

As well as the amulets for which she has a special fascination, Katya Miller-Wallin makes mezuzot as necklaces as well as for doors, Kiddush cups, Shabbat candelabra, and intriguing Hanukkah oil lamps in which little cups for oil are set into natural materials such as rough stone or tree branches. Brochure and price list are available.

KATYA MILLER-WALLIN, oil-burning Hanukkah lamp, hand pounded copper cups in a burl of wood, approx. 11" × 12", $75.

Myrna Balk Nathan
84 Salisbury Rd. • Brookline, Mass. 02146

Myrna Nathan is a sculptor who works primarily with forged and welded steel. She has developed a series of large, contemporary, menorah-form Hanukkah lamps, and also seven branched menorot. Write for more information about her lamps which are scaled for Temple or garden use.

MYRNA NATHAN welding.

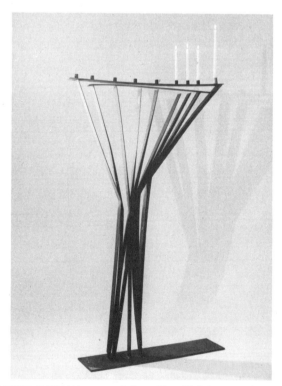

MYRNA NATHAN, menorah form Hanukkah lamp, corten steel, 33" wide, 60" high.

Harold Rabinowitz
Tobe Pascher Workshop
The Jewish Museum
1109 Fifth Avenue • New York, N.Y. 10028

It is not surprising that Harold Rabinowitz' work is reminiscent of that of Ludwig Wolpert and Moshe Zábari since Harold is a Fellow at the Tobe Pascher Workshop where both Wolpert and Zabari work and teach. Harold is also a teacher of jewelry and metal-smithing and has been chairman of the Art Department at the Usdan Center for the Creative and Performing Arts. He works in silver and other metals and often incorporates exotic woods and unusual stones in his work. He will accept commissions from individuals and institutions.

HAROLD RABINOWITZ, Torah ornaments—rimmonim, breastplate and yad (pointer), silver. (photo: Otto E. Nelson)

Chava Wolpert Richard
The Tobe Pascher Workshop
The Jewish Museum
1109 Fifth Ave. • New York, N.Y. 10028

Working in the Tobe Pascher Workshop, Chava Richard has created an interesting line of jewelry. It includes sterling silver mezuzot with beads, Stars of David in various designs, and three different Chai pendants. Write for her brochure with complete price list.

CHAVA WOLPERT RICHARD, sculptured silver Star of David, shown actual size.

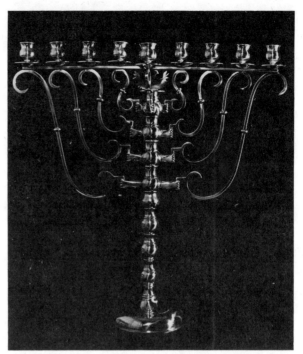

HAROLD ROGOVIN, menorah form Hanukkah lamp in bronze, 24" high, 26" wide; weight 30 lbs, $1250.

Harold Rogovin
P.O. Box 251 • Califon, N.J. 07830

At age 40, Harold Rogovin switched careers. Leaving behind missile guidance systems, he bought a small business which specialized in handmade lighting fixtures and "moved back into the 18th-century," working with simple hand tools. At the same time, he began an intensive study of silversmithing. Now, 14 years later, he has the capability of turning out a wide range of products for the home, all handmade in silver, brass, and bronze. Much of his apprenticeship in silversmithing was spent making reproductions of antique pieces, and some of his work has been sold through shops in the Metropolitan Museum in New York and other museum shops on the east coast. Some of his chandeliers are in the White House and the Library of Congress. His present group of products includes two menorahs and a Kiddush cup. In addition to his own pieces, he can make pieces from a customer's design or copy an existing piece from a photograph or drawing. He will do silversmithing demonstrations within 100 miles of his studio.

Schaefer Studios
9125 St. Marks Pl. • Fairfax, Va. 22030

This is a husband-and-wife operation. Rita Schaefer works with clay (see *Creating: Ceramics*) and Will Schaefer makes silver handwrought jewelry. He specializes in ½" wide silver band rings which have the word Shalom or L'Chaim cut out of the metal in Hebrew. He will accept mail orders and commissions as well.

Nancy Schön
291 Otis Street
West Newton, Mass. 02165

Nancy Schön's sculptures are lyrical expressions of subtle and powerful emotions caught in mottled and gleaming bronze. They beg to be touched and viewed from every possible angle. Nancy sketches

NANCY SCHON, "Minyan", unique bronze piece, 15" high, $10,000.

NANCY SCHON, rear view of "Minyan".

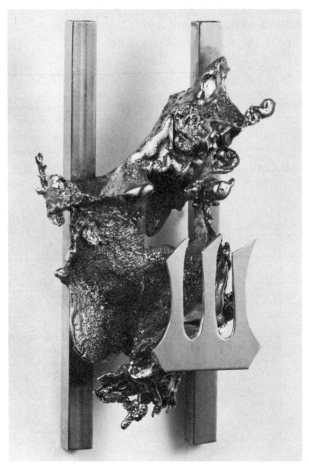

JEAN SCHONWALTER, mezuzah, 2" × 4½", bronze and brass. (photo: Bill Witte)

and sculpts in wax which is then burned away as the piece is cast in bronze (the lost wax process). Slides, biographical information, and black and white photographs are available to dealers or seriously interested individuals. These must be returned. She will accept mail orders and is interested in commissions (no portraits) up to life-size or a foot or two larger. Her prices range from $95 to $10,000.

Jean E. Schonwalter
1F Nob Hill • Roseland, N.J. 07068

Jean Schonwalter does religious and secular bronze sculpture, as well as lithographs and paintings, and has executed quite a few commissions for synagogues. She will correspond through the mail with prospective clients and has two brochures; these are helpful to get an idea of the style and approach of her secular work.

BARBARA W. STANGER, mezuzah wall sculpture with wall bracket, sterling silver, copper, cloisonné enamel, 3¼" high, ed. 25, $495.

Barbara W. Stanger
119 Maple St. • Summit, N.J. 07901

This gifted jeweler specializes in original designs in gold and silver. Sometimes, she will add a touch of copper. She makes a variety of different items, including adaptations of the traditional cere-monial wedding ring and *tallit* clips. In the last few years she has developed a series of mezuzot which are intricately modeled after fantasy towers. These, as well as impressive ceremonial wedding rings and pins (all variations of the tower form), are each more charming than the other and are illustrated in her brochure. Her prices range from about $125–$2,500. Her designs are produced in small editions and she will consider commissions for one-of-a-kind pieces.

LUDWIG WOLPERT constructing a duplicate of the silver and glass Seder plate he first made in 1930 in Germany, for an exhibit of Protestant, Catholic, and Jewish ceremonial art entitled *Kult und Form*. (photo: Mae Rockland)

Ludwig Wolpert, Director
The Tobe Pascher Workshop
at the Jewish Museum
1109 Fifth Ave. • New York, N.Y. 10028

"It is a perfection of form, material, and function, blended simply into one perfect whole." This statement by Frank Lloyd Wright (*New York Post*, November 12, 1958) defines in one sentence the extraordinary work of "the grand old man" of ceremonial Judaica, Ludwig Wolpert. In honor of his seventy-fifth birthday, the Jewish Museum in New York City had a retrospective exhibit of Mr. Wolpert's work in the spring of 1976. The show, which included slides of architectural designs as well as the silver-and-copper Sephardi-style Torah container presented by Chaim Weizmann to Harry S. Truman and lent by the Truman Library for the occasion, showed the incredible range of this gifted man who can create an intimate piece of jewelry or monumental doors for a chapel with equal facility.

One would imagine that a man of Mr. Wolpert's accomplishments and reputation would be totally unapproachable by the "ordinary person" seeking something nice for his or her home. Just the opposite is true. Mr. Wolpert is just as receptive to commissions from individuals as from institutions. For example, he recently completed a silver-encased drinking glass with the *Sheheheyanu* prayer to be given as a seventieth-birthday gift from a wife to her husband. At the bottom of the

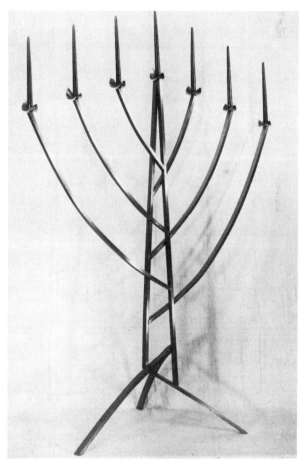

LUDWIG WOLPERT, menorah made for the International Festival of Arts, 1958.

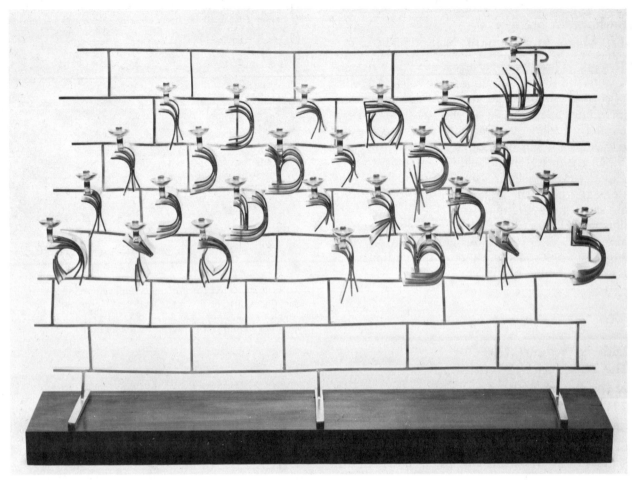

LUDWIG WOLPERT, Sheheheyanu commemorative lamp.

glass is the letter *ayin* which has a numerical value of seventy. He also has created certain domestic objects in editions, and he is willing to duplicate several other simple designs.

Moshe Zabari
The Tobe Pascher Workshop
at the Jewish Museum
1109 Fifth Ave. • New York, N.Y. 10028

Jerusalem-born Moshe Zabari is one of the three artists-in residence at the Jewish Museum in New York City. Working primarily in metal (often silver), Zabari creates ceremonial artifacts that simultaneously embody the simple elegance of contemporary design with the warmth of his interpretation of Jewish custom. Among the many important awards he has received was that of first prize in the international competition sponsored by the Yad Vashem Institute in Jerusalem for his design of the memorial lamp for the six million Jews who died in the Holocaust. I am particularly taken with his treatment of the concept of *tzedakah* (charity), embodied in a series of small collection boxes on view at the Jewish Museum. He accepts commissions from individuals as well as from synagogues and other organizations. Not only is Zabari an extraordinarily talented designer-craftsman, but as a teacher he passes on his knowledge to the students in his classes at the Tobe Pascher Workshop. A gifted graphic artist as well, Zabari has designed a number of important exhibitions for the Jewish Museum in New York and the Skirball Museum in Los Angeles, among others.

Pictures

BILL ARON, "Couple".

"A picture is worth a thousand words", so goes the old saying. I have a certain respect for cliches. They achieve that status because they embody perceived truths so concisely and so well; but they are repeated so often that they finally seem to be only platitudes—hollow, and stale expressions. Unfortunately, in the minds of many, Jewish pictorial art is thought to be nothing but a set of visual cliches: praying rabbis and dancing Hasidim painted on velvet—revered images made trite through repetition and sentimentalization.

The illustrations I've chosen for this section, and indeed for the book as a whole, show that Jewish pictorial art—even when it deals with traditional subject matter—can be as fresh and incisive as that of any other people. The artists whose work is represented in this chapter speak in a visual rather than a verbal language. For them, the test really is that they be able to communicate with one image what otherwise might take many many words. In these pages you will find graphic artists who are able to translate concepts into logos and posters, photographers and painters who record and interpret Jewish life and ideas, and papercutters who are reviving a traditional art-craft. This chapter is only a sample of the richness of the visual arts community; it is simply impossible to include even all of those artists I know about, let alone those I have not yet met. Many of the craftspeople in the other sections of *Creating* also paint, print, photograph, and papercut; and in the *Buying: Art Dealers* section you will find galleries representing even more artists. They can all be contacted for exhibitions and commissions.

Bill Aron
1227 Hi Point
Los Angeles, Calif. 90035

Bill Aron is a photographer and a sociologist, a photo-sociologist, if you will. He does in-depth photographic studies of people, events, times, and places—everyday people and events as well as those in which he has a special historical, sociological, or personal interest. His two year study of the Jewish community on New York's Lower East Side resulted in a portfolio of more than sixty photographs of surpassing beauty and sensitivity which chronicles Jewish life in an atmosphere that is at once familiar and fraught with jarring change.

Bill has recently done a study of the Jews of Cuba and another portfolio entitled "The Golden Age of Venice, California: Portraits of Life". He has prepared moving and informative slide lectures based on his work in Cuba and on the Lower East Side. Write to him for further information and honorarium. Traveling exhibits of his work (which is also available in signed limited editions), can be arranged through the Pucker/Safrai Gallery in Boston; see *Buying: Art Dealers*. For other examples of Bill's work, see *Learning, Playing* and *Observing*. He has been very generous in allowing me to use so much of his work and always seemed to come up with the right picture when I needed it. Bill would be interested in a commission to do a study of a period of time (day, week, month, etc.) in the life of a person, family, or other group. He would also agree to explore photographically a particular problem or event in a community. The product is a photo-essay. He also does regular commercial and portrait work.

Avrum I. Ashery
12212 Greenleaf Ave.
Potomac, Md. 20854

Avrum Ashery is a graphic designer specializing in logos, publications, posters, and exhibits for synagogues, organizations, and businesses. He is a master of Jewish iconography and has come up with many eye catching designs. He works on an hourly basis and offers a 10% discount to religious institutions and organizations (*not* to businesses). Compelling samples of his work are available on request.

BILL ARON, "Victor and Benjamin", from an exhibit entitled: "The Golden Age of Venice, California: Portraits of Life" commissioned by the Skirball Museum, Los Angeles.

AVI ASHERY created this design for B'nai Brith's New Year greeting, 1979/5740. It is reproduced here with permission.

Daniela Barnea
c/o Judah L. Magnes Memorial Museum
2911 Russell St. • Berkeley, Calif. 94705

Daniela Barnea is a talented young Israeli who works principally with etchings. She also does pen-and-ink illustrations and silkscreen. She accepts mail inquiries and orders and is interested in commissions such as book and magazine illustrations and posters.

Jane Bearman
30 Spier Dr. • Livingston, N.J. 07039

A versatile illustrator, Jane Bearman specializes in woodcuts, drawings, and collage paintings. She also does textile work and attractive greeting cards. See *Buying: Needlework.*

JANE BEARMAN, "Mothers of Israel" collage on canvas, 34" × 30", $1,000.

Sandra Bowden
143 Moe Rd. • Clifton Park, N.Y. 12065

In the endless discussion about what constitutes Jewish Art (a question only slightly less thorny than "Who is a Jew?"), it is often asked if a non-Jew can create "Jewish Art". My answer is *yes.* If the work

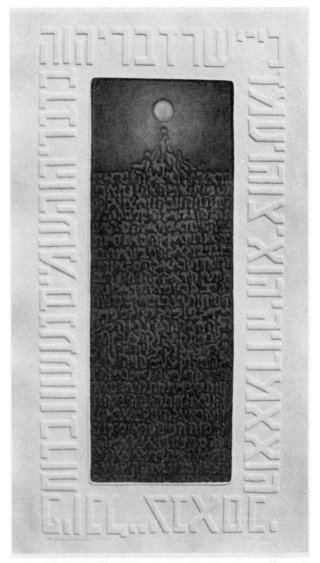

SANDRA BOWDEN, "He spake and it was done", collograph 18" × 30", buff Arches paper, deep green print, $150 unframed.

deals responsibly with Jewish themes and functions, then it is a part of the body of Jewish art. Several of the artists and craftspeople in these pages are not Jewish, but their products are. Sandra Bowden's paintings and prints fall into this category. A deeply religious woman, she writes: "I see the physical earth as a celebration by the Creator. I paint the earth's beauty and truth, and to me, this is the reflection of God." Biblical influence is evident throughout Sandra's paintings and collographs, which use a rich vocabulary of contemporary visual expressions. Her landscapes are inspired by references to the earth in the Book of Psalms. Hebrew calligraphy is often blended into an overall pattern that contrasts with layered strata, reflecting her interest in archeology and geology. Her work is very reasonably priced from $45–$200 for collographs and $300 and up for paintings. Her well-illustrated and elegant brochure is a treat to handle.

Rose Ann Chasman
6147 North Richmond • Chicago, Ill. 60659

Rose Ann Chasman is fascinated by the folkloric. Many of her designs are based on old amulets and mizrahim; she makes them in sizes to accomodate standard plastic box frames. She has also learned how to make a besamim (spice) holder from the lulav, and fills it with myrtle leaves, cloves, and cinnamon sticks. (See also: *Creating: calligraphy; Playing: Travel;* and *Buying: Cards, Gifts and Collectibles.*)

ROSE ANN CHASMAN, paper-cut mizrah, 12" × 16". (photo: Williams and Meyer Co., Chicago)

Stuart A. Copans
44 Putney Road
Brattleboro, Vermont 05301

I wish I could come to some profound conclusions as to why two of my favorite Jewish illustrators are also medical doctors. I leave that for the reader to figure out; but it is curious that Stuart Copans like Mark Podwal is also an M.D. by profession. Their drawings, however, are quite different. Copans uses an almost unbroken wirelike line to create fantastic, almost mystical, images. They are inspired by and infused with intense religious convictions, yet they are tranquil, subtle, and very often humorous. Touches of clear color and an occasional well-placed fingerprint add to their charm and impact. (See *Learning, Buying, Playing,* for more of his drawings.) He accepts commissions for almost anything and would very much like to do some work for synagogues, either working with a congregation or with an architect and congregation to plan a synagogue where the decorations will be created by members themselves.

Frank J. Darmstaedter, Curator
The Photographic Archive of the Jewish
Theological Seminary of America
Broadway and 122nd St.
New York, N.Y. 10027

The Jewish Theological Seminary has an extraordinary collection of photographs dealing with just about any Jewish subject imaginable. Prints are available to scholars and other individuals on a special-order basis.

Detail from an Oppenheim painting. Picture from the photographic archive of the Jewish Theological Seminary of America, N.Y. Frank J. Darmstaedter.

Lois Parks De Castro and Michael De Castro
80 Justin Drive
San Francisco, Calif. 94112

Both De Castros produce work on Jewish themes, together and separately. She is a communications designer and he is a photographer.

Raphael L. Eisenberg
379 Crown St. • Brooklyn, N.Y. 11225

Contrary to what Chaim Potok would have us believe from his novels, painting is not that alien an activity for the contemporary religious Jew. Like Zalman Kleinman, many of Raphael Eisenberg's paintings have religious themes. He handles this material in a very personal way in oil and gouache. He accepts commissions for portraits from life and will consider other requests if they are consonant with his manner of working.

Martin Farren and Joan Benjamin-Farren
43 Locke St. • Cambridge, Mass. 02140

Joan Benjamin-Farren, a graphic designer, and Martin Farren, a music theorist, are married and so is their work. Together they produce a variety of Jewish crafts. Most recently they have taken up papercutting. She designs, he cuts. Based on traditional images and midrashic symbology, their work is meticulously crafted and elegantly framed. Many of their papercuts are produced in limited editions. I don't, however, fully understand their method of pricing. It seems the second example of a paper cut will cost more than the first, and the third will be even more expensive. Their general price range is from $50–$900 (Dec. 1979). They will also accept commissions for ketubot, anniversary, Bar/Bat Mitzvah, and holiday pieces. Write for their free brochure.

JOAN BENJAMIN-FARREN and MARTIN FARREN, "When the King saw Queen Esther standing in the court, she won his favor" (Esther 5:2). Work in progress, 12" × 20½", © the artists.

Susan Fleischman
75 Nottinghill Rd. #3
Brighton, Mass. 02135

Susan Fleischman spent a considerable time in Israel taking interesting and intimate photographs. These are for sale as signed prints and for magazine and newspaper illustrations. She is available for a wide variety of photographic work and will entertain any requests. See *Playing: Travel* for an example of her work.

Neil H. Folberg
Ma'alot Dafna 139/13
Jerusalem, Israel
Telex: 26144 Att'n Folberg 7121 (BXJM IL)

Neil Folberg is known to many as the sensitive photographer who poetically documented the North American Lubavitch community. He has contributed many photos from that series to this book. In 1976 he and his wife made aliyah and are now settled in Jerusalem with their young son. For the last year or so, he has been working exclusively in landscape photography in color in the Sinai. He makes his living by the sale of original signed photographs to museums, galleries, and individuals. Prices start at $100 a print. They are available from him and from Douglass Elliot Inc. and Braunstein Gallery in San Francisco, and Daniel Wolf Inc. in New York city. He will take mail orders from people who know his work and know what they want. He writes that a lot of tourists coming to Israel call him and visit him at home to see his

NEIL H. FOLBERG, Sinai, from a color original, © the photographer.

work. He loves to meet people and says they shouldn't be shy about calling if they are interested in seeing the work, whether or not they plan to buy. He occasionally does work for organizations and encourages inquiries; anyone who is interested should give him an idea of what they want and how much they want to spend. He is efficient and reliable and his work is exquisite. I wish it was possible to reproduce his color work here. Remember to look all over the book for more of Neil's photographs.

NEIL H. FOLBERG, "Pidyon-ha-Ben", © the photographer.

Barbara Gingold
Dor Vedorshav 8
Moshava Germanit • Jerusalem, Israel

Barbara Gingold is a graphic designer as well as a photographer. She also writes and combines her many skills as the editor of *Young Judean* magazine. She does a wide variety of freelance work, from designing New Year's cards to producing a photo exhibit or complete book. Send a letter of inquiry including deadlines and budget for the project you have in mind. She can also guide tourists to artists' studios and places of interest for those looking for Jewish crafts in Jerusalem. Fee arranged on the spot.

BARBARA GINGOLD, © the photographer.

Renanah Halpern
6801 University Drive, Apt. 2W
University City, Mo. 63130

Like a number of the other calligraphers, Renanah has turned her hand to papercuts, all of which are

RENANAH HALPERN, papercut 9″ × 10″, yellow-gold cut paper on brown background.

based on Jewish themes and Hebrew verses. She has a repertoire of designs which she will copy on a limited basis and she will make new designs on commission. She knew she was serious about papercuts when she started buying X-acto knife blades in boxes of 100 instead of boxes of 5! Papercuts begin in price at $70. See *Calligraphy* for more about her.

Roslyn Hollander
Box 99 • Newton, N.J. 07860

Ms. Hollander designs and prints interesting poster-style bar and bat mitzvah invitations. Brochure available.

ROSLYN HOLLANDER, bat mitzvah invitation #106, "Persian", 9″ × 12″.

Zalman Kleinman
1612 Carroll St. • Brooklyn, N.Y. 11213

I am intrigued with Kleinman's work. It is honest and forthright, and, unlike so many paintings on similar themes, is not maudlin but appropriately exuberant and poignant. Kleinman will "always" accept commissions for illustrations and "sometimes" for paintings. If you are interested in his work, I suggest you write to him for more details.

Edmund Jan Kounitz
K & K Space and Toy Co.
146 Chambers St.
New York, N.Y. 10007

The photographs of Edmund Jan Kounitz are highly personal interpretive statements; sometimes humorous, often haunting, always poetic and provocative. Prints of Kounitz photographs are available in different sizes. Mr. Kounitz will accept commissions and present his portfolio upon request.

Jacob Landau
Lake Dr. • Roosevelt, N.J. 08555

Originally from Philadelphia, Jacob Landau lived in New York and Europe before choosing the congenial atmosphere of Roosevelt as a place to live in 1955. A few years ago, he moved his studio to a geodesic dome where he creates lithographs, woodcuts, watercolor paintings, and designs for stained-glass windows. I had been an ardent admirer of Landau's work for years before finally meeting him at a peace benefit art exhibit during the Viet Nam conflict. Because his work dramatically and poignantly touches many of the painful and even bitter sides of the human experience, I had anticipated meeting someone much more flamboyant and hostile than the soft-spoken, joking man I was introduced to. I soon realized that it is precisely his warmth and concern for humanity that infuses his graphics and paintings with such

intensity. The illustration shown here is from a portfolio of limited-edition lithographs commissioned by the Union of American Hebrew Congregations, entitled the "Holocaust Suite." A number of these prints are still available by contacting the artist. Landau has recently completed work on ten stained-glass windows, entitled "The Prophetic Quest," for Congregation Knesset Israel in Elkins Park, Philadelphia. He is currently at work on a new suite of lithographs based on the designs for these magnificent windows. Information about these prints can be had from the artist. Mr. Landau will accept commissions from industry as well as from public or private sources for art services, prints, drawings, and paintings.

Rita Kurtz Lewis
6631 W. 83 St.
Los Angeles, Calif. 90045

Using her own darkroom techniques, Rita Lewis creates single prints and limited editions of "photoart". These are signed and numbered. Prices start at $100, including frame, shipping, and

JACOB LANDAU, "The Geography of Hell", lithograph from the "Holocaust Suite". (photo: Richard Speedy)

RITA KURTZ LEWIS, "At One with the Wall", photo art.

insurance. Anyone buying an artwork from Rita also gets a wonderful penpal. We've never met but have been corresponding since her fan letter about my first book years ago. Her brochure is free, but send a generously stamped, self-addressed envelope.

Polly Ann Marson, Educational and Arts Director • Jewish Community Center
3960 Montclair Rd.
Birmingham, Ala. 35223

Ms. Marson does blockprints and drawings and accepts commissions.

Stefan Martin
48 Pine Dr. • Roosevelt, N.J. 08555

Ben Shahn considered Stefan Martin to be a superb printmaker and they collaborated on many editions. Shahn was amazed at Martin's ability to transfer and interpret his autographic brush-and-ink drawing into the precise medium of wood engraving. The Estate of Ben Shahn authorized Stefan Martin to print an edition of 100 signed and numbered prints, plus five artist's proofs of these three wood engravings known as the Ecclesiastes series. All the details of printing were worked out between Martin and Shahn before the latter's death. The prints are available from Kennedy Galleries in New York City or directly from the artist's Roosevelt studio.

Shulamith W. Miller
168 Tullamore Road
Garden City, N.Y. 11530

Shulamith Miller paints in oil, etches, and produces kits to embroider. Her paintings have a moody and haunting quality. She will lecture and has a flyer available.

David Moss
1235 Peralta • Berkeley, Calif. 94706

The proof of a true master is his willingness and ability to move on. David Moss has established a

STEFAN MARTIN, "Rex," wood engraving in black, paper: 14½" × 10½", image: 9⅜" × 6½". Signed in the block by Ben Shahn, initialed by Martin. Signed and numbered below by Martin in pencil. This print, particularly, shows Martin's interpretive skill with Shahn's lines.

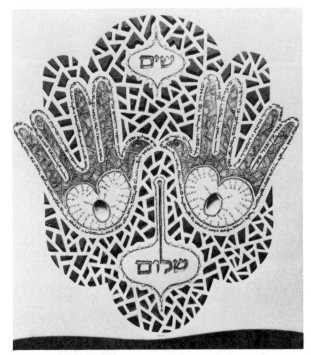

DAVID MOSS, peace amulet, 10" × 12", papercut with micrography, gold leaf and jewels. Courtesy Nathan Mead Gallery, San Francisco.

reputation as one of the country's best and most innovative ketubah artists (See: *Calligraphy*) and now, he writes: "I got into these amulets and they have really been doing well. They are small (usually about 5" × 8") and very delicate. They use micrography, cut-outs, gold leaf, sometimes jewels. All are on vellum. They sell for $400–$500 and I can't keep up with the demand. I will be getting out some similar things as limited edition graphics. I've also been doing large works: mizrahim, texts, maps, etc. I'm really enjoying doing these things—they offer me freedom that the ketubot don't. I've also been doing some interesting layered papercuts. Only time constraints limit what I can do, alas." David also lectures and gives slide talks and Hebrew calligraphy workshops. He has also recently written and illustrated a book on Shabbat (*Invitation to Shabbat*, SBS Publishing Inc.) I can't wait to see what he will produce in the coming years.

Michoel Muchnik
1406 Carroll St. • Brooklyn, N.Y. 11213

Michoel Muchnik's work simultaneously reflects his training at the Rhode Island School of Design and at the Rabbinical College of America, a Lubavitch yeshiva. Michoel is steadily gaining recognition as an outstanding Hasidic artist. He works principally in watercolors and pen and ink, specializing in folkloric scenes, mizrahim, charming village landscapes, and Hebrew letters. His most recent endeavor is an extraordinarily fine portfolio of four *"pochoirs"* (hand-colored prints). These are beautifully drawn and detailed in brilliant colors and metallic inks. They can be purchased separately or as a complete portfolio ($100). He has two posters available, one of which is shown here, which are quite similar to the prints. Michoel is remarkably energetic and prolific and has designed toys for Torah Toys, written and illustrated several childrens books, and still produces fine, limited edition engravings. Individuals and dealers are encouraged to contact him.

Mark Podwal
343 E. 30th St. • New York, N.Y. 10016

Mark Podwal skillfully uses the tension created by the juxtaposition of tautly drawn, fine pen-and-ink lines with sparingly used dramatic brush strokes and bold washes to create drawings of great visual appeal, even as they poignantly carry contemporary political messages. He is most widely known for the illustrations he did for a Haggadah entitled *Let My People Go* in which he writes in the introduction: "The land of Egypt becomes the Soviet Union, and Pharoah suddenly bears striking

MICHOEL MUCHNIK, "Alef", full-color poster, printed on heavy glossy stock, $3 plus postage and handling.

MARK PODWAL.

resemblance to the Czar Nicholas II" (Darien House, Inc., 1972). His original drawings are in many museum collections and have been used as magazine, book, and newspaper illustrations. Drawings can be purchased directly from him and he is available for commissions. See *Learning: Books*, and *Buying: Cards, Gifts and Collectibles* for more Podwal illustrations.

Peretz Prusan
P.O. Box 1665
Palo Alto, Calif. 94302

Peretz Prusan produces high quality screen printed posters for Jewish groups and events. The posters are designed by Peretz and are printed (often in several colors) in small quantities, 20–200. He will also sometimes produce a signed, limited edition of the posters which can then be sold by the organization as a fundraiser.

Mae Shafter Rockland
106 Francis St. • Brookline, Mass. 02146

Most of you know me as the author of this book and four others. Some realize that for most of the books I have done almost all of the artwork. This seems to be the place to say that I started out as an artist: prints, paintings, and textiles; that when I turned thirty I made a very conscious effort to integrate my Jewish, female, and artistic parts, and to deal with Jewish subject matter in my work. And, the more I worked in this direction, the more I found that my art enriched my Judaism and my Judaism enriched my art. Now everything is completely intertwined and to the patchwork I've added writing because it seems so necessary to verbalize the Jewish-aesthetic connection and to communicate with other artists and with other Jews.

At first my prints and paintings dealt primarily with Holocaust themes and that is a subject to which I return periodically. But most recently I've become convinced that, although we must never forget our history, our people has survived in order to celebrate rather than to mourn; and so now I turn to joyful and folkloric themes. In collaboration with my husband, Myron Tupa, a superb printmaker and technician, I am working on a suite of six story prints. Each one is based on a folktale, the text of which is incorporated into the design. The suite (and first print in the series) is entitled: "God Made Man Because He Loves Stories". They are printed on 100% rag paper in

MAE ROCKLAND, "Three Silver Spoons," silkscreen print, image size 21½" × 16½", brown on white, from the suite "God Made Man Because He Loves Stories."

signed, numbered editions of 100. They can be ordered from me for $85, postage included. These and other prints are described in my illustrated brochure, which is available for $1—refundable on first order. I will accept commissions for prints, paintings, and papercuts on special themes. Dealer inquiries are invited. (See also *Textiles* and *Learning: Programs*.)

Laurence Salzmann
3607 Baring St. • Philadelphia, Pa. 19104

LAURENCE SALZMANN, from "Last Jews of Radauti".

Laurence Salzmann is a photographer and filmmaker who spent 20 months as a Fulbright Fellow capturing on film the last Jews of Radauti, a town in northeast Romania. The town was once a busy trading post along the route between Russia, Romania, and Poland, and before W.W.II the Jewish community of about 8,000 played an important part in its commercial and cultural life. About 2,000 Jews of Radauti survived the Holocaust, but many of these have emigrated and today there are only 230 Jews in the town of 22,000. Salzmann returned from his trip with a wealth of photographic material which he offers in a number of ways. Forty framed and captioned prints are available for month-long rental as a show appropriately entitled "The Last Jews of Radauti". Each show comes with 25 complimentary copies of Salzmann's "Last Jews of Radauti" portfolio, plus ten exhibition posters. He has also produced a poetic book of photographs of male nudes entitled *La Baie/Bath Scenes*. The photographs for this book were taken in the baths owned by the Jewish community and used by them as well as by the other townspeople.

Besides these still projects, Salzmann has also made a film about Radauti *shtetl* life entitled "Song of Raduati". It is available for rental ($50) or purchase ($250). Write for more information and illustrated brochures; please send a stamped self-addressed business-size envelope. Salzmann is also available for lectures and will take on photographic assignments. (See *Learning: Media* and *Observing* for more of his images.)

Emanuel Schary
536 Kirby Rd. • Elmont, N.Y. 11003

Emanuel Schary is one of the few artists I would trust to depict *tallit*-draped, bearded, elderly men at prayer or study. All the characters that populate his paintings and lithographs are so warm and human that one is captivated and drawn (a bit sentimentally) into their world. Schary has a well-illustrated brochure available and will accept commissions. He has, for example, produced original lithographic editions for charitable organizations; and if his work schedule permits, he will also do commissioned paintings.

EMANUEL SCHARY, original lithograph.

ILYA SCHOR, "My brother Eli gets married", wood engraved illustration for Sholom Aleichem's *The Adventures of Motel the Cantor's Son,* black on buff rice paper, image 4½" × 4". Available from Resia Schor.

Ilya Schor's Wood Engravings and Graphics available from Resia Schor
164 W. 79th St. • New York, N.Y. 10024

Long before the fiddler on the roof became almost as familiar as the Yankee drummer boy, Ilya Schor was populating a world of ceremonial objects and paintings with the now-beloved shtetl folk. Trained as a metalsmith and jeweler before leaving his native Poland, he used these skills as a means of support while he pursued his primary interest in painting—both in Paris and in this country, where he moved in 1941 and lived until his death in 1961. His interest in pictorial art is abundantly evident in the silver and metal objects he made. Every surface is encrusted with marvelous folkloric figures going about the business of getting married, praying, or just living. Mr. Schor illustrated five books, including Abraham Heschel's *The Sabbath* and *The Adventures of Mottel the Cantor's Son* by Sholom Aleichem. Three wood engravings from limited editions of illustrations for the Sholom Aleichem book can be purchased from Mrs. Schor for $100 each, postage paid. She can also be contacted about other of his limited-edition graphics ($100–$200) and paintings which were shown at Yeshiva University Museum in a retrospective show from November 1975–January 1976.

Richard Sobol
1161 Commonwealth Ave.
Boston, Mass. 02134

A photographer-photojournalist who has worked on assignment for national news magazines, Richard Sobol has, during three visits to the Soviet Union, extensively recorded Jewish life in Moscow, Leningrad, Kiev, Kharkov, Odessa, and Vilna. These photographs (which had to be smuggled out of the country) include portraits of refuseniks, unofficial Hebrew classes, and Jewish cemeteries and landmarks. Photographs from this Russian collection have been organized into a traveling exhibition entitled "Portraits of Exile." Mr. Sobol also has a slide program of these photographs which he narrates. These programs are available as a package or individually. They offer a rare opportunity to get a moving, first-hand, visual experience of what Jewish life is like in the U.S.S.R. While much of his work is journalistic and documentary in nature, he also at times exhibits an ironic sense of humor. This is evident in the photographs he made while traveling through the U.S. He is equipped to handle commercial and individual work as well as special lighting situations. Write for further information about future commissions and projects, as well as for fees for his traveling exhibit and slide presentation. Look for other photos by him throughout the book.

© RICHARD SOBOL

Bernard Solomon
The Boxwood Press
P.O. Box 2362 • Statesboro, Ga. 30458

Bernard Solomon makes fine prints and portfolios (wood engravings, linoleum cuts, and lithographs, all black-and-white). He will accept commissions for individual blocks, cards or bookplates. He has a very well-set-up surface printing demonstration and travels extensively. Flyer available.

Charles J. Stanley
P.O. Box 1132, Peter Stuyvesant Sta.
New York, N.Y. 10009

The 14 murals at the Gustave Harman YM-YWHA were the first thematically Jewish works Charles Stanley ever painted. It was during the four months that he worked on the murals that Stanley, who had grown up in a Reform home, became Orthodox. He was befriended by the painter Zalman Kleiman, who suggested that he write to me for inclusion in this book. I am delighted to present his work because it is thrilling to see a practiced and developed artistic talent turned to the expression of the richness and vibrancy inherent in Jewish subject matter. (See also: *Creating: Art for Architecture.*)

CHARLES J. STANLEY, detail from a mural at the Gustave Hartman YM-YMHA, N.Y.

Sue Stember
8 Honey Brook Dr. • Princeton, N.J. 08540

Sue Stember is interested in gathering photographs of Jewish activities in synagogues and community centers. Suburban, non-Orthodox Jews are often less immediately identifiable as Jews than their Orthodox brethren, but their activities are also in need of documentation. She accepts mail orders and commissions.

Jack and Jean Tetalman
1913 Staunton Rd.
Cleveland Heights, Ohio 44118

Jack and Jean Tetalman are husband-and-wife artists who met in a highschool art class and have been working alongside one another ever since. (And, judging from their letters, it has been a long time.) They do work in painting, printmaking, graphic design, and paper sculpture, but most recently have become almost totally involved with papercutting. Jack writes that many of his inspirations for papercuts come while he is singing with the Temple choir, which he has done for 30 years. Jean's Judaism has been reinforced by working as an art director in a religious school for many years, guiding young people through various art forms to express the joys of Jewish life. Though both are absorbed in papercuts, they work differently and separately. Jack designs with bold strong cuts while Jean's papercuts have a softer, sometimes Hasidic feeling. Their prices vary according to design and size and they have made papercuts for reproduction on Bar/Bat Mitzvah and wedding invitations.

JEAN TETALMAN, "Mazel Tov", papercut, 20" × 26".

FREDERICK TERNA, "Twenty-Two Elementary Particles", 40" × 40", acrylic on canvas.

Frederick Terna
115 E. 89th St. • New York, N.Y. 10028

The expressive abstract interpretations of Judaic themes by Frederick Terna are created from a combination of acrylic paint with sand in various textures and weights. Vienna-born Terna took up sand painting as a medium of expression during the three and one-half years he spent in concentration camps during World War II. Sketches done in the sand with a stick could be quickly erased if a guard came by. Since 1952, he has lived in New York City. A graphic artist as well as painter and muralist, his work is in many private and public collections. He does accept commissions for synagogue as well as private work.

Lila Wahrhaftig
13320 Skyline Blvd. • Oakland, Calif. 94619

Intaglio (etchings and engravings) prints, many with biblical subjects as inspiration; suite of seven prints on the seven days of creation.

Tsirl Waletzky
80 Knolls Crescent • Bronx, N.Y. 10463

There is nothing derived about Tsirl Waletzky's papercuts; she is a papercutter's papercutter! She uses the techniques of traditional Jewish papercuts to interpret traditional themes in a totally personal and contemporary way. Her narrative series of papercuts illustrating the story of Ruth is a superb example of a modern interpretation of an ancient story. She is presently concentrating on ketubot with papercut borders, as well as prints and, of course, papercuts. She has several designs which can be easily mail-ordered. She lectures and leads workshops. Write for more information.

TSIRL WALETZKY, from "Book of Ruth", series of 14 papercuts, layered rice paper.

Beatrice Wool
21 May St. • Marblehead, Mass. 01945

Beatrice Wool has produced a series of multicolored screen prints based on Biblical themes. They are priced between $35 and $90. She has a color flyer available which shows three of the prints.

Malcah Zeldis
80 N. Moore St. • New York, N.Y. 10013

Malcah Zeldis' paintings have the brightly colored, flat-patterned look that we usually associate with folk art. She adeptly uses this approach to portray events of great personal significance to herself, and by abstracting them in this folkloric manner, they become universalized and important to us as well. She is a superb colorist, using heightened flesh tones—which have the effect of totally integrating her people with the objects and activity they are engaged in—to add greatly to the emotional impact of the work. She paints in oils and watercolors and does ceramic sculpture as well. She has illustrated a children's Haggadah, the Song of Songs, and various biblical and Jewish stories. See *Observing: Charity* for another Malcah Zeldis illustration.

MALCAH ZELDIS, "Wedding", 32″ × 48″. (photo: courtesy Jay Johnson's Folk Heritage Gallery)

Textiles

SUE SCHULTZ and detail of applique ark doors, B'nai Israel, Rochester, Minn. (photo: Jerry Alson)

The tailoring business was so bad that Feitelberg said to his partner, "Only the Messiah could help us."

"How could even the Messiah help us?" asked the partner in despair.

"Why," said Feitelberg, "he'd bring back the dead, and naturally they'd need new clothes."

"But some of the dead are tailors," the partner observed gloomily.

"So what?" asked Feitelberg. "They wouldn't have a chance! How many would know this year's styles?"

From A Treasury of Jewish Folklore

Along with calligraphy, the textile arts have been practiced for so long in Jewish history that the tailor and seamstress have made it into our repertoire of anecdotes and folklore. No matter where we have been in Diaspora, or what other guilds we might have been excluded from, there were always those among us who worked with fiber and fabric; sometimes, as the story above shows, eking out only a sparse existence. In recent years, our museums have fortunately begun to pay more attention to collecting and preserving our textile heritage, and fabric, the poor relation of the arts for so long, is finally beginning to be taken seriously. The textile artists whose work is shown here employ a wide variety of approaches and techniques to their medium. Some of them will design a work for your group to complete and will oversee the work and the installation. *(See Buying: Needlework.)*

Ita Aber
One Fanshaw Avenue • Yonkers, N.Y. 10705

Ita Aber restores and repairs old needleworks, sells antique embroideries and curved needles. A meticulous and knowledgeable needleworker, she accepts commissions for synagogues and public institutions. Her best works have been designed by Tsirl Waletzky and Ami Shamir. She is a well-known lecturer and workshop leader in the field of textile conservation and restoration.

Rebecca F. Conviser
The Rug Works
519 S. Fifth Ave.
Mt. Vernon, N.Y. 10550

Art school and factory trained Rebbeca Conviser produces custom rugs, tapestries, wedding canopies, and banners. On specially adapted industrial machines she will make rugs to fit just about any interior. An artist who is fluent in many styles of expression, she can be counted on to come up with a solution for a variety of design needs. She also does stenciled floors and designs for stained-glass. Most of her work is on a commission basis.

REBECCA CONVISER, rug detail.

REBECCA CONVISER, rug detail.

LYDIE EGOSI with her work in the Art and Design Atalier where she sells Judaica by other artists as well as her own works

Lydie Egosi
Main St. • Sag Harbor, N.Y. 11963

The meticulous craftsmanship which characterizes the appliqué wall hangings of Lydie Egosi reflects the intensity with which she approaches Biblical and ritual themes. Her designs are simple and clear, her colors fresh and bold. She makes careful use of variously textured materials, tastefully adding a spangle or two when appropriate. She accepts commissions for ark curtains, *shulhan* covers, Torah mantles, and wedding canopies, as well as for wall hangings, and she will send color photos and written descriptions to potential clients.

Lillian Elliot
1775 San Lorenzo Ave.
Berkeley, Calif. 94707

Lillian Elliot's expressive textiles are included in many major collections across the country, in-

LILLIAN ELLIOT, wall hanging, detail.

cluding the Museum of Contemporary Crafts in New York City and the traveling Johnson's Wax Collection entitled "Objects U.S.A." She has been the recipient of grants from the Tiffany Foundation and from the National Endowment for the Arts. She will accept mail orders and commissions, but like many of the artists in these pages, she emphasizes the individual quality of her work and insists that potential patrons be familiar with her approach, either through correspondence and slides or in person.

Joan Goodman Ganz
6 Sylvan Ave. • Delmar, N.Y. 12054

Joan Ganz weaves, embroiders, and appliques wedding canopies, talitot, Torah mantles, and hallah and matzah covers, using a variety of colors, symbols, and styles. She is eager to talk to people about the background of traditional Jewish crafts and to encourage them to make their own ritual implements. Write for buying and lecture information.

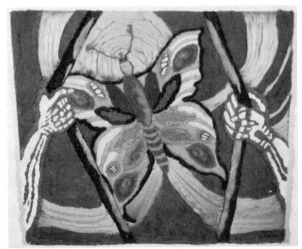

JOYCE S. GLASER, "Shcharansky's Hope: Next Year in Jerusalem", handsewn fiber. (photo: Samuel Poliakoff)

Joyce S. Glaser
25 Hoffman Ave. • Elmont, N.Y. 11003

Because of its unique surface quality, Joyce Glaser's work has often been identified as fiber painting or fiber sculpture. She uses needlepoint canvas as a backing for the traditional stitches which have been elongated, twisted, unravelled, wrapped, and even tied with invisible thread to create three-dimensional forms. She uses fibers from all over the world, choosing them for color and texture.

Ina Golub
366 Rolling Rock Rd.
Mountainside, N.J. 07092

Ina Golub has a brochure available describing her work as a "creator of Jewish ceremonial textiles."

Ann Harris
42 Harding Dr. • South Orange, N.J. 07079

Ann Harris designs and makes appliqué and embroidered ark curtains, Torah mantles and breastplates, as well as wall hangings with Judaic themes. She accepts commissions both for her own work and for work to be done in conjunction with the women's association of the commissioning institution. That is, she will design a work and present it in kit form. After the sections are completed according to her directions, she assembles the parts and directs the installation. Upon request she will send two brochures of work done in this way for a New Jersey congregation.

Andrea Hartman
9547 Saddlebag Row • Columbia, Md. 21045

A batik specialist, Andrea Hartman makes both decorative and functional pieces. As well as a line of hallah covers in muted colors, she also does wall hangings. (See *Observing: Holidays and Ceremonies*)

Dorothy Harwood
2258 Shore Hill Drive
W. Bloomfield, Mich., 48033

Dorothy Harwood's appliqué banners and wall hangings incorporate beads, jewelry, embroidery, leather, and fur. She accepts commissions from individuals and synagogues.

Gladys Hoisington
1227 S.E. 12th Terrace
Deerfield Beach, Fla. 33441

Gladys Hoisington is well known for the B'nai Or (Children of Light) tallit she designed with the inspiration of Everett Gendler and Zalman Schachter (see *Observing: Mitzvot*). But that is not the only thing she does. When we last spoke about her, Rabbi Gendler referred to a poem by D. H. Lawrence, saying in effect that Gladys' weaving is so alive because there is always something of her soul in it. Gladys is one of those righteous gentiles whose gentleness of spirit infuses the Jewish ceremonial things she makes with as much spirit as does her artistry. As well as the tallit pictured in the *Observing* section, Gladys designs and makes ark curtains, Torah mantles, wedding canopies, lectern covers, and wall hangings.

GLADYS HOISINGTON at her loom.

Phyllis Kantor
250 E. 38th St.
Eugene, Oreg. 97405

A 16-harness loom allows Phyllis Kantor a large range of possibilities to create woven patterns. She

PHYLLIS KANTOR, "Jerusalem, Day and Night", double weave, $150.

is experimenting with decorative double woven items such as the "Jerusalem Day and Night" in the photograph, and a verse from Isaiah in Hebrew and English, also in double weave. This technique can also be used to embellish a tallit with a blessing or name and to make some pretty special table linens. She is available for craft fairs in the Northwest. Write for more details.

Deborah Kelman
5173 Coronado Ave
Oakland, Calif. 94618

Deborah Kelman's mastery of painting and drawing with hot wax makes her finished batik designs look effortless and elegant. As well as delightfully fresh hallah and matzah covers and afikoman envelopes, she makes unique mezuzah containers which are the perfect solution for certain contemporary architectural situations where a small traditional mezuzah would be lost. She would like the opportunity to do more commissioned work:

DEBORAH KELMAN, mezuzah, 3½" × 12", cotton velveteen, batiked and quilted. Wood, coconut shell, brass, clay, buffalohorn, silver and copper bead signify the bond between the earth and its creator. There is a pocket in back to hold the scroll, which is not included. Available in earthtones, blues, greens; $30 , allow 3–5 weeks for delivery.

DEBORAH KELMAN, batik wall hanging, 26" × 27".

huppot, tallitot and wall hangings. (See *Observing: Holidays and Ceremonies.*)

Elisa Sandra Lottor
427 10th St. • Santa Monica, Calif. 90402

Elisa Lottor writes that she is a "fiber and fabric artist" who is very much "into" soft-sculpture at the moment. She makes dolls as well as other soft-fiber and fabric creations. These "dolls," however, are not the run-of-the-mill, toy-store variety. They are expensive (upwards of $900), but they are individual, interpretive sculptures by a craftsperson with a delightful sense of humor. These soft-sculptures are completely hand-sewn, many are costumed in fine old lace, silks, furs, plush velvets, and 14 K gold jewelry. Elisa also gives workshops for groups, clubs, and organizations on how to make these wonderful dolls as well as other divine creatures. Sign me up!

ELISA LOTTOR, with some of her special dolls. (photo: Tony Yarboro)

Carola Michael
35–11 169th St. • Flushing, N.Y. 11358

Carola Michael was born in Hamburg, Germany and lived in Seattle, Washington until 1952 when she took up residence in New York. Her woven and knotted textiles are characterized by a rich range of color and an inventive use of texture and form. Some of her wall hangings are so dense they can also be used as rugs, and her loosely woven silk mobiles are unique. She will design and

CAROLA MICHAEL, wall hanging, "Luminary", 48" × 38".

handweave any type of textile or wall hanging. Slides of her work can be seen in the Architectural Reference Library of the Union of American Hebrew Congregations and the Research and Education Department of the American Crafts Council in New York City.

JOANN ORANSKY and MARIE GALLAND, one of a series of letter greeting cards, 4½" × 6", $1.50 each or 6 for $7.50.

JoAnn Oransky and Marie Galland
38 Montrose Ave. • Portland, Me. 04103

Working in the summer in Marie's barn-studio and in the winter in JoAnn's basement-workshop, these two women are producing some very interesting collaborative work employing Marie's skills as a batik artist and JoAnn's as a silkscreen printer. They make fabric and paper items ranging in size from greeting cards to wall hangings. Write for more information and price list.

Mae Shafter Rockland
106 Francis St.
Brookline, Mass. 02146

Participating in the procession of two Torah scrolls to the Jewish Center in Elmont, New York, was one of the most emotionally rewarding experiences of my life. I had just completed the appliqué-and-embroidered huppah under which the scrolls

MAE ROCKLAND, "The Lion and the Dove", cotton patchwork, appliqué and embroidery on wool, ark curtain.

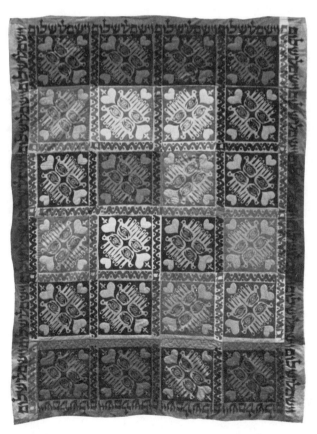

MAE ROCKLAND, "And Grant Thee Peace", bed quilt, screen printed fabric and hand quilting, 90″ × 106″, reds, blues, and purples, $1000. (photo: Richard Speedy)

were being carried, and I felt intense joy at seeing my work floating against the sky over the Torah. I felt privileged to be a Jewish artist and to have contributed to that event.

I'm sure the sunshine and the music in the streets helped, and maybe experiences never repeat themselves exactly, but I know that I continue to get special satisfaction from the work I do for synagogues and other public places. In recent years, my textile work has grown to incorporate printing and dyeing in addition to the appliqué and embroidery work I've done for a long time. Textile work is notoriously time consuming and underpaid. "Labor intensive" they call it. Nevertheless, even though it is a very hard way to make a living, I have rarely turned down a commission. I love the excuse to work with fabrics; it is almost self-indulgent, and when the work goes into a place of worship it becomes the embodiment of my prayer and will outlive me. So, I will gladly discuss new commissions; details can be arranged by mail, phone, or visits to my studio.

Sue Schultz
RR 2, Box 53A • Alma, Wis. 54610

Sue Schultz, the fabric artist in the photo at the beginning of this chapter, lives with her husband Allen, a cabinet maker, and their three children, in an old farmhouse on top of a hill in rural Wisconsin. They both grew up in the Chicago area and have degrees from large universities, yet they have chosen the hard work and daily struggles of life in the country because they feel that it allows them the freedom and space, physically and mentally, to create beautiful pieces of furniture and art, and to be healthy. Although lots of time and energy is put into daily survival chores, like growing several large vegetable gardens to feed their vegetarian family, and gathering firewood for the three wood stoves which are their only source of heat for the house and the shop, Al and Sue feel that the physical work is a good balance for the creative energy they put into their crafts. Can a Nice Jewish Family Find Happiness and Fulfillment Living in the Country? Read more about the Schultzs, their philosophy and lifestyle, in the next chapter on *Wood;* now it's time for a commercial. Using a technique reminiscent of Victorian pieced-velvet lap robes, Sue creates soft stained-glass, i.e. architectural pieces that look like windows. She will make ark curtains and also upholster ark doors (see photo in *Wood*). She also makes wedding canopies, Torah and bimah covers, wall decorations, matzah and hallah covers, and tallit bags. In their immediate area, the Schultzs do a lot of bartering their work for their neighbors'; through the mails, ordinary currency might be better, but if you can suggest something, I imagine that Sue and Allen would be agreeable to a trade. (See *Learning* and *Observing* for more family photographs as well as *Wood* for more about Allen's work.)

Halleluyah, art tapestry for S.A.R. Academy, Riverdale, N.Y. Design and supervision by Ami Shamir. Needlework and beads by Ita Aber.

Aviva Urbont
82 N. Chatsworth Ave.
Larchmont, N.Y. 10538

Almost all of the needlework done by Aviva Urbont is by custom order. She will make a wide assortment of ceremonial articles using a variety of needlepoint stitches. She exhibits her versatility in this medium by making Havdalah spice boxes and mezuzot, as well as ark curtains, Torah mantles, matzah or hallah covers, kippot, tallit bands and tallit bags. An accomplished textile artist, she designed the woven pattern, "The Twelve Tribes of Israel," for the F. Schumacher & Co. "A La Carte Collection" (#980378). She will accept mail orders if the instructions are specific enough.

Wood

ALLAN SCHULTZ turns a Kiddush cup on a lathe; watching are sons David and Joshua. (photo: Dr. Victor Youcha)

Allan Schultz writes: "Often I cut my own wood. My wife and I have timber land of our own and also log other people's land. Over the next few years the bulk of my wood will be from my own logging. Logging is a strange feeling. You walk the woods, enjoying the fresh air, wildlife, and trees. Yet you cut them down—the whine of a chain saw is not romantic, it's dangerous, grubby work. A beautiful tree, eighty years in growing, lies prone on the forest floor after maybe 10 minutes of cutting. I feel more like a *shochet* than a woodsman—doing a necessary but unpleasant job—but doing it with the utmost reverence, for it is the taking of a life. To be sure, I follow rules of sound forest management to ensure that another generation will have its forests, and even cull diseased trees to improve the health of the rest. Yet the bottom line is killing trees. When stepping up to cut a full-grown healthy tree, I offer a prayer and

an apology. It then becomes my responsibility to see that proper use is made of this gift, whether for 2 × 4's or the finest furniture. To deliver a piece of furniture built from trees one has felled oneself offers completeness; the life force of the tree and the craftsman are in harmony. I treat the forest as my brother, we care for one another. In the back of my mind is the feeling that one day God will harvest us to serve His purposes in much the same way."

Allan Schultz, about whom you will read more later in this chapter, eloquently expresses the almost symbiotic feelings many of us have about wood. The artists in this chapter use the inherent beauty and warmth of the material to create art objects for (and about) Jewish life. Wooden Toys can be found in the *Playing: Toys and Games* section.

Joan Carl
4808 Mary Ellen Ave.
Sherman Oaks, Calif. 91423

Joan Carl works in bronze, stone, welded steel, and mosaics, as well as in wood. She does representational and abstract sculptures and portraits. She is open to the challenges of commission work and feels that "it is up to the artist to create the desired pieces to meet the aesthetic demands of the client and to come up with a solution to fit his/her budget."

JOAN CARL, "Temptation of Eve", ligrumvitae wood.

Murray Dewart
96 Brook St. • Brookline, Mass. 02146

The son of an Anglican minister, Murray Dewart is at ease with narratives of a religious nature. *The Stand of the Rabbi* shown here is from a series of wooden relief carvings on the theme of religious persecution. Philip Fisher of Brandeis University

MURRAY DEWART, "Stand of the Rabbi", basswood, 36" × 36".

has praised his work as "rich with spiritual images of great force and humanity." He has exhibited his sculpture throughout New England and welcomes inquiries.

The Dreidel Factory
2445 Prince St. • Berkeley, Calif. 94705

From the folks who brought you redwood dreidels a few years ago, two inexpensive and nicely crafted wooden Hanukkah lamps. Send for illustrated brochure.

THE DREIDEL FACTORY, handmade hardwood Hanukkah lamp, $12.

Ted Egri
Taos, N.M. 87571

Ted Egri works in a wide range of materials including stone, synthetics, welded metals,

TED EGRI, ark, walnut, 8' high; lecturn, walnut, 4' high. Har Zion Congregation, Phoenix, Arizona.

stained-glass, and mosaics, producing dynamic ritual sculptures for synagogues and homes. However, his most intriguing work is in wood. He has a brochure and works almost entirely by commissions to fit specific locations.

Charles Garrett
2603 Angell Ave.
San Diego, Calif. 92122

Charles Garrett writes that his "primary thought in creating small sculpture of Hebraic themes is that these pieces will find their way into homes that reflect proud Jewish heritage; and hopefully will bring an added dimension by blending contemporary art with ancient traditions." Many of his sculptures take the form of Hebrew letters beautifully carved from hardwood. Each letter takes on an inspiring sculptural life of its own. The sculptures range in size from 11 to 15 inches and are available by special order in larger sizes. Prices vary with the size and complexity of the forms. His handsome and well-illustrated brochure also shows 6½" wooden *mezuzot*, a Sabbath candelabrum (16", zebrawood), and examples of work he has done on commission. He will accept mail orders for duplicates of most of the work shown in the brochure and is open to commissions for large pieces of sculpture and ceremonial pieces for

synagogues, organizations, and individuals. Twenty-one of his pieces comprise a complete exhibit, which is available to temples throughout the country.

CHARLES GARRETT at work.

Sark Gould
48-B Penn Park Apts.
Morrisville, Pa. 19067

Sark Gould inlays exotic woods from all over the world to create pictorial wood parquetry. Most of his work has been for walls, from 12" × 14" to mural size. He is also interested in inlaying doors with decorative motifs. His prices begin at $125, which includes shipping, packaging, and insurance. He is willing to try his hand at any theme and will send preparatory sketches as well as photos of previous work to prospective clients.

SARK GOULD, portrait of Einstein.

RICHARD FELDMAN/ELLIOT LANDES, spice boxes, 2″ × 2″ × 9″. (photo: Robert Reiter)

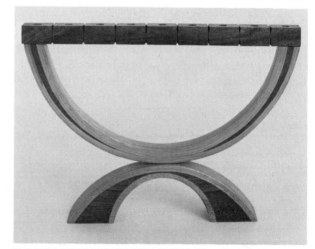

RICHARD FELDMAN/ELLIOT LANDES, Hanukkah lamp. (photo: Robert Reiter)

Martin Kessler
26 Tyler Rd. • Lexington, Mass. 02173

Martin Kessler is a rabbi who sculpts in wood and metal. He makes Jewish ceremonial objects from olivewood imported from Israel, as well as from walnut and rosewood. These include Hanukkah lamps, candlesticks, mezuzot, and Havdalah sets. He will accept mail orders and commissions for these objects or their equivalents made in brass or combinations of brass and wood.

Elliot Landes & Richard Feldman
2500 Market St. • Oakland, Calif. 94607

Partners, Richard Feldman and Elliot Landes are full-time craftsmen who have been making ceremonial objects since 1976. Their business started, like so many others, by accident. Elliot made a spice box (very crude by their current tastes) for his grandfather. Richard's parents saw it and wanted one to give as a gift. Soon interest mushroomed and they were selling to stores, temples, and museums. As well as spice boxes ($38), they also make candle holders ($25), menorahs ($60–$200), and mezuzot ($10–$25). Send for their brochure and ordering information. They are interested in dealing with shops as well as individuals, and would like very much to make large ceremonial pieces for synagogues and centers; their work is so warm and elegant it would be a beautiful addition to any home or place of worship.

Allan Schultz
Master's Cabinet Shop
RR 2 Box 53A • Alma, Wisconsin 54610

When I wrote about Sue Schultz, Allan's wife, in the *Textile* section of this chapter, I promised another installment in this saga of *A Jewish Family Living a Life of Deliberate Simplicity as Artisans*. Let Allan tell it:

"To be the only Jewish family in an entire county, and yet to be part of everyday rural America is an experience new to the American Jew and to Jewish art. Our original impetus came with the 'back to the land movement' of the Vietnam era; but we have not burned our bridges, we've reinforced them. We unequivocally identify ourselves as Jews to our neighbors, and even though the nearest temple is 50 miles away, this simply heightens the importance of our visits. Yet we learn from our neighbors. Most of the wood used isn't bought; we fell our trees, heat our home with whatever isn't sawn into lumber, and mulch our garden with the sawdust. The craftwork that arises from our lifestyle can never be a commodity, it is part of ourselves. Though our outward life is similar to our neighbors', the Jewish element is a supple, unbreakable thread, woven through the entire fabric of our lives. We are not like the great traditional Jewish artisans, with their almost Talmudic elaboration and attention to minute detail. Nor are we like the modern Jewish artisans with their soaring statements of Judaism. We are a natural voice from the hills and forests, a Judaism that can also feel at home in a cool stream or sweet clover field. It is a voice that has always been there, but has often been muted by the exigencies of survival in the Diaspora. God has been kind to us; we may speak freely in this land, and our statement as Jewish artists can partake of the natural beauty and breadth of America. Can't the Torah be lived in the open air, and its pages be turned with calloused hands?"

Allan and Sue are truly inspiring, for they are managing to do what many of us only daydream about; to carve their lives out of time and space

ALLAN AND SUE SCHULTZ, ark, walnut, with soft "stained-glass" upholstered doors and front. B'nai Israel Synagogue, Rochester, Minnesota. (photo: Pearl Sheps)

with a precision and commitment worth aspiring towards. When the archaeologists dig up and evalute 20th century Jewish life in America, they will find in the strata of Alma, Wisconsin, examples of the authentic, hyphenated Jewish-American dream. When Allan isn't logging, working in the garden or teaching his family Hebrew (see *Learning: Courses*) he is busy making furniture, wooden domestic articles, and Jewish ceremonial objects. For synagogues he will make arks, bimahs, and memorial plaques; for home use he makes small ritual items such as Seder plates, Kiddush cups, candlesticks, Hanukkah lamps, and Havdalah sets. Write for brochure.

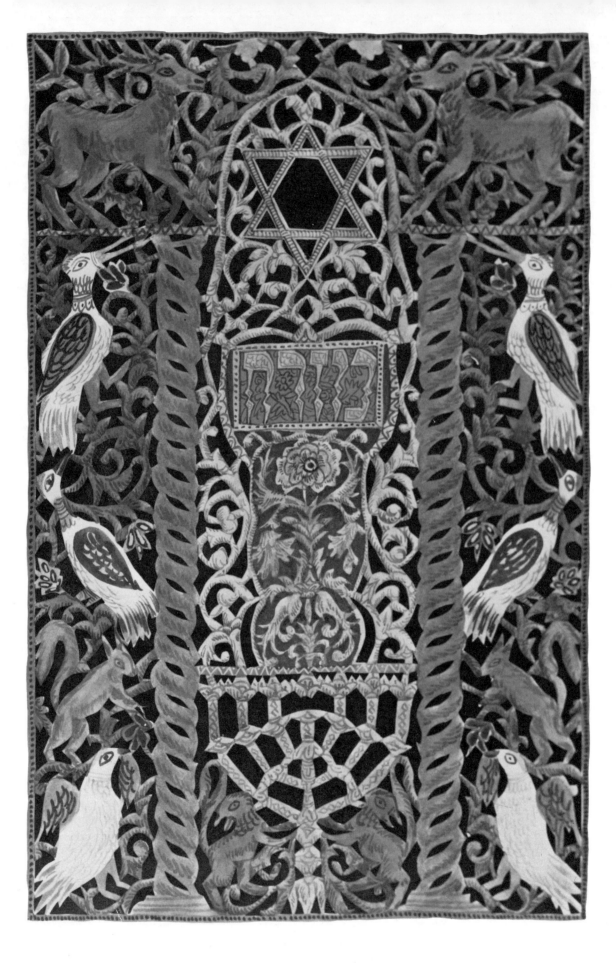

How to be a Jewish-American Folk Artist

Now that you have read about Jewish art objects created in many different media by some of the best artists and craftspeople in the country, some of you are probably impatient to try your own hand at making family heirlooms. We all have the desire from time to time to try one craft or another, but are sometimes easily discouraged, feeling that what we produce won't look "professional". Chances are that it won't; but that's alright. If you make something with your own hands, using whatever skills you possess, and do the work carefully with respect for the materials and for the function of the objects which you are making, the results may not mark you as an instant Picasso. But they will nevertheless be very satisfying and you will have become the creator of a piece of Folk Art.

In these pages you will find several suggested projects plus an alef-bet especially designed for this book by calligrapher-ceramist Joan Mesznik to use for projects of your own. It was designed, says Joan, with the home craftsperson in mind; the size is ideal for many needlework, wood appliqué, and ceramic projects. As a sampler, why not try your own version of the phrase:

SIMPLE AS אבג

Mizrah, late 19th or early 20th century papercut from Eastern Europe, brightly colored with watercolors.

JOAN MESZNIK'S ALEF-BET

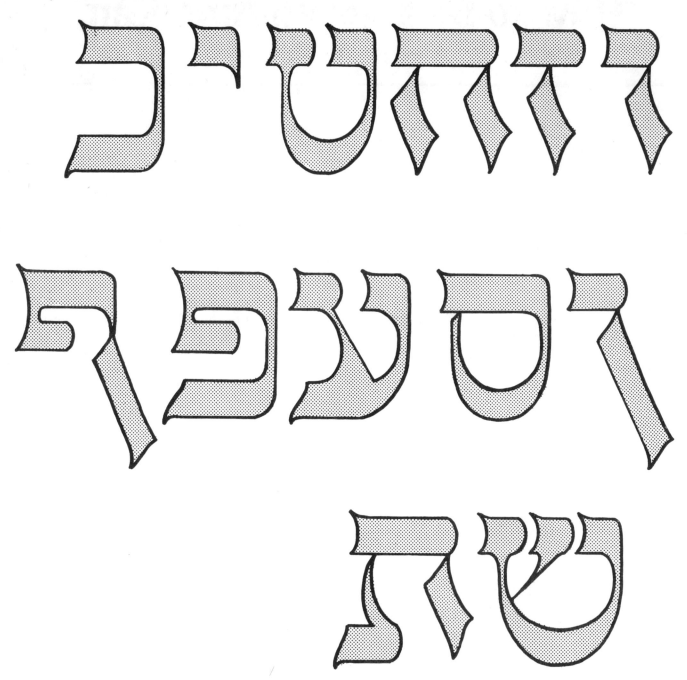

GENERAL CRAFT TIPS

1) Use skills you already have, whether recently acquired or lifelong, learned at your mommy's knee.
2) Make something functional; specific ceremonial things are easier because we know what we expect them to do. In papercutting, for example, try a mizrah or shiviti (devotional markers for Eastern walls) as a beginning project before you tackle interpretive or expressive pieces.
3) Avoid cliches—easier said than done; but try these hints:
   a) use less familiar symbols (read a lot! *The Jewish Encyclopedia* and the *Encyclopaedia Judaica* are treasure troves);
   b) repeat a motif over and over and it becomes a pattern, vary the pattern and it becomes a design;
   c) fill the space—an itty-bitty menorah in the middle of a hallah cover is boring and trivial; repeated, reversed, varied, enlarged, it takes on character.
4) Be patient—the investment of time and self into making something is what will breath life into the object and make it an heirloom worth treasuring.
5) Don't panic—if you can't draw (or think you can't), cut and tear paper shapes to come up with a design. Papercutting, which we know of as an art form in itself, is also invaluable as a design aid.
6) Use your favorite colors and textures (look at what you are wearing to see how *you* choose and combine colors).

MAKE YOUR OWN SOLID BRASS HANUKKAH LAMP FOR ABOUT $10
by Frann Addison

SUPPLIES:
9 solid brass guide hooks for toilet tank (hardware store; plumbing dept.)
9 brass set screws, ⅞" long
⅛" brass tubing, cut to 6¾" length
⁵/₁₆" brass tubing, cut into 9 half-inch lengths (brass tubing is available at most hobby shops)
4" diameter Plexiglas cylinder, cut to 3" in length (see the Yellow Pages of your phone directory for plastic supply houses)
flat black spray paint
epoxy cement
standard size Hanukkah candles

TOOLS:
drill with #21 (.159) drill bit
flat file or medium to fine grit sandpaper
ruler and pencil

PROCEDURE:
When you buy the plastic cylinder, ask the salesperson to cut it in half lengthwise, making two U shaped pieces; you will only need one of the halves for the lamp base, save the other half for another project.

Drill a hole in the middle of one of the U shaped pieces. Spray paint with flat black.

When the paint has dried, slip the 6¾" long ⅛" diameter brass tube through the hole so that the bottom of the tube rests on the table when the plastic is in an inverted U position. Fix the brass tube in place with epoxy. Set aside, allowing the epoxy time to harden.

File or sand smooth the edges of the ⁵/₁₆" brass tubing sections. (If the store won't cut the tubing into half-inch lengths for you, do it yourself using a tube cutter or a jeweler's saw.)

Replace the small screws that came with the brass plumbing parts with the larger ⅞" screws you have purchased.

Place tubing sections inside circular area of plumbing part opposite screw. Turn screw until it holds the tubing securely in place with tension.

When the epoxy that cements the small tube into the Plexiglas has hardened, slip the small hole of the candle assembly over tubing, successively placing the 9 parts so that they form a spiral. And, voila, you have a Hanukkah lamp!

Note: Instead of the Plexiglas cylinder for a base you can use an exotic block of wood, driftwood, or anything else that will firmly hold the tubing and brass parts.

Metalsmith FRANN ADDISON, whose work can be seen in the *Metal* and *Glass* sections, designed this easy-to-assemble but elegant Hanukkah lamp.

2. Painted Plexiglas base with ⅛″ brass support tube glued in place. First candleholder in position.

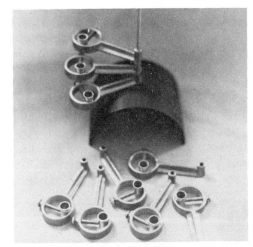

3. Three candleholders in position.

1. Brass guidehooks, ⅞″ set screws, ⁵⁄₁₆″ brass tubing cut into 9 half-inch lengths.

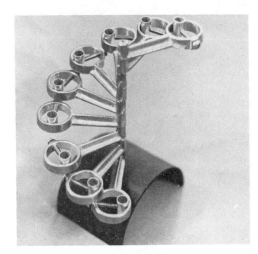

4. Finished lamp, ready for candles. (photo sequence: Frann S. Addison)

PAPERCUTTING

My mother started my fascination with paper-cutting when I was a child and she showed me how to make *royselekh* ("little roses"), the round papercuts they used to make in Poland and other parts of Eastern Europe to decorate the window panes for Shavuot. She said that the women used scissors to make their papercuts and men and boys usually used a sharp knife. With my mother's encouragement and my Great Uncle Layzer's example (he's still making papercuts at ninety), I've been making papercuts for years. For a while I thought I was the only one seriously involved with thematically Jewish papercuts. When I compiled the first edition of this book, not one papercutter contacted me; but this time there are quite a few craftspeople working almost exclusively in this medium, and even more who do papercutting alongside other crafts. It pleases me enormously that so many others have been as intrigued with the possibilities of this humble medium as I have. Perhaps the following "tips" for papercutters will encourage you to add your talents to the growing interest in this traditional craft.

For your first experiments, use any inexpensive paper that is firm and strong and will cut easily without a ragged edge; typing or shelf paper is fine, construction paper is a bit coarse. Later,

FOLD LINE

FOLD LINE

Design for papercut, note only ½ the Hannukkah lamp is drawn. The fold line is in the middle of the center candle.

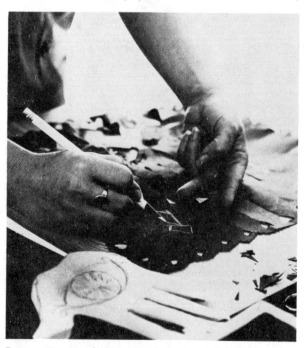

Papercutting as a design aid. (photo: Jane Kahn)

when you are concerned about your work lasting for centuries, you should look for 100% rag papers which will not darken and crumble with age. With these acid-free papers you will be somewhat limited in color selection, but there is still a great variety of weight, quality, and texture to choose from. The heavier paper is harder to cut; light-weight papers can be cut with scissors and pinking shears, as well as the favorite of most of the papercutters in this book—the X-Acto utility knife with a #11 blade. Many people start out doing their first papercuts with a scissors but as they master the use of the knife they use it almost exclusively. Jean and Jack Tetalman wrote reminding me to tell the novice that "a papercut takes a great deal of planning so that it all holds together. We believe that the papercutter must have a good design background and a thorough knowledge of

Judaism. We use the blade much as a brush or graphic tool and are constantly experimenting, sometimes using three colors at a time, as overlays.''

Don't attempt anything overly elaborate and intricate for your first papercut. Choose one or two clear symbols that show up well in silhouette. Fold the paper in half or quarters and lightly sketch ½ or ¼ of your design on the reverse of the paper. Make certain the forms touch enough, so that the whole thing won't fall apart in your hands as you're cutting, but are defined enough so that what they are is apparent in silhouette. It takes some practice; when the design is partly cut out you can open it and see what parts need more definition. When you decide to work with heavier papers which cannot be cut folded, you will have to draw the entire design on the reverse of the paper. Joan Benjamin-Farren and Martin Farren have worked out a careful system of doing their drawing on heavy tracing vellum (to allow for erasures); then, using Seral brand transfer paper, they trace their design to the back of the paper which will be cut. The Farrens are as concerned with the presentation and preservation of their work as they are with making the papercuts themselves. They say: ''Matting is essential to the preservation of paper

works. Because mat boards are made from both acid and rag materials, the choice of matting is as important as the choice of paper. When framed, a mat in front of the papercut keeps the paper away from the glass and prevents the build-up of condensation between the glass and the paper. The mat creates a space in which the paper may 'breath'—paper will expand and contract with the change in humidity from season to season. In addition to the front mat, we also use a mat behind the papercut. This serves two purposes: it creates a sense of depth and allows attractive shadows to be cast by the papercut onto the backing, and it allows us to use some of the colors available in non-acid-free mat boards. The rear mat keeps the papercut away from the acid surface of the backing. . . . Because of the space between the artwork and the glass, we caution you *not* to use non-glare glass. Non-glare glass will cause your work to look fuzzy and will distract from the clean line you have worked to cut.''

Study the papercuts in this book (and elsewhere), look for inspiration in silhouetted forms anywhere, and deepen your knowledge of Jewish themes and motifs. And hopefully soon, you too will be adding your papercuts to this growing branch of Jewish Folk Art.

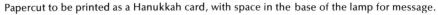

Papercut to be printed as a Hanukkah card, with space in the base of the lamp for message.

MAKING A HUPPAH

One of the most popular items I make is the huppah (wedding canopy) and many people write to me for advice about making one for their own use or as a gift. The huppah is basically a piece of cloth fastened at the corners to four poles. During the ceremony, the poles are either held by friends or fixed in stationary holders. The custom of using a wedding canopy probably goes back to the bridegroom's tent in which the marriage was consummated (Joel 2:16, Psalm 19:5–6). Today the huppah has come to symbolize the new home which is being formed by the couple.

The huppah design shown here is a variation of one which I have made in many color combinations and in a variety of techniques from batik to appliqué and embroidery. The Hebrew phrase קול ששון וקול שמחה says "voice of joy and voice of gladness", and is part of the seven benedictions which are recited after the groom places the ring on the bride's finger. These seven blessings are represented in the design as seven birds, some of which are wearing crowns to indicate their close relationship with the Divine. Another popular motif for a huppah design includes moons and stars to signify that the marriage is heavenly blessed.

This huppah is on the small side. It is just large enough for the couple and the officiating rabbi. If you want to have the entire family under the huppah, as well as many attendants, then you will have to enlarge the design or add many borders to it. This small size was chosen because it is so intimate and because the huppah can be used as a wall hanging when the wedding is over; or, in the case of a synagogue, between weddings. Specific directions for making this huppah are not given here because they will depend on which technique you choose. As I said at the beginning of this chapter, a folk artist uses the best skills he/she has. This design could be painted on cloth, worked in needlepoint, batik, embroidery, quilting or appliqué. But for any of them you will need to enlarge the drawing to make a working cartoon which you can trace onto your fabric. The simplest way to enlarge a drawing is to bring it to a photo-processing shop. Because the finished cartoon will be so large, the enlargement will have to be done in sections. If such a shop does not exist in your locality, or if it proves too expensive, the following grid method can be used.

On a large sheet of paper (tape wrapping paper together if you can't get super-large paper), mark the actual outside measurements of your huppah. Draw intersecting lines, horizontally and vertically, spacing them 1" apart. Count the number of squares you have drawn and draw a grid with the *same number of squares* over the huppah drawing. Then copy the pattern onto the large sheet of paper one square at a time. Start in one corner and work systematically by rows to avoid missing any of the squares. It may be helpful to have someone assist you by keeping your place. (If you use this method with a drawing that already has a grid over it just be certain that your enlarged grid has the same number of squares on it.)

Line the huppah with attractive matching or contrasting fabric and use brass shower curtain grommets at the four corners to reinforce the holes for the pole supports. Please note that the measurements are the finished dimensions; remember to add ½" to 1" seam allowance (for large objects I prefer a wider seam allowance) to all measurements. The loops, which appear as flaps in the drawing, measure 4" × 12" when they have been lined, but *before* they are folded in half and inserted into the seam at either end of the huppah. You will lose another two inches after they have been sewn between the lining and the top at both ends; this means that the *finished* loops add a *total* of 10" to the overall length.

Huppah detail, appliqué bird. (photo: Mae Rockland)

LEARNING

"Just as a tent cannot stand without pegs and cords, so Israel cannot stand without scholars."

Seder Eliyahu Rabbah

"Our most important investment as a people remains in our children's and in our own Jewish self-understanding. We must learn from each other and share our knowledge."

Moshe Dayan

Long before adult education became fashionable, Jews felt it was a religious obligation to gather for a study session every morning before beginning the day's work and again every evening when the ghetto gates shut out the world. We are known everywhere for our commitment to education and to the life of the mind. Indeed, precisely because we have contributed so much to world culture and in that way are so visible, people often confuse our intellectual contributions with political and economic power. Jews in America probably constitute the best educated segment of the population. Our intellectuals are active in every discipline, we support a great variety of cultural institutions, and the general Jewish population is quite well-informed. We are, in many ways, very like the Jews of pre-inquisition Spain. There too the Jews rose to intellectual and professional heights; there too the Jews were plagued by the problems of maintaining their Jewish identity even as they achieved more and more in the secular world. The answer now, as it was then, is education. Most of us have neither the desire nor the intention of making daily Torah and Talmud study part of our lives and yet, like the author of the country song, "Will the Circle be Unbroken", we worry about that circle and about what we will pass on to our children and grandchildren. Very simply said: we can only pass along that which we know and love.

Even if your Jewish education is minimal, it is never too late to add to it—Rabbi Akiba started at 40— and once your curiosity about your own heritage whets your appetite and you start with one course, book or film, it is like peanuts—impossible to stop. Learning opportunities exist all through this book; in this chapter I have gathered sources for appetizing educational materials for all ages and levels of previous knowledge.

"The more study, the more wisdom"

Hillel

Books

Israel Bookshop, Brookline, Mass. (photo: Bill Aron)

I am a bookoholic. I can't pass a bookstore or library without feeling a physical compulsion to go in, browse, fondle, and just plain breathe in book fumes; and it is rare that I can leave without something under my arm. More than 40,000 books are published annually in this country. A surprisingly large number of them have to do in one way or another with Jews. I am not talking only about the learned tomes or the specific books to be found in the Judaica sections of bookstores or libraries, but of the staggering number of popular works with Jewish characters and themes. Just a little while ago there was but a handful of Jewish publishers. Now, in addition to these, just about every major publishing house is looking for a broad variety of Jewish interest books. From cook-

books to Holocaust literature to spy thrillers, Jews figure significantly in the popular imagination. Is it any wonder that folks often assume there are many more of us in the world than exist in reality?

This section is a guide to book clubs, publishers, libraries, and councils which *specialize* in Judaica. This section will also introduce the work of two very different fellow bibliophiles, Will Eisner and Aryeh Kaplan, each laboring in different corners of the vineyard.

For a complete list of Jewish book publishers, write to:

The Jewish Book Council
National Jewish Welfare Board
15 E. 26th St.
New York, N.Y. 10010

BOOKSTORES

When I was a student at the University of Minnesota twenty years ago, I bought my first Jewish cookbook at Brochin's Bookstore which at that time also sold delicatessen, smoked whitefish, and lox. Since then, though the store retains the same name, it has moved across town, no longer sells food, and is run by Sybil Wilensky who makes it a wonderful place to browse, even if you can no longer walk out with a pastrami sandwich. There are countless Jewish bookstores and while I can't claim to have visited them all, many of them, I'm sure, have the special atmosphere which I associate with a place like the Israel Bookshop in Brookline, Mass. where I now live, or The Shtetl in Los Angeles, specializing in Yiddish and in used and out-of-print books.

Also in Los Angeles is J. Roth/Bookseller of Fine and Scholarly Judaica. In 1966 Jack Roth bought M. Harelick Books, then a small Yiddish-Hebrew bookstore. "Out of love and respect for Michael Harelick," who spent 35 years of his life in the store, Roth called his store Harelick and Roth Booksellers for more than ten years. But now that he has moved the store to a large and elegant location near Beverly Hills, the name has been changed to J.Roth/Bookseller. "The new store is what I have always dreamed of," he says. "I've enlarged, yet retained an old-world charm and flavor." Make friends with your nearest Jewish bookstore; I'm sure you will find it just that bit different from the supermarket atmosphere of so many of the chain stores.

Since most Jewish bookstores also sell a wide variety of holiday and gift items, I have included a representative list of them in *Observing: Holidays and Ceremonies.*

For a complete list of Jewish book dealers write to:

The Association of Jewish Book Publishers
838 Fifth Avenue
New York, N.Y. 10021

J. ROTH/BOOKSELLER
Los Angeles, Calif.

THE GRAPHIC NOVEL: WILL EISNER'S *A CONTRACT WITH GOD*

Until recently, although I fostered a nostalgic love for them, I thought that comic books were relics of my childhood and that the only people who were interested in them were today's children and teenagers. I knew nothing of the world of serious collectors until my husband, who teaches cartooning as well as printmaking, took me to my first comic book convention. Immediately I was bitten by a new collecting bug. I simply had to have an early *Wonder Woman*, and I fell in love again with the Classic comics that were my first introduction to some of the world's great literature. I kept looking for the old illustrated Bible stores I had loved as a child but couldn't find them (see Scarf Press below). By my third comic book convention I had learned how many fine artists, illustrators, story tellers, and political commen-

tators had their start in the comics, and how many more continued to be dedicated to that art form. I quickly shed my thin veneer of elitist prejudice against comic books and saw them once again as a potentially wonderful narrative medium. At that same convention I picked up a copy of *A Contract With God And Other Tenement Stories* by Will Eisner. What a treat!!

In his graphic novel, Eisner tells four poignant stories which vividly recreate the life of the tenements so many of us grew up in. In his preface he says: "I have attempted to tell how it was in a corner of America that is still to be revisited. The people and events in these narratives are compounded of people and incidents which I would have you accept as real. . . . It is important to understand the times and the place in which these

stories are set. Fundamentally, they are not unlike the world of today for those people living in crowded proximity and depersonalized housing. The importance of dealing with the ebb and flow of city existence and the overriding effort to escape seems never to change for the inhabitants."

In order to tell his stories more forcefully and poetically, Eisner has dropped the conventional panels associated with sequential (comic book) art and has allowed the narrative to design each page. He interlaces the text with the drawings, and the word balloons, when they are used, fit perfectly with both. This is a book which can be read for sheer enjoyment but because it deals sensitively and dramatically with the moral and religious issues it can, in my opinion, be used with great success by educators, both to illustrate recent Jewish American history and as a focal point for discussions. The book is rapidly gaining a wide audience and has been translated into several languages.

With Eisner, I feel that "the sequential art-comic is at the threshold of belonging to the cultural establishment. Now, in this climate warmed by serious adult attention, creators can attempt new growth in a field that formerly yielded only what Jules Feiffer, writing in *The Great Comic Book Heros*, referred to as Junk art." I hope Mr. Eisner continues to produce more books like this one and that others follow his lead. *A Contract With God*, 192 pages, is available for $4.95 in paper and $10.00 in cloth from:

Poor House Press
51 Winslow Road
White Plains, N.Y. 10606

For information about reprints of Eisner's "The Spirit" comic strip, write to:

Krupp Comics
P.O. Box 7
Princeton, Wisconsin 54968

See *Learning: Programs* for more on Eisner.

JANET KAPLAN, bookplates designed by various Israeli artists (see *Buying: Gifts and Greeting Cards*).

DISCOVERING TREASURES

Aryeh Kaplan is an Orthodox rabbi with a graduate degree in nuclear physics. He has written over twenty books and teaches a class in Kabbalah every Monday night in his home. But to hear him talk about it, it is obvious that his favorite pastime and consuming passion is collecting antique Jewish books. He was once invited to take any old books of interest from a synagogue in Bayonne that was closing down. When he got there, there were close to a hundred people rummaging through the shelves. A quick discerning glance, and he pulled out his first choice—a rare first edition printed in 1702. Another time he spotted a pile of old volumes on the floor in the back of a Jewish book store. The bottom book looked "different" and he bought it for $10. The title page was missing, but a little research revealed that he had a Hebrew Tanach (Bible) printed in 1523. The cover of another old book that he had bought had a funny feel to it. When he opened it he found some old pages which turned out to be from the first edition of the Mishnah, printed in Naples in 1492.

"But", he says, "even when finds are not that spectacular, there is much to be discovered—in basements, in old synagogues, in sacks designated for burial. Old Hebrew books represent a link with a world that no longer exists. And in the average synagogue one can find many such books; in some cases, books over 100 years old may be fairly common." Here are some "tips" from Aryeh for discovering your own treasures:

1. The best place to start looking is in a synagogue basement that has not been used for a while. Before World War II, most Hebrew books came from Europe and among them there were many old books. People also brought family heirloom books that eventually found their way into synagogue storerooms. You will often find boxes of books stored for burial some day. Sometimes, in the most unpromising pile, you might find your first 200-year-old treasure.

2. The date a book was printed is usually found on the title page in Hebrew. Sometimes the date is given in the form of a Biblical verse, with the pertinent letter-numbers in large type. This is especially true of older books, but with a little practice, it is easy to figure the dates out.

3. Paper can help identify the age of a book even when the title page is missing. If the paper is brown and brittle, the book was probably printed after 1860. But if it is white, soft, and old-looking, the book is probably over 150 years old—and you may have a real treasure.

4. Don't forget your own attic or basement. And, as is true for collectors of anything, don't let a friend or relative discard a possible gem without giving you a peek first.

If you suspect that you have something wonderful, but cannot tell what it is, send a photocopy of the title page to Rabbi Aryeh Kaplan, 413 East Third St., Brooklyn, N.Y. 11218, and he can probably identify it for you. I asked him if he does this as a mitzvah or charges for this service. He says that for now it just makes him feel good and he is always fascinated by what other people may turn up. Obviously if he is inundated with requests or a project becomes very involved he would have to be hired on a consulting basis. If you are going to ask his help in identifying a book, I think it would be only polite to provide him with a stamped self-addressed envelope. Happy Hunting!

American Biblical Encyclopedia Society
24 W. Maple Ave. • Monsey, N.Y. 10952

The Society publishes biblical books, among which is the *Encyclopedia of Biblical Interpretation*.

American Jewish Committee
165 E. 56th St. • New York, N.Y. 10022

In addition to its other activities, the American Jewish Committee is a publisher of some significance, particularly of a multitude of pamphlets, but also of book-length studies. A catalog of its publications is available.

Association of Jewish Libraries
c/o Mrs. Mildred Kurland
808 69th Ave. • Philadelphia, Pa. 19126

The goals of the Association are to promote librarianship and improve library services and professional standards in the field of Judaica; to serve as a center for the dissemination of Jewish library information and guidance; to promote publication of literature which will aid the Jewish library; and to keep members abreast of the latest developments in Jewish librarianship. The A.J.L. puts out occasional publications on Jewish librarianship.

(photo: © Neil Folberg)

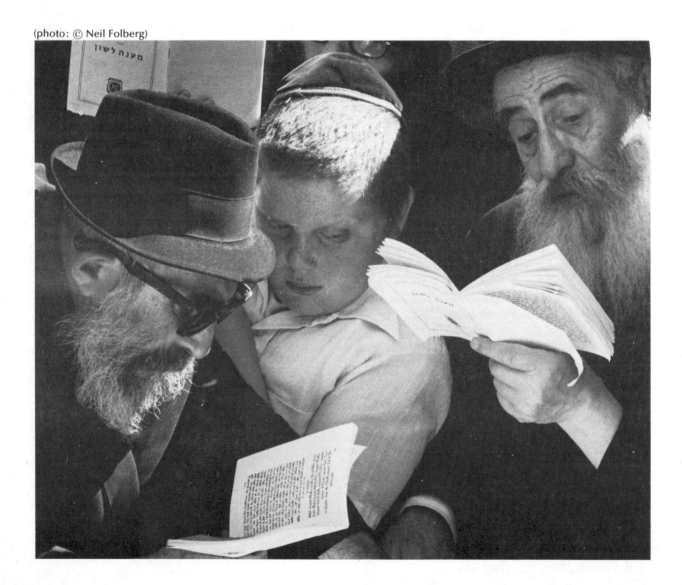

Behrman House, Inc.
1261 Broadway • New York, N.Y. 10001

Behrman House specializes in the publication of educational Judaica on all levels, including the Library of Jewish Studies and curriculum-development services for religious schools. Behrman House is also a bookseller. A catalog is available.

Biblio Press
P.O. Box 22 • Fresh Meadows, N.Y. 11365

The Biblio Press began in 1979 to publish and distribute books about, for, and by Jewish women (with a feminist perspective). They are looking for non-fiction manuscripts by experienced and/or published writers, male or female, on a variety of subjects. Query first with outline and sample pages of writing. As well as their own publications they also distribute books of other publishers which are of interest to women. Write for their folder.

Bloch Publishing Company
915 Broadway • New York, N.Y. 10010

This firm was founded in 1854 by Edward Bloch (the great-grandfather of the present president Charles Bloch) and Rabbi Isaac Mayer Wise, and justifiably prides itself on 125 years of service to the Jewish community. Subjects range from women's studies, through philosophy, religion, and children's books. Write for brochures and lists.

B'nai B'rith Adult Jewish Education
1640 Rhode Island Ave.
Washington, D.C. 20036

In addition to its many other activities, B'nai B'rith operates a book service, selling quality Judaica paperbacks at reduced prices. B'nai B'rith also functions as publisher of the Jewish Heritage Classics Series (in twelve volumes) and the Jewish Great Books Series (in five volumes). It also recently began to publish *Jewish Heritage Review*, a periodical devoted to the arts.

Burning Bush Press
155 Fifth Ave. • New York, N.Y. 10010

Burning Bush Press is the publishing arm of the United Synagogue's National Academy for Adult Jewish Studies. Catalogs are available.

Central Yiddish Culture Organization
25 E. 78th St. • New York, N.Y. 10021

C.Y.C.O. is the major Yiddish-language publishing house in the United States. It also is a book-distribution center for books in Yiddish. A catalog is available.

Congress for Jewish Culture
25 E. 78th St. • New York, N.Y. 10025

The Congress publishes books in Yiddish. Catalog is available.

Jonathan David Publishers
68–22 Eliot Ave. • Middle Village, N.Y. 11379

This publisher also runs the Judaica Book Club which offers special discounts on popular Judaica. Write for more information.

Encyclopaedia Judaica
Sadot Agencies Ltd.
14 West Forest Avenue
Englewood, N.J. 07631

The 16-volume *Encyclopaedia Judaica* is the most authoritative and comprehensive reference work on Judaism. Write or call toll-free (800-631-2564; in N.J. 201-569-8700) for details of easy payment plans.

Enjoy-A-Book Club
25 Lawrence Ave. • Lawrence, N.Y. 11559

Yaacov Perseil, the president of Enjoy-A-Book Club, comments that while Jewish children are book-oriented, their leisure reading is almost invariably devoid of Jewish content. Most children and parents don't know where to look for quality, exciting, and fun Jewish books. To remedy this situation Peterseil has designed his club which offers a wide selection of the best in Jewish fiction and non-fiction books for children, from nursery through eighth grade. There are no membership fees or annual book purchase requirements and all books are discounted. All books are tested for their age level and every brochure will have at least 20 new books on it. Send for the introductory illustrated brochure which describes the available books.

Philipp Feldheim Publishers
96 East Broadway • New York, NY. 10002

Feldheim publishes Jewish religious books. It also has a huge bookstore, which specializes in rare and out-of-print titles. Catalog available.

Hebrew Publishing Co.
100 Water St. • Brooklyn, N.Y. 11201

Well-known for liturgical and related books as well as textbooks of Hebrew. Under its Sanhedrin Press imprint it publishes Anglo-Judaica, and children's books under its Bonim Books imprint. Catalogs are available.

The Jewish Book Club
165 E. 56th St. • New York, N.Y. 10022

Some years ago, *Commentary* magazine branched out into the Jewish Book Club, an exciting way to keep up on new Jewish books and to purchase them at reduced prices. Like any book club, there are special introductory offers whereby one can obtain free books or books at greatly reduced cost in exchange for purchasing a certain number of other offerings. The Jewish Book Club also offers limited-edition etchings on Jewish themes, such specialty items as mizrahim, and postcards and greeting cards for holiday occasions.

The Jewish Book Council of the National Jewish Welfare Board
15 E. 26th St. • New York, N.Y. 10010

The Jewish Book Council is by any reckoning the one institution central to the vitality of Jewish books and publishing in the United States. It publishes the *Jewish Book Annual,* the work on Jewish books published during the previous year. The Council is also the best source for bibliographies of selected books on Judaic subjects. The Council awards citations to Jewish libraries and sponsors the National Jewish Book Awards to the best Jewish books in various categories. The Council also sponsors Jewish Book Month and supports it by helping organizations arrange programs to stimulate the reading of Jewish books, by providing posters, dramatic materials, bibliographies, program suggestions, and library aids.

The National Jewish Welfare Board is also a major publisher, not only of a multitude of pamphlets, but of book-length works as well. Write for its catalog.

THE JEWISH BOOKSHELF.

A gift from:

For the collection of:

The Jewish Bookshelf P.O. Box 434 Teaneck, N.J. 07666

The Jewish Bookshelf
P.O. Box 434 • Teaneck, N.J. 07666

This family-run business offers an interesting solution to the problem of finding satisfying reading of Jewish content for young people and the problem of gift-giving. They offer a gift subscription plan in which the youngster who is enrolled will receive four quality hardbound books selected especially for his/her age group by the Bookshelf staff. The first book arrives with a gift card telling the child that more books will be coming, and each book has a bookplate with the child's name on it, as well as that of the giver. Their attractive brochure explains the service more completely and gives a partial list of the books they choose from. An interesting and useful idea since it is often so difficult to find quality Jewish books for young people, and they have really researched and rounded up the best that is available.

Jewish Literary Market Place
B. Arbit Books
8050 N. Port Washington Rd.
Milwaukee, Wis. 53217

A directory of Jewish booksellers, publishers, newspapers, periodicals, and related organizations in the U.S. and abroad. Send a check for $7.95 (incl. shipping) with your order.

Jewish Publication Society of America
117 S. 17th St. • Philadelphia, Pa. 19103

J.P.S. has published some eight hundred Judaica titles during its eighty-eight-year history, covering all facets of Jewish religion, history, literature, and culture. It offers a membership plan to individuals and libraries that allows for the selection of books at substantial discounts. Write for its catalog.

Judaic Book Service
3726 Virden Ave. • Oakland, Calif. 94619

This is a book service specializing in Hasidic and Kabbalistic books. Twice a year it publishes *Tzaddikim*, a catalog of its books.

Judaica Book News
303 W. 10th St. • New York, N.Y. 10014

Judaica Book News is published twice a year, in October and March. It contains listings of forthcoming Jewish books of all kinds, articles on Jewish writers, artists, and museums, and advertisements for Jewish products. A *must* item for the Jewish bibliophile.

Kar-Ben Copies
11713 Auth Lane • Silver Spring, Md. 20902

Kar-Ben Copies, a cottage industry (two mothers, two basements, two station-wagons, four children) was founded in 1975. They started with ''My Very Own Haggadah'' and have since expanded to ten inexpensive children's books and have more in the works. Write for brochure with single order and bulk order information.

Ktav Publishing House
75 Varick Street • New York, NY. 10013

Ktav is one of the larger publishers of Judaica in America, with a list varying from juveniles to textbooks and other scholarly works. Write for a catalog.

Mesorah Publications Ltd.
1969 Coney Island Ave.
Brooklyn, N.Y. 11223

The Art Scroll Series, elegantly produced translations, commentaries, and background "overviews" on scripture and classics of traditional Jewish literature, is published by Mesorah Pub-

MESORAH PUBLICATIONS LTD., ArtScroll Tanach Series. (photo: Menachem Adelman)

lications Ltd. Write for their free brochure. They will also notify customers by mail of forthcoming publications, bookclub style.

Mayan
P.O. Box 246 • Sudbury, Mass. 01776

Mayan calls itself "a well-spring of Jewish books" and "a bookstore without walls." Founded by two Jewish women, Mayan sets up mini-bookfairs and helps meet the needs of congregational libraries.

Ner Tamid Book Distributors
P.O. Box 10401 • Riviera Beach, Fla. 33404

Ner Tamid is a mail order distributor of books dealing with Judaica. They handle a large list of publishers' remainders which includes children's and adult books, both paper and hardbound. As well as supplying libraries, schools, individuals, and religious institutions, they also supply book fairs. Catalog available.

Reconstructionist Press
15 W. 86th St. • New York, N.Y. 10024

Reconstructionist Press, an arm of the Jewish Reconstructionist movement, publishes prayerbooks, cantatas, books on reconstructionism (Mordecai M. Kaplan's works), and other books related to the work of the movement. Catalog available.

SBS Publishing Inc.
14 West Forest Ave. • Englewood, N.J. 07631

When European publishers started subsidiary companies in the U.S.A., they came with capital—lots of it—and lists of books that were a result of many years of work. When an Israeli publishing company (Masada Publishing) opened its new subsidiary in the U.S.A., its main assets were good will (or "chutzpah") and an unconventional way of tackling things (again "chutzpah"). Well, it works: the first SBS title, *Jewish Days and Holidays*, was selected by the Book of the Month Club and they are publishing *this* book, aren't they? Write for their catalog of adult, how-to, childrens, and reference books.

SBS PUBLISHING INC.

Scarf Press
58 E. 83rd St. • New York, N.Y. 10028

When I began going to comic book conventions, one of the first things I looked for was a well-remembered book of Bible stories in comic book form. I was finally directed to Mark Levine who, after unsuccessfully looking for this same comic to give to his niece and nephew, formed his own publishing company in order to republish the book himself. *Picture Stories from the Bible: The Old Testament in Full-Color Comic-Strip Form* is a 224-page, hardcover book, telling familiar Bible stories from Adam and Eve to Jonah and the whale in the brightly colored, text-in-balloons format generally associated with superheros like Batman rather than Samson. I still love the book; my 7-year-old niece, 13-year-old daughter, and 19-year-old son also thought it was terrific. It is available directly from Scarf Press by sending a check for $10.95, which includes postage and handling.

Schocken Books Inc.
200 Madison Ave. • New York, N.Y. 10016

One of the foremost publishers of Judaica, Schocken has a wide offering in hardcover and paperback books, both in non-fiction and fiction. A catalog is available.

Sepher-Hermon Press
175 Fifth Ave. • New York, N.Y. 10010

Sepher-Hermon Press publishes high-quality Jewish books, with special attention to the arts and history.

SCARF PRESS.

photo: Bill Aron (see *Creating: Pictures*)

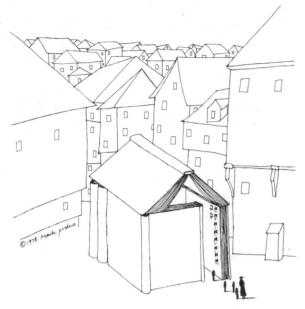

MARK PODWAL (see *Creating: Pictures*).

Union of American Hebrew Congregations
838 Fifth Ave. • New York, N.Y. 10021

The publisher of a wide variety of juveniles, textbooks, social action, and history volumes, and materials designed especially for religious schools in Reform Judaism. Catalog available.

United Synagogue Book Service
155 Fifth Ave. • New York, N.Y. 10010

Publishes a wide variety of materials, especially books for religious schools. Catalogs and sample book jackets are available on request.

Vilno in Pictures Inc.
34–40 93rd St.
Jackson Heights, N.Y. 11372

Vilno in Pictures publishes books about Jewish history, literature, theatre, opera, and art in Eastern Europe. Their most notable publication is the three-volume set "*Jerusalem of Lithuania, Illustrated and Documented*". It covers all aspects of 500 years of traditional and secular life and creativity (till after the Holocaust) in Vilna, which was known as the "Jerusalem" of the destroyed Yiddish shtetl civilization. Recipient of the National

Jewish Book Award. Write for more information and impressive brochure.

Women's League for Conservative Judaism
48 E. 74th St. • New York, N.Y. 10021

The Women's League publishes a number of books for children and for adults, especially for women. It also produces a series of records. Catalogs are available.

MARK PODWAL (see *Creating: Pictures*).

I'm really getting into the Talmud!

© STUART COPANS (see *Creating: Pictures*).

Workman's Circle
45 E. 33rd St. • New York, N.Y. 10016

Along with its many other activities and educational programs, Workman's Circle publishes and sells English books on Yiddish topics, sheet music and songbooks, program materials for groups on holiday celebrations, and Ghetto memorials and program materials.

World Zionist Organization
Publications Department
515 Park Ave. • New York, N.Y. 10022

The W.Z.O. publishes a variety of materials concerned with Israel and Jewish topics. Catalogs are available.

Yesod Publishers
75 Prospect Park West
Brooklyn, N.Y. 11215

Yesod specializes in the publishing of books on Jewish mysticism.

CINDY BENJAMIN, bookplate (see *Creating: Calligraphy*).

Courses

ALLAN SCHULTZ teaching Sue and the children Hebrew in Alma, Wisconsin. (See *Creating: Textile and Wood*; photo: Dr. Victor Youcha)

No matter how knowledgeable we are, there always seems to be room for a little more. Sometimes taking a course adds to an already rich storehouse of facts and sometimes a new course opens a window for us into a totally new world. Recently, colleges, universities, adult schools, and even local high schools across the country have been offering many more courses and whole programs of study in Jewish subjects, so look into what is available in your area. For the most part the courses offered by these institutions are secular; for formal religious study, the best source is *The American Jewish Yearbook*, published by the American Jewish Committee, which lists the many seminaries and institutions available. Most of the materials included here are meant for informal home study by individuals or study groups. Courses on cassettes offer an excellent way of learning for those of us who spend a lot of time at home or in traffic commuting to and from work or chauffeuring children (also see *Learning: Media*).

The Academy for Jewish Studies Without Walls
165 E. 56th St. • New York, N.Y. 10022

The Academy for Jewish Studies Without Walls is part of the worldwide movement to bring higher education to those who cannot experience it in a conventional setting.

The offerings of the Academy are varied and exciting. Some of the most outstanding scholars in Jewish studies were commissioned to design the courses and write the accompanying texts. Examples of the courses available are: Bioethical Issues in the Rabbinic Tradition; History of American Jewry; Hasidism; Jewish-Christian Encounter; and Zionism: History and Ideology.

ADELANTRE!
The Judezmo Society
4594 Bedford Ave. • Brooklyn, N.Y. 11235

Ladino, also known as Judezmo, also known as Judeo-Español, is the interest of this small society, which was founded only a few years ago but has already accomplished a lot. Ladino is basically medieval Spanish written in Hebrew letters, the language of Sephardic Jews. Founded by two young men, David Bunis and Steven Levy (who writes poetry in Ladino), the Judezmo Society has a library archive and a bibliography (card file) on the Sephardim, and maintains correspondence with scholars the world over. ADELANTRE! has published *A Guide to Reading and Writing Judezmo* and *Problems in Judezmo Linguistics*. Those interested in more information on Sephardic Jewry and Ladino will also want to contact the American Sephardi Federation, 515 Park Ave., New York, N.Y. 10022.

Alternatives in Religious Education
3945 Oneida St. • Denver, Colo. 80237

Alternatives in Religious Education offers a series of interesting mini-courses on such themes as: bar and bat mitzvah; death, burial, and mourning; Jews in Spain; who is a Jew?; the Jewish calendar; and the Holocaust. Prices range from $8–$20 per course. These are excellent courses for religious school leaders to investigate.

American Association for Jewish Education
114 Fifth Ave. • New York, N.Y. 10011

Viewpoints is a series of study guides to a ten-part course on Israel which the Association offers for

ALTERNATIVES IN RELIGIOUS EDUCATION.

teachers and schools. The activities of the Association are too diverse to list here. Suffice it to say that it is the primary institution to turn to with curriculum problems and questions concerning Jewish studies.

The Commission on Jewish Affairs
American Jewish Congress
15 E. 84th St. • New York, N.Y. 10028

The American Jewish Congress offers a two-record LP album entitled "Invitation to Yiddish," which comes with a 112-page manual-dictionary. Its price is $7.99. This superb Yiddish language tool is now available on cassette also.

AMERICAN JEWISH CONGRESS, "Hebrew Through Conversation," a set of two long-play records with fourteen lessons.

Heinle & Heinle Enterprises
29 Lexington Road • Concord, Mass. 01742

Heinle & Heinle are publishers of language learning materials in Hebrew. They offer multi-media courses on the adult and adolescent level for use in public schools, religious schools, community centers, and colleges, and Hebrew audio-visual courses designed to appeal to elementary school children. These can be used in the classroom but are especially useful for families who want to learn Hebrew together. On the simplest level is their workbook "How to Read Hebrew (and love it)". (See also *Buying: Collectibles.*)

THE JEWISH CENTER FOR SPECIAL EDUCATION. (photo: Eliezer Greenstein)

The Jewish Center for Special Education
430 Kent Avenue • Brooklyn, N.Y. 11211

The Jewish Center for Special Education (Yeshiva Bais Limudei Hashem) is an Orthodox school for learning-disabled children with an extremely innovative program. Although the school is based in New York, it is open to children from out-of-state who live with foster families while they attend the school. Whether a child is accepted to the school depends only on whether the program is appropriate for the individual child and there is space available. Unfortunately there is a long waiting list. The director, Rabbi Aharon H. Fried, and other staff members, have served as consultants to the beginnings of various Jewish special education programs across the country, and continue to do so. Their most recent effort involved the establishment of a branch in Jerusalem at the request of parents and the Minister of Education. Interested parties should write to Dean Fried for more information.

Jewish People's University of the Air
30 West 44th St. • New York, N.Y. 10036

During 1979 and the beginning of 1980 radio station WEVD in New York broadcast courses of Jewish interest which were so enthusiastically received by listeners that they were put into cassettes which can be mail-ordered from the above address. The courses include such subjects as: *The American Jewish Experience, Yiddish Fiction in America,* and *The Holocaust in Retrospect.* Each is taught by noted authorities in their field

JEWISH PEOPLES UNIVERSITY OF THE AIR.

such as Dr. Hayse Cooperman and Professors Henry Feingold and Nora Levin. Each course consists of 8–13 lectures, an annotated course outline, and a recommended reading list, as well as suggestions for the most effective ways to use the course. The cassettes are packaged in a convenient sturdy case. One can listen to the cassettes on an *à la carte* basis or carefully pursue the full course of study. After sampling several lectures from various courses, I find my appetite whetted and I am looking forward to making a systematic study in several areas. It is nice to know that more courses are in preparation. Send for course listings, prices, and ordering information.

National Council on Art in Jewish Life
15 E. 84th St. • New York, N.Y. 10028

While not offering any art courses per se, the National Council on Art in Jewish Life has compiled a most interesting bibliography of books and pamphlets on Jewish art. These are available from the Council by mail. Send for its listing.

National Federation of Temple Sisterhoods
838 Fifth Avenue • New York, N.Y. 10021

NFTS, the women's agency for Reform Judaism, involves 630 sisterhoods in 16 countries with some 100,000 members. The agency publishes a considerable amount of adult education materials

Samizdat materials, Soviet Union. (photo: © Richard Sobol, see *Creating: Pictures*)

Sabbath Study Group, Moscow, July 1978. (photo: © Richard Sobel, see *Creating: Pictures*)

including items for home observance, all of which are designed to be used by individuals or groups without the aid of an educator or Rabbi. Write for syllabus, course descriptions, and prices.

Rabbinical Alliance of America
156 Fifth Ave. • Suite 807
New York, N.Y. 10010

The Rabbinical Alliance produces and sells tapes for Talmudic learning in English and in Yiddish. It accepts mail orders and will provide a list of its tapes, including prices.

Spertus College of Judaica
618 South Michigan Avenue
Chicago, Ill. 60605

Spertus College of Judaica awards a Bachelor's or Master's degree in Judaica (Bachelor of Jewish Studies, Master of Arts in Jewish Education or Jewish Communal Service). Schools might be interested in affiliating with the consortium, a program in which Spertus students may fulfill general educational requirements at any accredited college or University, with their Judaica major at Spertus. Spertus presently supplies the Judaica Department for 18 colleges and universities in the metropolitan Chicago area and is affiliated with Hebrew University in Jerusalem and Oxford University in England.

Tarbuth Foundation
129 W. 67th St.
New York, N.Y. 10023

The Tarbuth Foundation, which devotes itself to the advancement of Hebrew culture, has produced a number of audio-visual aids for use in connection with Hebrew language instruction. Among the materials available are: three courses in Hebrew (described under the World Zionist Organization listing in this section); two thirteen-part series of half-hour television segments, "To Israel with Hebrew," a combination of travelogue and instruction in functional Hebrew, and "Israel Culture Caravan"; and three television lecture courses ("Portrait of a Century—The Seventeenth Century in Jewish History," "Art and the Jewish Experience," and "The Music of the Jewish People"). The television programs are offered by Teleprompter Cable TV. Tapes (video or audio) are available from Tarbuth.

Union of American Hebrew Congregations
838 Fifth Ave. • New York, N.Y. 10021

The Union of American Hebrew Congregations has put together a complete kit for teaching Hebrew in religious schools. It is meant to enrich the Hebrew in the Mah Tov series of children's books and covers every phase of Jewish life. The kit includes twelve Super-8 sound-on-film cartridges, twelve two-volume textbooks, a teacher's guide, and a Super-8 self-threading sound movie projector.

World Zionist Organization
Publications Department
515 Park Ave. • New York, N.Y. 10022

"Hebrew Through Conversation," fourteen conversational lessons in elementary Hebrew covering a basic vocabulary of more than 250 carefully selected words, can be ordered from the World Zionist Organization. The lessons are presented on two LP records, which are accompanied by an extensive student manual.

The World Zionist Organization also distributes three courses in Hebrew on both tape and cassette. The first is entitled "Let's Talk Hebrew," the second, "Let's Talk More Hebrew," and the third, "Let's Advance in Hebrew." These are ideal for individuals, groups, and schools. The courses are produced by the Tarbuth Foundation and are also available from them at 129 W. 67th St., New York, N.Y. 10023.

The W.Z.O. also offers Ta-Kol, a Hebrew "Home Ulpan," through cassettes and correspondence. The course is based on a new full-planned combination of listening, speaking, and writing. One may acquire a conversational vocabulary of one thousand words with this course.

Yeshiva University
Rabbinic Alumni Office
500 W. 185th St. • New York, N.Y. 10033

Cassettes of lectures by some of Yeshiva University's leading scholars, including some by Rabbi J. B. Soloveitchik ("The Rav"), may be ordered through the mail at $5 each. The topics range from weighty philosophical questions to discussions of problems in Jewish law. Write for a list.

Holocaust

SIMON WIESENTHAL CENTER FOR HOLOCAUST STUDIES, Los Angeles, Calif. Memorial Plaza adjacent to the museum area, a spacious walled courtyard in black on black for gatherings or for quiet meditation. (Design of court and sculpting, Ami Shamir, see *Creating: Art for Architecture;* photo: Vanguard Photographs.)

At last the stories are being told. The last few years have seen a mushrooming of material about the Holocaust. Survivors and their children want to be heard and researchers are looking for reasons and facts. Perhaps earlier, the horror was too close at hand and now we have begun to realise that the penalty for forgetfulness could be another epoch of terror. Books like *The Hoax of The Twentieth Century* written by Northwestern University Professor Arthur Butz, which maintains that the Holocaust never happened, have convinced many survivors of the importance of speaking out and telling of their experiences. In this section I have put together a sampling of some of the ways in which we can learn more about what happened and can hopefully wrest some meaning from it as we work towards what we hope will be a saner future. Other sections of the book will also direct you to yet more sources for Holocaust studies.

RESCUING TORAH SCROLLS

The Jewish Museum in Prague is the largest of all Jewish museums. The background of this incredible collection of artifacts is mass murder. At the same time that the Jews of Bohemia and Moravia were transported to concentration camps their belongings, too, were rounded up. Their shoes ended up in warehouses in Auschwitz and Maijdanek; their cultural and religious artifacts went to the "secret" museum in Prague which, infused with antisemitism, was to be presented to a Judenrein Europe as a salute to the great Nazi accomplishment of having eliminated the Jews. Now the museum stands as a mute testimony to the longevity and variety of Jewish cultural life in Czechoslovakia and as a memorial to the way in which that community met its death. So much was collected that, after the war when the accumulated material was resorted, some of it was made available to foreign buyers. In 1963, an English art connoisseur, Erik Estorick, went to Prague looking for art and antiques to bring back to England and was offered instead 1564 Torah scrolls in various conditions which were being stored in the Michle synagogue. It was agreed that the scrolls should pass in trust to a responsible, non-commercial body, and Mr. Estorick returned with them to London where the Memorial Scrolls Committee was organized at the Westminster Synagogue.

In 1973 when Frank Waldorf, now the rabbi at Temple Sinai in Brookline, Massachusetts, was serving congregation Beth El of Winchester, Virginia, a member of the congregation acquired a Torah rescued from the synagogue in Humpolec (pronounced: Hoom-po-letz) from the Memorial Scroll Committee of the Westminster Synagogue. "Through some research we did, aided by the Society for the History of Czechoslovak Jews," recalls Rabbi Waldorf, "we discovered amazing similarities between our congregation (a small group of Jews living in a rural area some distance from a large urban center) and the town of Humpolec. A committee of the congregation worked closely with me in creating a very moving dedication ceremony in which we pointed out the parallels between our tiny congregation and theirs. We pledged ourselves to carry on with faithfulness the

Bat mitzvah Keren Rockland with Torah scroll originally from the Pinkas Synagogue in Prague, now at Temple Sinai, Brookline, Mass. (photo: Mae Rockland)

Judaism that they were no longer able to promulgate.

"As I prepared to move to Temple Sinai of Brookline, I was determined to help the congregation achieve a similar emotional experience. Again the Memorial Scroll Committee obliged our need, this time by sending us a scroll from a small congregation in the midst of a large urban Jewish community, very much like Temple Sinai in the Brookline-Boston area. Our congregants researched the history of Prague Jewry and from a woman who was married in the Pinkas Synagogue in 1924 we were able to reproduce a clear photograph of 'our' synagogue. For the dedication ceremony, the synagogue was draped with computer tape punched with one million holes. A crystal urn filled with tiny paper punches made real the figure of six million. Instead of the *hakafot* of Simhat Torah, we arranged a *hakafa* in which the people stood around the periphery of the synagogue, and the new scroll was handed from person to person. In the four years since the Pinkas scroll has been in the synagogue, several dozen b'nai and b'not mitzvah have used this scroll for the celebration of their bar or bat mitzvah ceremony. Students at young ages are taken into the synagogue and told the story of the scroll.

"Persons wishing to acquire scrolls may apply to the Memorial Scroll Committee of the Westminster Synagogue, Rutland Gardens, London, S.W.7. Many of the scrolls are not in usable condition. Temple Beth Elohim in Wellesley has used a clear lucite case in order to display its damaged scroll in the vestibule outside of the synagogue. It is a constant reminder of the Holocaust and our obligations to keep Judaism alive."

NOTE: A major source of information on the history of Czechoslovak Jewry is Robert Eisner, 121 81st Avenue, Kew Gardens, N.Y. 11415.

Alternatives in Religious Education, Inc.
3945 S. Oneida St. • Denver, Colo. 80237

This relatively new, innovative company, which is rapidly becoming a leader in the field of Jewish education, offers a mini-course entitled "The Holocaust: A Study in Values." The student man-

ALTERNATIVES IN RELIGIOUS EDUCATION, a game of values and survival.

ual includes five interviews with personalities from the Nazi Era, discussion questions, and decision-making forms. The leader guide includes teaching strategies, projects and resource material, a history of anti-semitism in Germany, and more. The course is suitable for grades 7–12 and useful at the college and adult level as well. Students will never forget what they learn in this course. A.R.E. also has a teaching game entitled "Gestapo". (See: *Playing: Toys and Games.*) Write for catalog and buying information.

David Bergman
23011 Parklawn • Oak Park, Mich. 48237
or
Rememberance Educational Media
P.O. Box 37111 • Oak Park, Mich. 48237

David Bergman was twelve-years-old when he was deported from his hometown in the Carpathian Mountains in Eastern Europe and is one of the few children that survived the extermination camps. Much of what he experienced can never be put into words, but after 33 years of making notes and compiling material from memory he has completed a book-cassette program which movingly recounts his story. He says: "I was fortunate to have survived, I will finish the stories for the ones who did not." His program has recently been accepted by major school systems in Michigan for use in classroom study. The book is well-illustrated with photos of sculptures and other art objects about the Holocaust and with maps of all the geographical locations discussed in the book and of the locations of the major concentration camps. The cassette is 50 minutes long; music and sound effects such as that of trains heighten the impact of Bergman's compelling narration. The book-cassette program can be ordered by sending a check for $22.45 to Rememberance Educational Media (Michigan residents add 4% sales tax). David Bergman is also available for lectures with a slide and tape program on the Holocaust.

Board of Jewish Education
426 W. 58th St. • New York, N.Y. 10019

One of the better things produced by the Board of Jewish Education is "We Who Survive", a docu-drama on cassette with accompanying student-teacher guide and the complete script of the play which is professionally performed on the cassette. Students can also act out the roles of David and Rachel, as they struggle to survive, and of Moyshe, Rachel's cousin, whom we do not meet until 1951 in Israel. The cassette, because it is like a radio drama, is immediately absorbing to teenagers (tested in my living room) and with the guide and script should be a helpful teaching tool. Packaged in a durable case. Write for ordering information.

Canadian Jewish Congress
1590 Ave. Dr. Penfield
Montreal, Que. H3G 1C5

The National Holocaust Rememberance Committee of the Canadian Jewish Congress is an invaluable Holocaust study resource. They have published an annotated Holocaust bibliography ($3) and offer free-of-charge a catalogue of audio-visual materials available from their library. They also have produced a "Janusz Korczak Kit," a "Yom Hashoa Kit", and a "Programming Guide on the Holocaust for Summer Camps", $1 each. There is no charge for their Rememberance Newsletter. They also distribute in Canada other related materials which are not produced by them.

Facing History and Ourselves Resource
Center
25 Kennard Road • Brookline, Mass. 02146

The resource center is a place where students, teachers, administrators, and any interested

PROGRAMMING GUIDE ON THE HOLOCAUST

FOR SUMMER CAMPS

NATIONAL HOLOCAUST REMEMBERANCE COMMITTEE, Canadian Jewish Congress.

community residents can find a myriad of readily available services and materials in an atmosphere conducive to sharing ideas, experiences, and advice. Under the direction of Margot Stern Strom, curriculum materials on 20th-century genocide, using the Holocaust and Armenian genocide to educate students and teachers about the meaning of human dignity, morality, law, citizenship, and human behavior, were assembled and introduced effectively into the Brookline school system on the 8–12 grade level. The impressive and thorough inter-disciplinary curriculum guide is available from the resource center. The staff is eager to hear from any schools seeking implementation support. They offer a wide variety of services from lending materials to teacher training workshops in awareness, content, and methodology. A very important project. Contact the center through the Brookline school system at (617) 734-1111, ext. 335 or 355, or write to the above address for more information and for help with integrating Holocaust material into your public school system.

International Books and Records
40–11 24th St. • Long Island City, N.Y. 11101

As we study and remember the Holocaust, we must also recall the other peoples who suffered and we must celebrate those who saw our pain, and who helped, and commiserated. I would like to draw your attention to a Greek musical recording which movingly deals with themes from W.W.II., Mikis Theodorakis' (of "Zorba" fame) recording of "The Ballad of Mauthaussen". Even without understanding the Greek lyrics, which are movingly sung by Maria Farandouri, the music powerfully expresses the terror and agony of the concentration camps and its effects on the minds and bodies of the inmates. One of the best-known of the four songs is *"Asma Asmaton"* (Song of Songs) which tells of the anguish of a prisoner when he hears that his beloved has just been taken to the gas chamber. The record is #2j062-70204 on an EMI ODEON label. Write: attention Anna.

Jewish Identity Center
1453 Levick St. • Philadelphia, Pa. 19149

The Jewish Identity Center is a one-man, basement museum operated by Yaakov Riz, who is attempting to create a miniature Yad Vashem. He has a program called "Operation Truth," which disseminates information in support of Israel and the Jewish people. Write for more information.

Jewish Media Service of J.W.B.
15 E. 26th St. • New York, N.Y. 10010

"The Holocaust: Media Materials", a comprehensive filmography, is available from the Jewish Media Service for $2.

Jewish People's University of the Air
30 W. 44th St. • New York, N.Y. 10036

"The Holocaust in Retrospect", a course on cassettes, is taught by Professor Nora Levin of Gratz College. Dr. Levin's verbal presentation is as thorough and informative as her books. The course is presented in 13 lectures in a 6 cassette album and is available for $41.45, including postage. It is an excellent focus for study group use.

Judaic Research Institute
747 Livingston Road • Elizabeth, N.J. 07208

The Judaic Research Institute is a non-profit research center and publishing house which publishes works dealing with Judaica, ethics, and the Holocaust. Its founder and editor-in-chief, Dr. Lester Eckman, is a survivor of the Holocaust and is available for lectures on such topics as : "The Meaning of America to a Holocaust Survivor" and "Jewish Resistance Against the Nazis in World War II". Write for brochures describing his work and lecturing more fully.

Phoenix Films
470 Park Avenue South
New York, N.Y. 10016

"In Dark Places", a film produced and directed by Gina Blumenfeld, explores the attempts of a few individuals to come to terms with the Holocaust. Unlike similar films, "In Dark Places" does not attempt to reconstruct the history of the period; rather it concerns itself with the present and with the ways in which we absorb and echo the past. Gina Blumenfeld writes: "As a filmmaker and the

"In Dark Places" by Gina Blumenfeld, available from Phoenix Films.

daughter of Holocaust survivors, my primary goal was to make a film about the memory of this historical tragedy—about how we remember such an experience—and why we might try to forget." The 16mm color film lasts 58 minutes. It is available for one-day rental ($65) and purchase ($650). Gena Blumenfeld is also available as a lecturer.

Rosenbush Productions
6033 N. Sheridan Rd., Suite 43 D
Chicago, Ill. 60660

"The Legacy: Children of Holocaust Survivors" was made by Chicago filmmaker Mimi Rosenbush. The film was shown at the First International Conference of Children of Holocaust Survivors held in November, 1979. Write for brochure.

Spertus College of Judaica
618 S. Michigan Ave. • Chicago, Ill. 60605

Dr. Byron L. Sherwin, a professor at Spertus, is available for lectures on "Encountering the Holocaust", which is also the title of a resource book edited by him and Susan G. Ament. Grace Cohen Grossman, who serves on the Advisory Board of the President's Commission on the Holocaust, is available to speak on "The Experience of Children during the Holocaust".

Simon Wiesenthal Center for Holocaust Studies
9760 West Pico Blvd.
Los Angeles, Calif. 90035

Names for the renowned Simon Wiesenthal who has devoted his life to bringing Nazi criminals to justice, the Center for Holocaust Studies is engaged in research into all aspects of the Holocaust, from the origins of Fascism and Nazism to accounts of those who risked their lives to save people from the Nazis. The Center is collecting documents, photographs, and oral history which form the foundation for educational programs and which also serves as a memorial to those who were lost in the Holocaust. Their public outreach educational programs have been presented in high schools, churches, and synagogues and before civic groups. A multi-media presentation utilizing five screens, three film projectors, 25 slide projectors, and multi-channel sound, all controlled by a central computer, draws upon material gathered from libraries and archives all over the world and includes an original musical score and narration. The Center hopes to reach millions of people with this absorbing program. The Wiesenthal Center also played an important role in abolishing the statute of limitations against Nazi war criminals. The work being done by the Simon Wiesenthal Center deserves our support. Write to them for information about their programs and to find out how you can help.

SIMON WIESENTHAL CENTER FOR HOLOCAUST STUDIES in Los Angeles. "The World That Was Silent" exhibit depicts some of the staunchest proponents of freedom, including England, the United States, and the Vatican, who looked the other way during the early stages of the Holocaust. (Museum design and mural by Ami Shamir; see *Creating: Art for Architecture;* photo: Vanguard Photography)

"May the memory of the righteous be a blessing." Fragments of destroyed synagogues are part of the memorial to the victims of Nazism at Congregation Habonim, N.Y.C. (Emmanuel Milstein; see *Creating: Art for Architecture*; photo: Ronald G. Harris)

MOSHE ZABARI, Yad Vashem Memorial Light, 6"h. (see *Creating: Metal*).

Two Holocaust Libraries have just come to my attention; one on either coast. Write for full details.

Holocaust Library
216 W. 18th St.
New York, N.Y., 10011

Holocaust Library
613 14th Ave.
San Francisco, Calif. 94121

An eleven-year-old slave laborer shows an American journalist the oven in which his parents were cremated. From the slide lecture of Yaakov Spivak.

Media

From a program on missionaries and cults on New York's WOR-TV. From left to right: Julie Frank, Malcolm Hoenlein, Executive director of the JCRC and Rabbi Yaakov Spivak. (photo: courtesy Yaakov Spivak)

When the printing press was invented, the Rabbis quickly understood what a wonderful tool it would be for teaching Talmud. In our age of instant communications, when our senses are constantly bombarded with messages that come to us via invisible waves, flashing lights, and electronic devices, educators (I use that word very loosely) are also quick to use the new technologies. These pages will direct you to filmstrips, cassettes, tapes, slides, films, radio and television productions, and multimedia projects. Media items have also been listed in other parts of the book according to their subject matter. As yet I have heard nothing about Jewish video-discs, but I imagine that as soon as that system is in wide use they will be there.

SO YOU WANT TO BE ON TV?

It cannot be denied that television is the communications medium which most dominates the popular imagination. Everyone wants to see themselves or their group on the tube. "The intricacies of the media are not as mysterious as they may seem, and opportunities exist for ordinary people to be involved", says Julie Frank, director of broadcasting for the New York Board of Rabbis. "But," she adds, "they call for two things: *initiative* and *imagination!*" Here are Julie's recommendations for ways in which individuals and groups can gain know-how and make meaningful contributions to the T.V. world:

1. Instead of trying to exploit the medium by using the T.V. camera as a pulpit and trying to sell religious propaganda, folks might find a wide circle of support from both the government and the broadcasting industry by exploring the whole communications process.

2. The religious denominations, Catholic, Pro-

JULIE FRANK.

(photo: Yaakov Spivak)

testant, and Jewish, have been given air time, technical assistance, studios, and cameras to tell their story. We must use this time to provide stations with something that brings pride to the *station* as well as to the Jewish community. Stations do not look well on yet one more boring religious program. If you are creative you can generate a tremendous amount of support from the local stations. Dramatize a Passover sequence, for example, by visiting a matzah bakery. (This seems obvious but too many religious programs just have people talking at the camera.)

3. Workshops can be set up where station representatives teach Jewish communal leaders how to get across their ideas using television and radio. Communities should use the talents of visiting artists, authors, musicians, entertainers, and already available quality films, and fuse the material to produce worthwhile programming.

4. Don't worry that programs will not be sufficiently intellectual; unfortunately, most Jews know little about Judaism. T.V. can achieve cognitive and attitudinal effects by presenting Jewish education to Jews in their homes using techniques and formats that are inherent to the T.V. medium, skillfully developed by fusing entertainment with education. Good broadcasting should serve to disseminate accurate information and project positive images about Jews and Judaism to the general community. Esoteric subject matter will just not do it!

5. Get to know local station managers, news directors, and public affairs directors. Encourage them to incorporate Jewish guests and features into regular programming. Have them contact you for reliable information. Become a *source*.

6. The best way to get into television is to produce mass-appeal programs for national distribution. In Flint, Michigan, "World of Wonder", an excellent children's show, is written by a nun. The Lutheran Church has an outstanding inspirational children's series, "Davey and Goliath", and has recently begun a project of providing local cable companies and churches with fifteen minute segments.

7. Sponsorship is another line to T.V. time, as is cable T.V. which has *free* public access. The FCC mandate of April 1972 says that every cable operating company in the nation must make two public access channels available. It is a pity to let them go unused. If you want free time in PATV call or write the cable company in your area. In reply you will receive an application asking for a description of your projected program and the time and day you would like it to be scheduled.

Julie will be happy to help with any Jewish T.V. project anywhere in the country. She is full of programming ideas and energy. contact her at:

The New York Board of Rabbis
10 E. 73rd St.
New York, N.Y. 10021

Alden Films
7820 20th Ave. • Brooklyn, N.Y. 11214

Alden Films concentrates on short films concerning Israel and a variety of Jewish subjects. It has a catalog and rents its films at nominal prices (as little as $5).

American Association for Jewish Education
114 Fifth Ave. • New York, N.Y. 10011

The American Associaion for Jewish Education offers a volume entitled *Multi-Media Resources on the Jewish Community*, an annotated listing of some nine hundred materials for teaching Jewish civics. Subject areas include "The American Jewish Community," "Trends and Issues," and "The World Jewish Community." *Multi-Media Resources* is available for $3.30. The Association also publishes *The Jewish Audio-Visual Review*, an annual catalog and evaluation of current Jewish audio-visual materials, which sells for $3.50. Further, it maintains a master index of audio-visual materials for Jewish schools. Finally, the Association sponsors the National Council on Jewish Audio-Visual Materials. The Council, comprising forty Jewish agencies that produce and utilize audio-visual materials, meets regularly to evaluate the work of the member institutions and to offer annual awards for outstanding productions. The Council issues periodic bulletins with information on new media products of Judaic content which it calls "Updates." It also makes available bibliographies of films on various Jewish themes.

American Jewish Congress
Commission on Jewish Affairs
15 E. 84th St. • New York, N.Y. 10028

With the American Association for Jewish Education, the A.J.C. publishes the invaluable quarterly, *Media Information Bulletin*. Annual subscription, $3.50.

American Library Color Slide Co.
P. O. Box 5810
Grand Central Station
New York, N.Y. 10017

This company sells selections of slides on ancient and contemporary Judaic art, the synagogue, and Jewish ceremonial objects. Write for descriptions and prices.

American Zionist Youth Foundation
515 Park Ave. • New York, N.Y. 10022

The American Zionist Youth Foundation aims at instilling in young American Jews a comprehension of their Jewish heritage and a deeper appreciation of the indispensable role of modern Israel in Jewish life. To further this aim, the A.Z.Y.F. has a wide-ranging program that includes printed materials—kits of articles, programming ideas, songs, games, stories, etc.—and excellent filmstrips and slide shows (with and without cassette tapes) on all subjects concerning Israel. The A.Z.Y.F. also publishes a "Guide to Programming Material," which is available free of charge.

Behrman House Inc.
1261 Broadway • New York, N.Y. 10001

Long-known in the field of Jewish book publishing, Behrman House now also produces sound-filmstrips and activity booklets to enrich the teaching of Jewish history. Write for brochure.

Robert Binder
B'yad Hayotzer
24 Warwick Ave.
Toronto, Ontario M6C 1T6

Rabbi Binder established B'yad Hayotzer in 1979 to create new media projects for Jewish education

BEHRMAN HOUSE INC.

and culture. Working with puppetry, drama, music, film, video, and art, the company develops original materials based on Biblical, Judaic, and Hebraic themes. Thus far, they have produced three films and a cable T.V. program. A specialty of the company is custom-made puppets of Jewish characters and ritualia. They accept commissions for new plays, films and videocassettes. Write for more information

Butterfly Media Dimensions
9431 Clair Ave.
North Ridge, Calif. 91324

Butterfly Media Dimensions was founded by two rabbis struck by what they thought to be a paucity of media materials of an exciting nature available to Jewish education. Their hope was to create a central source for rabbis', educators', and communities' needs in Jewish media materials. They have worked with film and filmstrips but their current emphasis is on cassette recordings. They distribute the "Famous Rabbis and Scholars in Living Voices" series for the Central Conference of American Rabbis and also have a subscription program through which one can purchase rare tapes of speeches and talks by leaders of the American Jewish community of the past. Their cassettes are used in adult education programs and by havurot, and include recordings of lectures by speakers at major Jewish conventions as well as Biblical and dramatic readings. Most of the recordings are in English, some in Hebrew, fewer in Yiddish, and to date nothing in Ladino. An interesting service they offer is to go to conventions and do on-the-spot recordings, making multiples of the cassettes available immediately. They welcome queries from convention directors. A brochure describing listings and related services is available.

The Center for Jewish Media Ltd.
48 Urban Ave. • Westbury, N.Y. 11590

The Center for Jewish Media produces and distributes cassettes, videotapes, and multimedia materials on the Jewish life-cycle and observances. Write for a list of lectures on cassette by well-known Rabbis, including several series by Rabbi Shlomo Riskin.

"JOE AND MAXI," a film by Maxi Cohen and Joel Gold; running time 80 minutes. 16 mm and 35 mm color.

Maxi Cohen
31 Green St. • New York, N.Y. 10013

Maxi Cohen is an independent video and filmmaker. Her most recent accomplishment is the feature-length film, "Joe and Maxi," an intimate and moving film about her relationship with her father after her mother's death from cancer. During the course of the film her father, too, is found to have cancer. While the complexities of the emotions and relationships in this slice-of-life film

MAXI COHEN, "My Buba, My Zayda", video, black and white, 15 minutes.

are universal (and the film has won national acclaim), the fact is that the film incidentally gives us a rare glimpse into the family life and work of a Cape May, N.J., Jewish family. Ms. Cohen is available for lectures and commissions. For film and video bookings and print sales, contact: Fran Spielman, First Run Features, 419 Park Avenue South, New York, N.Y. 10016.

Hadassah Program/Film Department
50 W. 58th St. • New York, N.Y. 10019

Hadassah, the Women's Zionist Organization of America, has a twenty-page booklet describing scripts, soundstrips, filmstrips, and movies. Prices range from 50 cents for resource materials to $10 for film rentals. Subjects include much of interest to Hadassah program committees and themes of general Jewish interest.

Hebrew Union College-Jewish Institute of Religion
Education Laboratory and Learning Center
3077 University Mall
Los Angeles, Calif. 90007

The Hebrew Union College's division in Los Angeles has set up an Education Laboratory and Learning Center open to the Jewish community at large. This is a unique institution for learning to use various media to produce Jewish materials of a wide variety. The Center offers short courses, which are primarily instruction in how to use basic hardware for producing filmstrips, videotapes, motion pictures, and sound and print media. The Center has a well-equipped workroom where either individuals or groups can learn and apply new media techniques.

International Film Exchange Ltd.
159 W. 53rd St. • New York, N.Y. 10019

"Best Boy," the remarkable Academy Award winning documentary film by Ira Wohl about his retarded 52 year-old cousin Philly, is available for rental and purchase from International Film Exchange Ltd. Ira Wohl can be contacted through them for lectures.

Jewish Book Council
The National Jewish Welfare Board
15 E. 26th St. • New York, N.Y. 10010

The Jewish Book Council publishes a very useful catalog featuring multimedia materials organized into chapters on thematic lines. Entitled *Aspects of American Jewish Life*, the catalog gives full details on where to obtain a wealth of materials, including films, slides, filmstrips, records, and cassettes on such topics as American Jewish history, the Holocaust, Israel, the High Holy Days, etc.

Jewish Community Relations Council of San Francisco
870 Market St. (Suite 920)
San Francisco, Calif. 94102

The Mass Media Project, directed by Sydnee Guyer, is a coordinated community effort to develop more effective and imaginative ways of utilizing electronic and print media. The project serves as a center of mass media activity for the Jewish community of Northern California.

Jewish Education Press
426 W. 58th St. • New York, N.Y. 10019

The Jewish Education Press, a division of the Board of Jewish Education, produces a great variety of materials, including books, filmstrips, cassettes, games, records, and even a Hebrew label maker. Write for its free catalogs. See *Learning: Holocaust* and *Programs* and *Playing: Music* for more details.

Jewish Media Service
The National Jewish Welfare Board
15 E. 26th St. • New York, N.Y. 10010

The Adult Program Services Department of the National Jewish Welfare Board publishes a newsletter that contains important listings of sources for media newly available to Jewish organizations. The Jewish Welfare Board also distributes a wide variety of filmstrips, tapes, and slide presentations on its own which are listed in the newsletter.

THE JEWISH STAR, "The Return: A Hassidic Experience." Tzipora and Michoel Muchnik, two of the growing number of newly traditional Jews, are featured in this Barry Ralbag and Yisrael Lifshutz documentary. (See *Creating: Pictures* for more on Muchnik.)

The Jewish Star
26 Court St., Suite 1211
Brooklyn, N.Y. 11242

The Jewish Star produces and distributes films of Jewish interest. Their first release, "The Return: A Hassidic Experience," introduced by Isaac Bashevis Singer, is a 27-minute color sound documentary about those who have opted for a Hasidic way of life. It was acquired by several PBS affiliates. Write for purchase and rental information about this and other films and videotapes.

Jewish Theological Seminary of America
Department of Radio and Television
3080 Broadway • New York, N.Y. 10027

The Jewish Theological Seminary, in cooperation with NBC, produces the "Eternal Light" radio and television programs (see National Academy of Adult Jewish Studies entry below.) Scripts of these programs are available from the Seminary. A catalog of radio scripts and a separate catalog of television scripts are also available.

THE JEWISH STAR, Diaspora Yeshiva Band interview with Richard Seigel; half-hour videotape.

JWB Lecture Bureau
The National Jewish Welfare Board
15 E. 26th St. • New York, N.Y. 10010

The Lecture Bureau of the National Jewish Welfare Board has a complete catalog of feature films, entitled *Selected Full-Length Feature Films of Jewish Interest*. All of these eighty-three films may be rented from the bureau itself. Subject categories in the catalog include Holocaust dramas, Israeli comedies and dramas, American-Jewish drama, Yiddish films, Biblical films, and feature-length documentaries on Israel. Probably any film of Jewish content you have heard of is in this catalog—and lots you may not know. Rentals are $40 through $200, depending usually on how current the film is. Financial arrangements also may depend on what use is to be made of the film.

Living Archives Ltd.
P.O. Box 86 • Barrington, Ill. 60010

Rita Jacobs Willens narrated and produced "Rozhinkes Mit Mandlin", a remarkable two-hour audio montage/documentary which has been honored with three National Broadcast Awards. This thoroughly enjoyable record (also available on cassettes) has such gems as Joel Grey's "Rumania, Rumania"—the original country song (eat your heart out Johnny Cash!)—interwoven with Aaron Lebedeff's amazing rendition of the same song; Isaac Bashevis Singer reading the final lines of "Gimpel the Fool"; Sophie Tucker singing "My Yiddishe Momme"; Giora Feidman's clarinet. Excerpts from speeches and readings by David Ben Gurion, Elie Wiesel, Abba Eban, Irving Howe, and many more, add to this sparkling patchwork of Jewish life, an entertainment that is an effective educational tool. "Rozhinkes Mit Mandlin" is available *only* by mail or phone: (312)381-3736. They ship UPS within 24 hours of receipt of your check and order; $25 for the two-record set includes all shipping charges (Master charge and Visa also accepted). They will send it with a gift enclosure according to your instructions.

Macmillan Audio Brandon
34 MacQuesten Parkway So.
Mt. Vernon, N.Y. 10550

Macmillan Audio Brandon rents, sells, and leases 16 mm entertainment and educational films in all price ranges from $15 for short subjects to $50 for late releases or feature films (these rates are rental, not lease or sale). Their mouthwatering catalog includes such popular films as "Operation Thunderbolt", "Lies My Father Told Me", "Jacob the Liar", and "Cast a Giant Shadow", as well as Yiddish and Israeli films.

Media Resources Center
University of Michigan • Educational Film Library
416 Fourth St. • Ann Arbor, Mich. 48109

Michigan Media, as they also call themselves, distributes 16mm educational films and videocassettes. Their catalog is $4 plus tax.

Barbara G. Myerhoff
Dept. of Anthropology
University of Southern California
University Park • Los Angeles, Calif. 90007

Dr. Barbara Myerhoff spent five years researching an elderly group of Eastern European Jews in Venice, California who, she says, will soon disappear as individuals and as a culture. They are the subject of her new book *Number our Days* and of her half-hour film by the same name, which won an Academy Award as Best Short Documentary. The 16mm color film, or ¾" video cassette, is available for a $75 rental fee ($55 classroom) or for lease at $450. It is distributed through Hackford/Littman, 6620 Cahuenga Terrace, Los Angeles, Calif. 90068. There is a study guide available. Barbara Myerhoff is also available as a lecturer.

National Academy for Adult Jewish Studies of the United Synagogue of America
155 Fifth Ave. • New York, N.Y. 10010

The National Academy for Adult Jewish Studies of the United Synagogue of America has a catalog entitled "Eternal Light—Library of Films." These films are produced by the Jewish Theological Seminary in cooperation with NBC and are presented initially on the "Eternal Light" television series. The films dramatize Jewish life and the teachings and spiritual values of Judaism. They are available for rental at nominal prices.

BARBARA MYERHOFF (left) in Venice, California, with some
of the people in her film, "Number our Days".

National Educational Television Film Library
University of Indiana Audio-Visual Center
Bloomington, Ind. 47401

All National Educational Television films are stored
at the University of Indiana. This is a vast resource
and, naturally, includes a fair number of films of
Jewish interest. A general catalog is available, or
you may write inquiring about listings in Judaica.

Neot Kedumim
770 Elder Court • Glencoe, Ill. 60022

This nonprofit corporation distributes original
educational materials created by Neot Kedumim, a
500 acre Biblical and Talmudic garden and educational center in Israel. The materials, including
vivid film strips, slides, teacher's guides, posters,
and pamphlets, give new insights into the ecological unity of the land of Israel, the Biblical heritage,
and the Jewish Festivals. Experienced lecturers are
available for illustrated talks throughout the
United States. The fee is a contribution of $125.
Brochure available (see *Playing: Travel*).

Phoenix Films, Inc.
470 Park Ave. So. (Suite 802)
New York, N.Y. 10016

Phoenix films distributes Gina Blumenfeld's film
"In Dark Places: Remembering the Holocaust".
They also have an extensive and interesting catalog
of other documentary, dramatic, educational and
children's films. Among their listings are several of
Jewish interest, including "The Arab Jews" which
deals with the problems of Jewish refugees from
Moslem countries.

Religious Media
Box 8626 • Rochester, N.Y. 14619

Religious Media's catalog describes a variety of slide/tape programs produced by them, games, posters, greeting cards, audio-visual equipment, and more.

Rocky Mountain Curriculum Planning Workshop
1110 Holly Oak Cir. • San Jose, Calif. 95120

The Rocky Mountain Curriculum Planning Workshop produces creative materials for Jewish learning environments designed by college students involved in Jewish education. Included among its products are records, bibliographies, and materials for creative approaches to Jewish holidays.

SOL RUBIN, "Among Sacred Stones", 7 minute, 16 mm color documentary. Music, dance, and poetic closeups earned this the "Best Film, Religion category" award at the Cannes Film Festival 1974. Available from Arthur Mokin.

Sol Rubin
Motion Pictures
P.O.B. 40 • New York, N.Y. 10038

Sol Rubin is an independent film maker and is available for lecture demonstrations. He has a two-hour program, including six Cannes Film Festival awards, mostly with works about the inter-racial-religious fabric of the U.S. He is best known for two films: "Trinidad in Brooklyn", and "Among Sacred Stones" which is distributed by Arthur Mokin, 17 W. 60th St., New York, N.Y. 10023.

"Tevye", 1939, starring Maurice Schwartz. Ruttenberg and Everett Yiddish Film Library.

Ruttenberg and Everett Yiddish Film Library
Brandeis University • Waltham, Mass. 02154

In 1976, the American Jewish Historical Society acquired the largest extant group of Yiddish languages films in the world. The most famous as well as the most important Yiddish films are in this collection. Most of the films were originally produced on nitrate stock which disintegrates into an inflammable powder in a few decades. With assistance from the National Endowment for the Arts and the American Film Institute, copies have been made with improved picture and sound quality and have been adapted for public use with English subtitles. The original nitrate films have been donated by the Society to the Library of Congress for preservation. Six films have undergone extensive restoration and are now available for rental. The series makes a marvelous film festival. Write for their brochure which describes the 1939 version of "Tevye", "Mirele Efros", and the others. Rental fees are scaled according to use. Contact: Sharon P. Rivo, Film Curator; Miriam S. Krant, Film Distributor.

Tarbuth Foundation
129 W. 67th St.
New York, N.Y. 10023

The Tarbuth Foundation, which concentrates on the advancement of Hebrew culture, places special emphasis on audio-visual aspects of Jewish education. It has produced filmstrips, television series, and Hebrew language tapes (see *Learning: Courses*).

Taryag Media Inc.
719 Crown St. • Brooklyn, N.Y. 11213

Taryag distributes the films of Zalman Jofen, "Prayer", and "Rituals and Demonstrations". Send

an SASE for their brochure. A study guide is available free with film rental (otherwise $1.50). Commissions are accepted for new work, depending on the project.

Union of American Hebrew Congregations
Commission on Synagogue Administration
838 Fifth Ave. • New York, N.Y. 10021

The Commission will rent its collection of slides on the synagogue—its architecture, art, and ceremonial objects—as well as the Jew's contribution to the world of art.

TARYAG MEDIA INC. Still photo from the film, "Prayer". (photo: Michoel Behrman)

Control room. Photo: courtesy of 3R Sound, Ltd., Brooklyn, N.Y., amulti-media production company.

Union of Councils for Soviet Jews
24 Crescent St., Suite 3A
Waltham, Mass. 02154

The Union of Councils for Soviet Jews has available for rental a 16mm film about Ida Nudel, a 49 year-old economist sentenced to 4 years of internal exile for "malicious hooliganism", filmed in Siberia.

World Zionist Organization
Publications Department
515 Park Ave. • New York, N.Y. 10022

The World Zionist Organization produces and distributes a series of color filmstrips with accompanying study guides. Each filmstrip sells for $7.95.

Titles include "A Study Tour of Israel", "Architects of the Hebrew Renaissance", "Dreamers and Builders of Zion", and "Israel: Holidays and Festivals".

YIVO Slide Bank
Max Weinreich Center
1048 Fifth Avenue • New York, N.Y. 10028

The YIVO Institute for Jewish Research is the repository of an incredible amount of visual material as well as books and ceremonial objects. Their slide collection is so extensive that their brochure only begins to list the available subject matter. They suggest that you write to them with your needs and they will try to fill them. Ask for more information about how to borrow the slides and rental fees. Bernice Selden is the slide librarian.

Jewish Cemetery Leningrad (photo: © Richard Sobol). From the travelling exhibition and slide presentation, "Portraits of Exile," see *Creating: Pictures* for details.

Mr. Lefkowitz makes the sign of the Cohanim (photo: ©
Laurence Salzman). From the film *Song of Radauti;* for rental
and purchase information see *Creating: Pictures.*

Zemeron Trading Inc.
MJK Productions
114 E. 25th St. • New York, N.Y. 10010

MJK Productions distributes Israeli films. Their
handsome, well-illustrated brochure describes
Israeli-made films on a variety of subjects. All but
two are in Hebrew with English subtitles: "Stan
Getz in Israel" is in English and "Rejoice and be
Happy", on the 1971 Hasidic song festival, is in
Hebrew.

Museums

Museums are no longer repositories of dead artifacts as many of us once thought of them. Fortunately these days museum curators and administrators see their institutions as places of education and even entertainment. The Jewish museums are no exception and have been working on making their collections more appealing to the public with lively, and sometimes participatory, exhibitions. As they should be, the museums have been encouraging the growing number of contemporary Jewish artists and craftspeople by sponsoring residencies and workshops, by their purchases, and by stocking current work in their museum stores.

This section also includes listings for historical societies. Although some of them occasionally have exhibitions, their primary function is the maintenance of archives and research facilities. Several of these institutions have material relating to the whole of the American Jewish community; most however, are regional in nature. Thus, if you are interested in learning about Jewish life on the Western frontier or in the southern United States you might consider writing to one of the local societies as well as to the larger organizations.

THE SPERTUS MUSEUM, Torah ark, mixed materials, Jerusalem, 1913–23.

American Jewish Archives
Hebrew Union College—Jewish Institute of Religion
3101 Clifton Ave. • Cincinnati, Ohio 45220

With the American Jewish Historical Society, the American Jewish Archives is one of the two principal centers for American Jewish historical research. It publishes *American Jewish Archives*, a journal devoted to the preservation and study of American Jewish historical records.

American Jewish Historical Society
2 Thornton Rd. • Waltham, Mass. 02154

The American Jewish Historical Society is *the* repository of information on the history of American Jewry. Publishing the distinguished journal, the *American Jewish Historical Quarterly* and occasional books, it also houses a large library and an abundant archive of primary materials for the scholar. It also functions as something of a museum, offering exhibitions of materials often

THE SPERTUS MUSEUM, "Isaiah's Messianic Vision," wool tapestry, Nazareth, Israel, 1965–66; after a painting by Shalom of Safed.

taken from its own extensive collections. In honor of the celebration of Boston's 350th birthday, the Society mounted an impressive and thoroughly researched exhibition of 330 years of Jewish life and culture in the Boston area. Parts of this show will travel, inquiries are invited.

The Jewish Museum
1109 Fifth Ave. • New York, N.Y. 10028

The Jewish Museum flourishes under the auspices of the Jewish Theological Seminary of America as the senior museum of Judaica in America. Its collection of ceremonial objects is the most extensive in the United States and is considered to be one of the three most important in the world. The collection ranges from archaeological artifacts of the Holy Land (first century B.C.E.) to ornate silver objects from seventeenth century Italy to American folk art of the twentieth century. In addition to its permanent collection, the Museum presents a continuing series of exhibitions (photography, sculpture, painting) as well as special events,

which range from walking tours of the Lower East Side to films and lectures and children's events. As an educational and cultural institution it provides an opportunity for learning and enjoyment to all its visitors—Jews, non-Jews, New Yorkers, and out-of-towners. It has an active membership program, which offers discounts on items in the Museum Shop (see *Buying: Antiques and Reproductions* and *Gifts*), invitations to exhibition openings, and, depending on the membership category, other services including Judaica appraisals. Write for further membership details and prices. The Tobe Pascher Workshop, which has three full-time artists-in-residence, is located in the Museum (see *Creating: Metals*, under Ludwig Wolpert and Moshe Zabari, and *Creating: Glass and Enamel* under Chava Wolpert Richard). The Museum also has an important program of traveling exhibitions (see *Learning: Programs*).

Judah L. Magnes Memorial Museum
2911 Russell St. • Berkeley, Calif. 94705

The Magnes Museum is the Jewish Museum of the West Coast. It has a fine collection of historical, artistic, and literary materials illustrating Jewish life over the centuries in different countries of the Diaspora. Particularly noteworthy is its collection of ceremonial textiles. The Museum was established in 1962 and is named for Judah L. Magnes,

THE SPERTUS MUSEUM, Hanukkah lamp, bronze, cast, Germany, early 20th century; artist: Benno Elkan (1877–1960).

founder of the Hebrew University in Jerusalem, who was born in the Bay Area; the Magnes Archives are housed in the museum. As well as concerning itself with cultural material of a national and international scope, the Museum serves a very important purpose regionally. It collects and preserves historical documents and landmarks of Western Jewry. The Museum also operates the Western Jewish History Center, which studies the influence of the Jewish population on the development, character, and culture of the far west. It has a research library and collects rare Jewish musical recordings and notations. At the same time that it actively encourages study of the past by making its facilities available to researchers and by publishing, it maintains a program of changing exhibits of Jewish painting, sculpture, and photography. The Museum supports an artist-in-residence program and commissions limited edition graphics and medals. Write for the Museum's list of publications and details on buying its commissioned art works and medals. The Magnes is an outstanding example of the "living museum" concept.

Skirball Museum • Hebrew Union College
3077 University Mall
Los Angeles, Calif. 90007

The Skirball Museum is attached to Hebrew Union College's branch in Los Angeles. It exhibits extensive collections of ceremonial art, archaeological artifacts, coins, paintings, sculpture, and textiles. The Museum has a gift shop which sells posters, antiquities, Israeli jewelry, ceramics, crystal, and metal crafts.

The Spertus Museum of Judaica
618 S. Michigan Ave.
Chicago, Ill. 60605

The Spertus Museum is part of the Spertus College of Judaica in Chicago. While not enormous, the exhibition space is handsome and pleasant. It has a distinguished collection of Judaica from around the world on which it draws to produce beautiful, informative exhibitions. As well as showing ritual and ceremonial artifacts, recent exhibits have included "Chagall in Chicago", and "Spiritual Resistance: Art From Concentration Camps,

1940–1945". It has an exceptionally fine gift shop from which gift certificates may be purchased; the merchandise is primarily Israeli art and craft items, much of it created exclusively for the Museum Store. (See *Buying: Antiques and Reproductions* and *Cards, Gifts and Collectibles.*

Temple Beth Sholom
Judaica Museum
Roslyn Road at Northern State Parkway
Roslyn, N.Y. 11577

Many temples and synagogues have entry ways which could be turned into mini-museums. Temple Beth Sholom has done just that. Architect Saul Silverman, who with his wife Nancy is co-curator of the museum, designed a glass and walnut display area which attracts upwards of 50,000 visitors annually. The museum has a permanent collection of over 100 ceremonial objects reflecting every facet of Jewish lifestyle and religious ritual experience. Periodically the museum displays exhibits on loan from major Jewish museums and private collectors. Several years ago it was the first synagogue museum in the United States to be privileged to display a loan exhibit from the Israel Museum in Jerusalem. Every year the museum has at least one major show devoted to current work by contemporary Jewish craftspeople. Temple Beth Sholom has set an example worth emulating.

Yeshiva University Museum
2520 Amsterdam Ave.
New York, N.Y. 10033

Yeshiva University opened its museum only a few years ago. It has an outstanding collection of Judaica and informative material encompassing art, architecture, and history. Its group of ten scale-model synagogues from different eras is especially interesting (see *Learning: Programs*). It recently had a retrospective exhibition of the works of Ilya Schor including his graphics and paintings as well as his metal work. (See *Creating: Pictures.*) Another provocative exhibition was entitled "Jerusalem Through the Eyes of Travellers and Settlers." Photographs of these and other exhibitions can be borrowed. (See *Learning: Programs.*) Its fine gift shop has exclusive Israeli art objects.

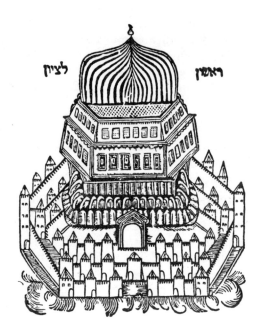

YESHIVA UNIVERSITY MUSEUM, "The Temple," a woodcut from Rabbi Haim ben Attar's *Rishon Le-Tsiyon* (1750), Yeshiva University, Strauss Collection. From the exhibit "Jerusalem Through the Eyes of Travellers and Settlers."

LOCAL HISTORICAL SOCIETIES

There are more local Jewish historical societies in the United States and Canada than I can list here. I am including a selection of them for the reader who in interested in doing research or in contributing to or communicating with the society in his area. For a more complete list, including many Canadian societies, write to the American Jewish Historical Society, 2 Thornton Road, Waltham, Mass. 02154.

JEWISH HISTORICAL ASSOCIATION OF GREATER ST. LOUIS
11001 Schuetz Rd. • St. Louis, Mo. 63141

GREATER BOSTON JEWISH HISTORICAL SOCIETY
2 Thornton Rd. • Waltham, Mass 02154

JEWISH HISTORICAL SOCIETY OF DELAWARE
701 Shipley St. • Wilmington, Del. 19801

INDIANA JEWISH HISTORICAL SOCIETY
215 E. Berry St. • Fort Wayne, Ind. 46892

JEWISH HISTORICAL SOCIETY OF GREATER HARTFORD
335 Bloomfield Ave. • West Hartford, Conn. 06117

JEWISH HISTORICAL SOCIETY OF GREATER WASHINGTON
701 Third St. N.W., • Washington, D.C. 20001

JEWISH HISTORICAL SOCIETY OF MARYLAND
5800 Park Heights Ave. • Baltimore, Md. 21215

JEWISH HISTORICAL SOCIETY OF MICHIGAN
163 Madison Ave. • Detroit, Mich. 48226

JEWISH HISTORICAL SOCIETY OF NEW YORK
8 W. 70th St. • New York, N.Y. 10023

RHODE ISLAND JEWISH HISTORICAL ASSOCIATION
130 Sessions St. • Providence, R.I. 02906

SOUTHERN CALIFORNIA JEWISH HISTORICAL SOCIETY
6505 Wilshire Blvd. • Los Angeles, Calif. 90048

WESTERN JEWISH HISTORY CENTER
2911 Russell St. • Berkeley, Calif. 94705

CHICAGO JEWISH HISTORICAL SOCIETY
618 South Michigan Ave • Chicago, Ill. 60605

JEWISH HISTORICAL PROJECT OF NORTH DAKOTA
P.O. Box 2431 • Fargo, N.D. 58102

JEWISH HISTORICAL SOCIETY OF OREGON
6651 South West Capital Highway • Portland, Oregon, 97219

JEWISH HISTORICAL SOCIETY OF SOUTH FLORIDA INC.
65 Lincoln Rd., Suite 600 • Miami Beach, Fla. 33139

ROCKY MOUNTAIN JEWISH HISTORICAL SOCIETY
c/o University of Denver, Center for Judaic Studies University Park, Denver, Col. 80208

CANADIAN JEWISH HISTORICAL SOCIETY
150 Beverly St. • Toronto, Ontario M5T 1Y6

JEWISH HISTORICAL SOCIETY OF WESTERN CANADA,
65 Academy Park Rd. • Regina, Saskatchewan S4S 4T8

Periodicals

(photo: Bill Aron; see *Creating: Pictures*)

That old quip "Two Jews, three opinions" is really evident in the world of periodicals. With our penchant for words, it seems that "Two Jews, four periodicals" is even closer to the truth. There are certainly far too many to list them all here; instead I am presenting a representative sampling. Some are old timers; others are only a few years or even months old. Hopefully all of those listed will still be publishing when you write for your subscription.

But you can be assured that if they are not, there will be another magazine along to take its place.

The periodicals listed here come from every segment of the Jewish community; a more complete listing of national and regional Jewish periodicals can be found in the *American Jewish Yearbook*, in the quarterly *Index to Jewish Periodicals*, Box 18570, Cleveland, Ohio 44118, and in *Jewish Literary Market Place* (see *Learning: Books*).

EMANUEL SCHARY, lithograph; see *Creating: Pictures.*

what you may be missing. Baat-Kol Promotions can also help in fund raising by selling subscriptions through Jewish organizations. Mark Roseman writes that "not enough Jews are aware of the dynamics of their people internationally; Baat-Kol Promotions is trying to improve upon that situation." Mail orders, MasterCard and Visa accepted.

The Biblical Archaeological Review
1737 H Street, N.W.
Washington, D.C. 20006

The Biblical Archaeological Review will appeal to many Jews fascinated by archaeological discoveries in the Holy Land. Annual subscription, $18, issued six times a year.

Commentary
165 E. 56th St. • New York, N.Y. 10022

An intellectual monthly published by the American Jewish Committee, edited by Norman Podhoretz. $2.50 per issue.

Congress Monthly
15 E. 84th St. • New York, N.Y. 10028

I have long felt that *Congress Monthly*, though unpretentiously printed, is one of the best small journals in covering events in Israel and the American Jewish community. It is also especially good on American Jewish literature. The Annual America-Israel Dialogues sponsored by the Congress and printed in the *Monthly* are a model of intelligent discourse on intellectual and artistic problems facing world Judaism. A one-year subscription costs $5.

American Jewish Historical Quarterly
2 Thornton Rd. • Waltham, Mass. 02154

The *American Jewish Historical Quarterly*, published by the American Jewish Historical Society, has been around for many years, but may not be known to a wide audience of American Jews. It is a scholarly journal that endeavors to expand our knowledge of the history of the American Jewish community.

Baat-Kol Promotions
206 Deerfield Road • Cranston, R.I. 02920

Mark Roseman, the founder and director of Baat-Kol Promotions, has created a clearing-house for Jewish magazines for Israel and the U.S. A wide variety of English language and Hebrew publications are available through his service—many at a discount. Ask for his brochure and find out

Genesis 2
233 Bay State Road • Boston, Mass. 02215

Genesis 2, "an independent voice for Jewish renewal", is a journal of news, opinion, and the arts. Subscriptions $6 annually. See *Creating: Art for Architecture,* for a sample of a *Genesis 2* interview.

From "Shmata", *Genesis 2's* annual Purim supplement.

Hadassah Magazine
50 W. 58th St. • New York, N.Y. 10019

In addition to its important work in Israel and for Israel in the United States, Hadassah, the women's Zionist organization, publishes a first-rate magazine. Along with informed reporting from Israel, *Hadassah Magazine* has marvelous photographs and other graphics and pays keen attention to the arts in Israel and in America. Published ten times a year, the subscription is $10.

The Holy Beggars Gazette
c/o Steven L. Maimes, Bookseller
3726 Virden Avenue
Oakland, Calif. 94619

The Holy Beggars' Gazette is published approximately twice a year by the House of Love and Prayer, Inc. and distributed by Steven Maimes, who also publishes *Tzaddikim*, a periodic listing of Hasidic and Kabbalistic books, and *Tzaddikim*

Holy Beggars' Gazette, a journal of Hasidic Judaism.

Review, a series of discussions of new Hasidic and Kabbalistic books and periodicals. *The Holy Beggars' Gazette* is priced by individual issue, with an average of $2. For $2 one can also obtain a subscription to *Tzaddikim* and *Tzaddikim Review;* four numbers of each of the two periodicals are issued each year. The *Gazette* and its associated publications are tastefully yet simply printed mystical journals that will turn the layperson on to Hasidism if anything will.

The Jerusalem Post
110 E. 59th St. • New York, N.Y. 10022

Assuming you do not read Hebrew but wish to keep up on current events in Israel, there is no better way than to subscribe to the overseas edition of *The Jerusalem Post*. A weekly, the English-language *Jerusalem Post* not only includes the weeks's top stories but all of the editorials from the daily issues as well. Cost is $30 per year.

The Jerusalem Quarterly
The Middle East Institute
P.O. Box 1308-Q • Fort Lee, N.J. 07024

This quarterly does not present "news" nor is it a "journal of opinion." The editors assume that its readers are quite well informed and are looking for indepth discussion of situations and events in the Middle East. Four issues $10.

Jewish Daily Forward
44 E. 33rd St. • New York, N.Y. 10016

When I gave my mother Nobel Prize winning Isaac Bashevis Singer's novel *Sosha* as a mother's day present a few years ago, she thanked me but with a superior smile said she had already read it in *The Forward*. This Yiddish language daily was founded in 1897 and is still alive and well. Every so often supplemental issues on special themes are published which have an English section as well. Singer has said that his primary job is as a writer for this paper since he has received a regular paycheck from them for decades, long before he was "discovered".

Jewish Folklore and Ethnology Newsletter
Max Weinreich Center for Advanced Jewish Studies
YIVO Institute for Jewish Research
1048 Fifth Ave • New York, N.Y. 10028

Fascinating newsletter, mostly involved with events in academia but also in contact with what the "folks" in folklore are doing. Eager for reports about or from outside the Eastern Seaboard area. *The Jewish Folklore and Ethnology Directory*, assembled by the newsletter, should appear shortly. Subscriptions to the Newsletter, $5 (1 year); $13 (3 years); single copy: $1.75.

Jewish Student Press Service
15 E. 26th St. (Suite 1350)
New York, N.Y. 10010

JSPS is an alternative source of articles dealing with current issues in the Jewish community from a variety of perspectives. It publishes a monthly packet of feature articles on all aspects of Jewish life. Student and community publications, libraries, and Jewish organizations of various types subscribe to JSPS services. Fees vary with type of organization and whether it has reprint rights. JSPS is also the national distribution center for Jewish student publications.

Why Did Golda Fight Feminism? The Politics Behind Ordaining Women Rabbis

Journal of Psychology and Judaism
Human Sciences Press
72 Fifth Avenue • New York, N.Y. 10011

This journal, a novel idea, addresses itself to the philosophical, clinical, and practical aspects of psychology and its relationship with Judaism. The journal focuses on psychological problems faced by Jews and seeks an appropriate philosophy to apply in the clinical context. Perhaps Sigmund Freud is not the only major example of the particular affinity between the psychological sciences and Jews.

Ke xaber? ('What's New?')
Adelantre! The Judezmo Society
4594 Bedford Avenue • Brooklyn, N.Y. 11235

Ke xaber? is a quarterly newsletter with articles and commentary in both English and Judezmo (Ladino). Insights into Sephardic history and contemporary culture. $5 brings you four issues, a Judezmo/English membership card, a membership directory and as a bonus, new members will receive *Adelantre!* broadside Number 1.

Lilith
500 E. 63rd St. • Suite 16C
New York, N.Y. 10021

Lilith is an exciting publication spawned by contemporary feminism, but, in this case, devoted entirely to the Jewish woman. A quarterly, *Lilith* is "named for our ancestor who insisted on equality with Adam", and it is dedicated "to changing the

consciousness of the Jewish woman". *Lilith* devotes its pages to such themes as "Analysis of the Oppression of Jewish Women", "Surviving Single and Jewish", "New Rituals for Jewish Women", "Jews ZPG and Abortion", "When a Jewish Wife Becomes a Widow", "Sexism in Jewish Textbooks and Children's Stories", "Our Abandoned Grandmothers in the Slums", "The Crisis of the Jewish Volunteer". Subscription price, $8 per year; single issues, $2.50.

Moment Magazine
462 Boylston St.
Boston, Mass. 02116

Moment is another major magazine published in recent years by and for the American Jewish community. Founded by Leonard Fein and Elie Wiesel, it is an extremely attractive periodical of a general nature; it is as interested in Israel as it is in the American Jewish community and the arts. Published ten times a year, subscriptions are $18.

Present Tense
165 E. 56th St. • New York, N.Y. 10022

Present Tense is a second major periodical publication effort of the American Jewish Committee, which also publishes *Commentary*. While *Commentary* is a monthly, *Present Tense* is a quarterly, and while the former only partially devotes itself to Jewish affairs, the latter is exclusively concerned with Jewish affairs, especially the international scene. A one-year subscription costs $10.

Shalom
Jewish Peace Fellowship
Box 271 • Nyack N.Y. 10960

The Jewish Peace fellowship is a pacifist organization, offering membership to like-minded people and the opportunity to express one's convictions through action and publications including the quarterly newsletter *Shalom*. Membership is $10 per year, ($6 for students); the newsletter is $3 per year, free to members and contributors.

The National Jewish Monthly
1640 Rhode Island Ave., NW
Washington, D.C. 20036

B'nai B'rith publishes *The National Jewish Monthly,* and it is a most attractive and interesting journal. It pays serious attention to American-Jewish artists, in addition to being a good general magazine on matters of Jewish interest. It is far more than the "house organ" one might expect.

Options
Box 311 • Wayne, N.J. 07470

Options calls itself "The Jewish Resources Newsletter." While dealing generally with new developments in the American Jewish Community, this monthly publication contains excellent discussions of new media projects and products being created around the country. A pamphlet describing *Options* is available from Betty J. Singer, its Editor/Publisher. The subscription rate is $12 per year.

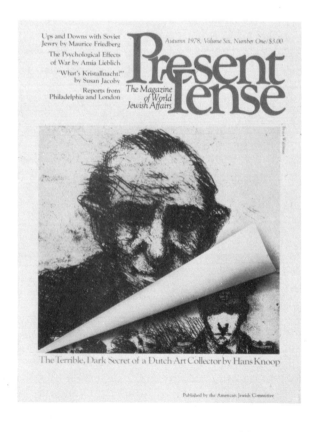

Sh'ma
P.O. Box 567
Port Washington, N.Y. 10050

Sh'ma describes itself as "a journal of Jewish responsibility." Edited by Eugene Borowitz, *Sh'ma* says that it is "too thoughtful for the unreflective and too practical for the mental snobs. It's too Jewish for the self-hating and too humanitarian for the chauvinists." *Sh'ma* is a small journal that courts controversy. It publishes short, provocative think pieces which ask the hard questions American Jews may normally prefer to ignore. It is kept lively by publishing anyone who has something new and exciting to say. At the same time, it has a distinguished group of contributing editors, including Elie Wiesel, Nora Levin, and Blu Greenberg. *Sh'ma* is published bi-weekly, except during the summer.

Tom Thumb
c/o Gottex Industries
1411 Broadway • New York, N.Y. 10018
or 9, Akiva Eiger St. P.O.B 28110
Tel Aviv, Israel

Tom Thumb is the Israeli children's magazine, recommended for the six-to-eleven year old. *Tom Thumb* includes a write-up on a Jewish holiday in each issue, a short Hebrew lesson, and stories and articles about Israeli and Jewish life. Subscriptions are $8.50 per year (group subscriptions available for schools) for ten issues. Also available are two bi-weekly Hebrew language children's magazines: *Etzb'omi*, for ages 7–12, and *Dubbon*, for ages 3–7. *Etzb'omi* is $30 per year and *Dubbon* $24 per year.

The Uforatzto Journal
770 Eastern Pkwy. • Brooklyn, N.Y. 11213

The Uforatzto Journal is published by the Lubavitch Youth Organization. It is a handsomely printed publication which best represents the Lubavitch Chassidim's philosophy and way of life as well as their outreach program. Issued four times a year; write for subscription information.

Yiddish
Queens College • Flushing, N.Y. 11367

Yiddish is a quarterly journal which prints scholarly and critical articles in the field of Yiddish language and literature, as well as translations of lesser-known writers with the goal of providing both a forum and a stimulus for new work. The editors are interested in receiving manuscripts. Write for information about this and for subscription rates.

Yugentruf
3328 Bainbridge Ave. • Bronx, N.Y. 10467

Yugentruf is a Yiddish student-quarterly magazine. It is dedicated to the continuation and propagation of Yiddish. It is a lively little publication, including fiction, poetry, music, etc. Subscriptions are $4 a year, $2.50 for students.

Programs

"If I were Rothschild," goes the fantasy, "I'd be richer than Rothschild; I'd do a little lecturing on the side."

A recent advertisement in *Moment* magazine was addressed to "SPEAKERS!" and offered 11,000 classified one-line jokes. We can appreciate the need for a stock of good one-liners from either side of the lectern, since at one time or another we have all been both bored and inspired by difficult cultural programs. Ideally, every program is stimulating and makes the viewer or participant eager for more. This chapter is designed to be helpful to groups and individuals in search of meaningful cultural, educational, and fundraising events. Fees are not discussed here but should be agreed upon as the arrangements are being made. Most speakers expect their travel expenses to be paid in addition to whatever the honorarium is. Also, be sure to see *Buying: Art Dealers* and *Playing: Dance* and *Music,* and don't forget to look in other sections of this book (particularly *Creating* and *Learning*) for the many talented individuals who also "do a little lecturing on the side." Look

(photo: courtesy C.A.J.E.)

for ♦ symbol throughout the book which indicates that the individual is available for programs.

♦ Meir Abehsera
1852 E. 7th St. • Brooklyn, N.Y. 11223

Moroccan born Meir Michel Abehsera is the descendant of a long line of Sephardic Jewish leaders. At 16 he left Morocco for France where he studied and worked as a civil engineer and a wrought iron craftsman. Plagued with illnesses since childhood, he regained his health through the intensive study and practice of nutrition and oriental medicine, and then became known through his writings and lectures as an expert in this field. He has published numerous authoritative books on natural food and medicine which are considered classics and have sold over a million copies combined. Abehsera was always close to his Jewish roots and in 1968 became a follower of the Lubavitcher Rebbe. He is presently teaching Judaism in America and Europe through his lec-

tures, and is known as something of a Pied Piper, an inspiration to young people who are drifting and confused. His lectures will often include a mixture of Sephardic, Israeli, and Hasidic music and dance. The demand for him is so great that he cannot fulfill every request, but those who meet him are invariably moved by the encounter.

♦ The America-Israel Cultural Foundation
4 E. 54th St. • New York, N.Y. 10022

The America-Israel Cultural Foundation will make available, on request, traveling exhibits dealing with the work of contemporary Israeli artists and craftsmen to community centers, synagogues, and for special Israeli events. Ample time must be allowed for such exhibits to be assembled. They are available both on loan and for sale

MEIR ABEHSERA. (photo: © George F. Meyers)

Suzanne Benton
22 Donnelly Dr. • Ridgefield, Conn. 06877

Using welded-metal masks of female Biblical characters, Suzanne Benton, sculptor, is available for ritual performances, lifestory workshops, exhibitions, and processions. See *Creating: Metal* for more details.

B'nai B'rith Lecture Bureau/Traveling Exhibit Service
1640 Rhode Island Ave., NW
Washington, D.C. 20036

Like the National Jewish Welfare Board, B'nai B'rith has a very complete and active lecture bureau, including Israeli as well as American speakers. Write also for information on subjects and availability of their various traveling exhibits.

American Jewish Archives
3101 Clifton Ave. • Cincinnati, Ohio 45220

The American Jewish Archives has traveling exhibits documenting the history of the Jew in the Western Hemisphere (mostly eighteenth and nineteenth centuries) as well as Jewish participation in the American Civil War and immigration from Eastern Europe.

American Jewish Historical Society
2 Thornton Road • Waltham, Mass. 02154

The American Jewish Historical Society maintains the Academic Council Speakers Service which includes distinguished university scholars and professional historians from all over the country. Write for brochure of speakers, their topics and fees.

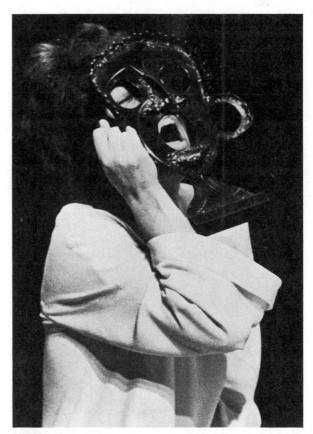

SUZANNE BENTON, "Hagar" mask, from the ritual tale, "Sarah and Hagar".

Board of Jewish Education
426 W. 58th St. • New York, N.Y. 10019

The Board of Jewish Education is the largest central agency for Jewish education in the world, serving some 110,000 children in 660 Jewish schools, and thousands of Jewish educators. It sponsors a wide variety of programs, such as seminars, workshops, and media labs, mostly in the New York City area—though some of its programs are also available nationally through the mails. The BJE is devoted to the principle of Jewish survival through education. Among its other activities it maintains a Jewish Education Hotline to put those seeking some form of Jewish education in touch with appropriate institutions (phone [212] 245-8390).

CAROL BAUMGARTEN, "Yankel the Glassman", soft sculpture ancestor portrait. (photo: Morris Wolf)

Carol Burstein Baumgarten
2040 NE 214 Terr.
North Miami Beach, Fla. 33170

Pratt-trained Carol Baumgarten is available to teach either child or adult workshops in a number of Jewish folkcrafts. She works with clay, paper, and fabric. One of her specialities is helping people make soft sculpture "ancestor portraits."

Abraham Carmel
Washington Jefferson Hotel (Apt. #504)
318 W. 51st St. • New York, N.Y. 10019

Abraham Carmel, the former Father Kenneth Cox, was received into Judaism by the Court of the Chief Rabbi of the British Commonwealth in 1953. He discusses such topics as ; Four Popes and the Jews", "The Compaints of a Convert", "Why a Priest Became a Jew", "Converting Jews to Judaism", and "Religious Roots of Anti-Semitism".

Rubin R. Dobin
"Jews for Jews"
17720 North Bay Road, Suite 8D
Miami Beach, Fla. 33160

The purpose of "Jews For Jews", directed by Rabbi Dobin, is to help and counsel families whose members have become involved with cult groups or missionary organizations. They are in contact with parent and family groups all over the country and are prepared to bring people together for the purpose of self-help. "Jews for Jews" serves as a clearing house for information on all newly-formed cults. No charge is made for any services that the organization provides. A list of experienced speakers in various parts of the country is maintained.

Will Eisner
51 Winslow Road • White Plains, N.Y. 10606

Will Eisner is best known as the creator of "The Spirit" comic strip which first appeared in the forties when the superheros, Batman, Superman, etc., were also introduced. Eisner's character, "The Spirit", wearing an ordinary overcoat and hat but sporting blue gloves and a mask, is a compromise: part superhero and part very human crime fighter working just beyond the reach of the law. The strip is a combination of fantasy, adventure, and humor highlighted by the author's keen insight into people. When I asked him if "The Spirit" has a *Yiddishe neshamah* (Jewish soul), he laughingly replied that Jules Feiffer, who assisted him for a few years with the strip, started that rumor. He then went on in a more serious vein to say that "The Spirit's" view of crime and the criminal was in many ways Talmudic; the villain is never a total criminal and crime is not necessarily absolute. In recent years Eisner has done a lot of work on the use of sequential art (comic books) for special education. He will lecture on this, on "Jews in Comic Books", and possibly other related subjects presented to him. Contact him for availability and fees. See *Learning: Books* for more on Eisner.

David Fishof Productions Inc.
250 W. 57th St. • New York, N.Y. 10019

David Fishof Productions represent many of the best-known stars such as Hershel Bernardi, Sam Levenson, Theodore Bikel, Roberta Peters, and more. They are especially helpful in arranging fund-raisers. Brochures available.

Susan Fleminger
565 First St. • Brooklyn, N.Y. 11215

As coordinator of exhibits for the UAHC, Susan Fleminger has acted as an art consultant for synagogues and community centers and has organized and set up many shows. She is available to help organizations arrange for art exhibits.

Lynn Gottlieb
12 E. 64th St. • New York, N.Y. 10021

Lynn Gottlieb graduated from Hebrew University in Jerusalem and presently serves as rabbi to two congregations of deaf people in New York City. She has been involved with theatre and puppetry since childhood and founded the Bat Kol Players. Her combination of both rabbinic and theatrical background allows her to offer a variety of programming possibilities. She will give talks, offer workshops, be a scholar-in-residence, and conduct services in sign language. A talented woman, an invaluable resource!

Allan Gould
31 Glen Rush Blvd.
Toronto, Ontario M5N 2T4

Allan Gould lectures on Jewish literature, history, sociology, and religion. Several of his talks are slide presentations as well. Some of his topics include: "The Jewish Joke and Jewish Humor", "Trials and Errors: A series of Great Jewish Court Cases", and "The Fourth Commandment: Remember the Sabbath Day. Keep it Wholly?"

Daniel Grossman
Arden Heights Blvd. Jewish Center
1766 Arthur Kill Rd.
Staten Island, N.Y. 10312

Dan is a Rabbi who has developed programs and material on the Jewish deaf. He presents an evening of Music and Jewish sign language which is simultaneously moving and informative.

Israel Showcase Department
American Zionist Federation
515 Park Ave. • New York, N.Y. 10022

The Israel Showcase Department of the American Zionist Federation provides kits for Israel fairs, concentrating on acquainting the public with Israeli products.

The Jewish Museum
1109 Fifth Ave. • New York, N.Y. 10028

The Department of Circulating Exhibits of The Jewish Museum has several traveling exhibits available. These exhibits are easy to install and are especially designed for schools, libraries, colleges, synagogues, and centers. A handsome, illustrated brochure giving details of all the exhibitions, their rental fees, and other information is available by writing to the Registrar at The Jewish Museum.

The Jewish Teacher Center
161 Green Bay Rd. • Wilmette, Ill. 60091

The Jewish Teacher Center is a resource organization, the first of its kind for teachers. Though most of its activities are in-house, it publishes flyers with exciting ideas for special programs in Jewish schools and centers.

Joint Commission on Synagogue Administration of the Union of American Hebrew Congregations and Central Conference of American Rabbis
838 Fifth Ave. • New York, N.Y. 10021

The Commission has a very handy free pamphlet entitled "Sources for Traveling Exhibits and Illustrated Lectures on Judaica and Synagogue Architecture".

JWB Lecture Bureau
The National Jewish Welfare Board
15 E. 26th St. • New·York, N.Y. 10010

The National Jewish Welfare Board Lecture Bureau is the single most important repository of information on Jewish performing artists, lecturers, and other programs of a general nature. Write for its catalog, which includes "The Jewish Arts: A Directory of Artists and Theater", "Young Israeli Concert Artists", and "Learning for Jewish Living" (which covers lecturers, educators, and performers available for forums, debates, recitals, symposia, institutes, concerts, and courses). The Adult Program Services Department of the JWB also publishes a newsletter with information on current lecturers and audio-visual services.

Sydney Kellner
41 Montclair Ave. • Montclair, N.J. 07042

Art historian Sydney Kellner presents a series of illustrated lectures dealing with archaeological topics such as: "Archaeology of the Holy Land", and "New Light on Ancient and Modern Israel; the Archaeological Explosion".

Lilith Magazine
250 West 57th St. (Suite 1328)
New York, N.Y. 10019

Lilith, the feminist Jewish magazine, has an active speakers bureau; its editors are also available to lecture and travel.

Judah L. Magnes Memorial Museum
2911 Russell St. • Berkeley, Calif. 94705

The Judah L. Magnes Memorial Museum has various traveling exhibits available. Write for details.

Larry Mandell
6720 Paseo Redondo • El Paso, Texas 79912

Larry Mandell produces films for the U.S. Army and can arrange for showings of especially interesting films such as the official army films of the Nuremberg trials.

Network
15 E. 26th St. • New York, N.Y. 10010

Network is the coordinating organization of Jewish university student activities nationwide. It is the source of a wealth of programming ideas and materials. It publishes *Network,* the newsletter of the Jewish student movement, and *The Guide to Jewish Student Groups;* it maintains the Jewish Student Press Service; it has a field worker project (the field worker visits Jewish students on campuses around the nation and endeavors to plug them into *Network*); it organizes regional conferences; it houses the New Jewish Media Project; it manages a speaker's bureau; it maintains a resource center.

VELVEL PASTERNAK at the Conference on Alternatives in Jewish Education. (photo: Mae Rockland)

Velvel Pasternak
29 Derby Avenue • Cedarhurst, N.Y. 11516

Velvel Pasternak, who has the largest mail order catalog of Israeli, Hasidic, Yiddish, Cantorial, and Ladino sheet music, recordings, and cassettes, is available for lectures anywhere in the country. Not only is he incredibly knowledgeable about Jewish music but his presentations are enhanced with snatches of recorded music (he sings a few bars from time to time as well). His presentation of history is anecdotal and humorous and thoroughly enjoyable.

Mae Shafter Rockland
106 Francis St. • Brookline, Mass. 02146

I try to do everything that I can to promote the growth of Jewish crafts and art in America. My time is divided between my own art work (see *Creating: Pictures* and *Textiles*), writing books, and "a little lecturing on the side". My topics include: "Jewish Art is Alive and Well in America", and "How to Be a Jewish-American Folk Artist", using your own skills and life experiences to create heirlooms. Slides and show-and-tell of actual objects accompany these talks. I also run day-long workshops on "Designing and Making Jewish Things". These are hands-on demonstrations and/or participatory instruction in batik, papercutting, and printing without a press: silkscreen and stamp-pad with Jewish symbols and colors in mind.

Sylvia Rothchild
19 Hilltop Road • Brookline, Mass. 02146

Sylvia Rothchild is an able and interesting lecturer and panel participant in literary and Holocaust related areas. Her most recent work is a compilation of oral history interviews with Holocaust survivors about what they did *after* their W.W.II experiences.

Zalman M. Schachter
B'nai Or
6723 Emlen St. • Philadelphia, Pa.

Zalman Schachter is well known as a guru for many people. He will lead retreats and weekends. Brochures and cassettes on various Jewish topics are available.

Peninnah Schram,
POM Records
525 West End Avenue (Suite 8C)
New York, N.Y. 10024

Peninnah Schram is a storyteller who keeps audiences of adults and/or children spellbound as she gracefully retells folk tales, legends, and parables. If you can't arrange to hear her in person (which is a treat), I heartily recommend her record "A Storyteller's Journey", a collection of five Molly

MAE ROCKLAND and students at screen printing workshop sponsored by Brandeis University Hillel. (photos: courtesy Brandeis University)

PENINNAH SCHRAM, story teller.

Cohen stories, available for $5.95, plus .65¢ postage (N.Y. residents add sales tax); cassettes, $6.95, from the address above.

Danny Siegel
c/o Dr. and Mrs. Julius Siegel
1600 S. Eads St., 712-N
Arlington, Va. 22202

Danny Siegel is a favorite of Hillel Directors everywhere; and no wonder. His poetry presentations are as amusing and moving as they are intellectually stimulating. His talks on such diverse subjects as "Tzedakah: the Privilege, Joy, and Dignity of Giving"; "Ugliness and Beauty in the Jewish Tradition"; "Loneliness: Angels in our lives"; "Goofing-Off for the Sake of Heaven: Applied Simha"; and "The Grandeur of Old Age in Poetry and Midrash", are informed, scholarly, and inspiring. Danny has a way of dissecting daily life and getting to the core of Jewish values that are (or are not) present. He also has slide programs on Soviet Jews and synagogues and on "Poland (Warsaw, Maidanek, Auschwitz, Cracow): Aftermath of the Holocaust". Whether your group wants him for a "serious but light" or a "light but substantial" program, you will not be disappointed. An encounter with Danny is exhilarating. Read more about him in *Observing: Charity*.

Skirball Museum of the Hebrew Union College
3077 University Ave.
Los Angeles, Calif. 90007

The Skirball Museum has several traveling exhibits of Judaica available. Write for details.

Spertus College of Judaica
618 South Michigan Ave.
Chicago, Ill. 60605

Some of the Spertus College of Judaica faculty are available for lectures to groups and organizations. Speakers and topics include: Rachel Dulin: "Archaeology and Its Relevance for Understanding the Bible"; Warren Bargad: "Twentieth Century Hebrew Fiction"; Martin Goldman: "The Talmud and Contemporary Society; Medical Issues, Poverty, Psychology"; Monford Harris: "Life in the Community of the Devout, a medieval Jewish Community"; Mayer Gruber: "Dance and Body Language in the Bible"; Moses Shulvass: "The Jewish Experience: History of The Jewish People." David Weinstein, the president of Spertus since 1964, is also available for talks on "Judaic Studies on the College Campus," and "The Future of the Private Institution of Higher Learning." Contact Ruth G. Silverman, the Public Relations Coordinator, for more information about individual speakers and subjects.

Yaakov Spivak
P.O. Box 122 ● Monsey, N.Y. 10952

As well as a slide presentation on "The Holocaust," Rabbi Spivak has other fascinating lecture slide shows including one on "Jewish Marriage and Divorce," and another on "The Missionary Movement Against the Jews" which discusses the history of the missionary movement and also presents suggestions to parents concerned about protecting their children from various fringe groups. Write for illustrated brochure describing his programs.

Synagogue Rescue Project, Att: Eric Byron
2067 Broadway, (Suite 27)
New York, N.Y. 10023

Eric Byron is urban anthropologist, specializing in Jewish ethnicity. He is available for lectures about the work of the Synagogue Rescue Project which is trying to preserve the remnant of Jewish culture on the Lower East Side of Manhattan. Recently a synagogue was purchased which is now in the process of being restored and which will eventually house a library and museum. The project is also branching out into other N.Y. suburbs. The project's work, as described by Byron, is a source of inspiration for communities all over the country trying to preserve a bit of Jewish-American culture as it once was.

Tora Dojo Association
192 Beechmont Drive
New Rochelle, N.Y. 10804

The Tora Dojo Association was founded by Chaim Sobor who teaches Modern Hebrew and Archaeology at Yeshiva University. The association is the only Jewish Karate federation and has 20 schools located throughout New York, Connecticut, and New Jersey. Chaim Sobor is available for lecture demonstrations.

Arthur Waskow
1747 Connecticut Ave., N:W.
Washington, D.C. 20009

Arthur Waskow is available as a Shabbaton leader and a *sheliach tzibbur* for services using body-movement in connection with the Siddur. He will also speak on such topics as "Godwrestling", "The Havurah: New Form of Jewish Life?", and "Before There was a Before: Stories of the Creation for Children and Adults".

SYNAGOGUE RESCUE PROJECT: Anshe Slonim, the oldest synagogue building in N.Y.C. (photo: © Bill Aron, see *Creating: Pictures*)

BILL ARON, "The Lower East Side and Brooklyn by night, from the air". See *Creating: Pictures* for more about Aron's travelling exhibitions and slide show.

The Workman's Circle
45 E. 33rd St. • New York, N.Y. 10016

Joseph Mlotek, Workmen's Circle Education Director, can be contacted for information about Yiddish entertainers.

Yeshiva University Museum
185th St. and Amsterdam Ave.
New York, N.Y. 10033

The Yeshiva University Museum has extensive materials available about the history and development of Yeshiva University. Selections from this enormous resource can be borrowed. Also available are photographs of exhibitions held at the Museum. Depending on the subject in which you may be interested, the Museum can also help with materials and photographs of objects from its considerable permanent collection, which includes the Torah Scroll of the Baal Shem Tov. Contact the Public Relations Department for detailed information.

Joseph Young
1434 S. Spaulding Ave.
Los Angeles, Calif. 90019

The multidimensional artist, Joseph Young, who has created many impressive art works for Jewish institutions (see *Creating: Art for Architecture*), has an extensive slide library on contemporary Jewish art throughout the world. He uses this material in multimedia lecture presentations and seminars on Jewish art.

Yugentruf Youth for Yiddish
3328 Bainbridge Ave.
Bronx, N.Y. 10467
and
200 W. 72nd St. (Room 40)
New York, N.Y. 10023

Yugentruf (Call to Youth) is a worldwide organization of Yiddish-speaking youth founded in 1964 to give young people an opportunity to come together to speak Yiddish, read and study Yiddish works, and write, sing, dance, act, and create in Yiddish. Only minimal fluency is required for membership.

Yugentruf has two offices, its Resource Center in Manhattan and its Youth for Yiddish office in the Bronx. *Yugentruf* magazine (see *Learning: Periodicals*) is published at the Bronx office which also distributes tee shirts which say "YIDDISH" in Hebrew letters (blue or red), as well as buttons which say (in Yiddish) "Speak to me in Yiddish." (See *Buying: Gifts and Greeting Cards.*) Yugentruf has a full-time field worker who will travel anywhere in North America to provide ideas, programs, and bibliographies to help establish Yiddish clubs and courses, particularly on campuses.

Finally, Yugentruf maintains a speakers bureau and a list of instructors of Yiddish language, literature, and culture.

Zion Talis Manufacturing Co.
48 Eldridge St. • New York, N.Y. 10002

The Zion Talis Manufacturing Co. has a traveling exhibit that traces the history of the prayer shawl through the ages. It is available on request to organizations, institutions, and congregations for a maximum of two weeks. Freight charges to be borne by those requesting the exhibit. Write for more information.

Teaching Aids

Levy Teitlebaum learning the alef-bet, Montreal. From "Portfolio One", © Neil Folberg.

While it is my hope that all the sections of this book will be helpful to educators, the sources listed here have been assembled especially for the religious school teacher who is continually involved with the problems of Jewish education and is always on the lookout for ways of enlivening the classroom. All the firms in this section are particularly committed to the production of exciting classroom materials; check the index for listings of specific products by some of these outfits. Write for catalogs and descriptive literature.

Alternatives in Religious Education, Inc.
3945 S. Oneida • Denver, Colo. 80237

Ask for information about *The Jewish Teacher's Handbook*, edited by Audrey Friedman Marcus, and their stimulating catalog.

B. Arbit Books
8050 N. Port Washington Rd.
Milwaukee, Wis. 53217

Interesting catalog describes rub-on Hebrew lettering for paste-ups, posters and labels, cloth-mounted maps of Israel, game-making kits, and more.

Behrman House Inc.
1261 Broadway • New York, N.Y. 10001

Seymour Rossel, vice-president at Behrman House, writes that the publisher is "now in the process of planning new classroom materials to meet the needs of students and teachers in a new decade". He welcomes comments and criticisms from interested educators "including peeves and hopes". Ask about Debbie Friedman's charming

BEHRMAN HOUSE INC., "Alef Bet", musical curriculum for *Hebrew and Heritage.*

"Alef Bet" record which accompanies the *Hebrew and Heritage* series.

Board of Jewish Education
426 W. 58th St. • New York, N.Y. 10019

See multiple listings throughout the book. Their audio-visual catalog lists "My Life or Yours", an original audio-drama about the contemporary relevance of the Talmud. Geared to teenagers it was the gold medal winner at the AMER Festival and when I tried it out informally on students and teachers it was very well received and generated a lot of lively idea exchanges.

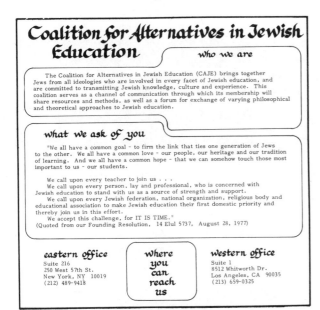

Coalition for Alternatives in Jewish Education

who we are

The Coalition for Alternatives in Jewish Education (CAJE) brings together Jews from all ideologies who are involved in every facet of Jewish education, and are committed to transmitting Jewish knowledge, culture and experience. This coalition serves as a channel of communication through which its membership will share resources and methods, as well as a forum for exchange of varying philosophical and theoretical approaches to Jewish education.

what we ask of you

"We all have a common goal - to firm the link that ties one generation of Jews to the other. We all have a common love - our people, our heritage and our tradition of learning. And we all have a common hope - that we can somehow touch those most important to us - our students.

We call upon every teacher to join us . . .
We call upon every person, lay and professional, who is concerned with Jewish education to stand with us as a source of strength and support.
We call upon every Jewish federation, national organization, religious body and educational association to make Jewish education their first domestic priority and thereby join us in this effort.
We accept this challenge, for IT IS TIME."
(Quoted from our Founding Resolution, 14 Elul 5737, August 28, 1977)

eastern office
Suite 216
250 West 57th St.
New York, NY 10019
(212) 489-9418

where you can reach us

western office
Suite 1
8512 Whitworth Dr.
Los Angeles, CA 90035
(213) 659-0325

Everyone who has attended any of the first four CAJE conferences has come away stimulated and enriched by the sharing of ideas with people from every corner of Jewish education. It is an experience not to be missed.

Educational Horizons
15445 Ventura Blvd. (Suite #10)
Sherman Oaks, Calif. 91316

Educational Horizons specializes in electronic learning games for Jewish education. Write for their catalog and a free introductory copy of their newsletter "Chicken Soup".

Educational Resources
24010 Oxnard St.
Woodland Hills, Calif. 91367

Their catalog shows a variety of teaching aids such as finger puppets, time-telling board games, posters, and cassettes.

Heinle and Heinle Enterprises
29 Lexington Road • Concord, Mass. 01742

Everything offered in Heinle and Heinle's catalog is as visually attractive as it is useful.

Kohl Jewish Teacher Center
161 Green Bay Rd. • Wilmette,ill. 60091

Mail orders accepted for subscription to "Jewish Teacher Center in a Bag". For $20 you will receive three "Bags" of classroom materials for primary and intermediate groups.

The Learning Plant
6950 Country Place Road
West Palm Beach, Fla. 33411

Illustrated catalog available.

(photo: Richard Speedy)

Union of American Hebrew Congregations
838 Fifth Avenue • New York, N.Y. 10021

I imagine that most teachers are aware of the wealth of material offered by the UAHC, from *Keeping Posted*, the student magazine which for twenty years has been a marvelous tool in Jewish education (I still have some of the early issues which I've saved from my days as a Sunday school teacher at the Temple of Aaron in St. Paul) to *Compass*, the teacher's magazine. Rabbis Dan Syme and Steve Reuban, National Director and Associate Director of Education, respectively, are eager to have open lines of communication with educators all over the country and are always looking for fresh approaches and ideas for books and projects.

BUYING

Here we are in the middle of an inflationary recession, which the best minds in the country are having difficulty diagnosing, and I am writing a book full of places to spend money. "Well," says the brilliant young economist David Rockland (my son), "Mom, that may not be a bad idea. What this country needs is two Hanukkah-Christmas buying seasons. If you could convince folks that there was another big shopping time coming up in July, why they'd all rush out to beat the crowds, start spending like mad, and that would jack up the economy and solve the unemployment problem right there!"

David is no doubt right, but there has to be some other redeeming reason besides salvaging our confused economy for buying the things described in this book. More than any of the others, this section of the book reflects the secular side of Jewish-American life. In our super acquisitive society we very often feel indifference rather than enjoyment when we buy the very things that are advertised as pleasure producing. Especially when we are very carefully watching our pocketbooks, it makes intellectual as well as emotional sense to have that money which we allocate for the "little luxuries" perform double service by giving us that warm ethnic glow that comes from acquiring something with the possible hallmarks of an heirloom.

Antiques and Reproductions

Collecting antique Judaica is usually a very emotional business. I have bought my share of genuine fakes complete with stories. When I lived in Spain I naively believed I was rescuing pieces of my past from the Inquisition, and when traveling in Israel I was duped by storytelling "antique" dealers. Yet, even though I felt silly afterwards, I am still happy with my purchases because they are beautiful objects which I enjoy living with and they are worth what I paid for them in terms of materials and artistry. The "stories" were a dispensable bonus. If I had been buying for investment I would probably hate myself. The serious collector of pre-Columbian art, French furniture, oriental rugs or what have you, is probably equally spurred by love of the beauty and craftmanship of a particular period as he is by thoughts of investing. With Judaica collectors, investment is rarely the motive for a purchase; rather it is a love of heritage and a feeling that each addition to the "collection" is yet another link with our past. We tend to use the word "investment" as a cover for gut-level enjoyment. Nevertheless it cannot be denied that Jewish antiques, especially because of their rarity, are indeed a very sound investment and pieces of exquisite artistry comparable to any other field of antiques are available (albeit at very respectable prices) in Judaica. It is always wisest to consult an expert—not necessarily one in the field of Judaica but someone knowledgeable about the period you *think* you are buying from. A silver or print appraiser, for example, can help you date and evaluate a piece even if he is ignorant of the particular Jewish iconography. With my admitted history of having been burned, all I can say is: beware and enjoy.

The antique dealers listed here are very careful of their reputations and knowledgeable about the Jewish antiques they handle. Antiques, by their very nature, are one-of-a-kind objects and the artifacts shown here are meant only as examples of possible purchases. Reproductions and almost antique "collectibles" are available in greater quantity and can also be a very satisfying and less expensive way of linking us with a bygone era.

MORIAH, Havdalah spice box, German.

Brobury House Gallery
Brobury, Herefordshire, England

The Brobury House Gallery sells original antique prints. They have a good selection of Judaica and old Palestine views and maps. An illustrated general catalog of old prints is available for $3; lists of Palestine views, maps, and Judaica (not illustrated) are free on request. They accept mail orders all the time, restore, mount, and frame prints, and are generally very accomodating. If you are searching for a particular print they might very well be able to help you find it.

Degen Enterprises
P.O. Box 1557 • New Brunswick, N.J. 08903

Degen Enterprises specializes in an area which is not really antique but still of interest to the collector of oldish things. They deal in old photographic images and have many of the Holy Land, both hand-tinted and black-and-white from 1900–1930. Their annual fully-illustrated catalogue is $4.95.

Grand Sterling Silver Co.
345 Grand St. • New York, N.Y. 10002

The Grand Sterling Silver Company manufactures and imports all types of sterling silver items from throughout the world. It specializes in reproductions of old Judaica art pieces and has an enormous line of different objects. One can easily spend hours poring over their profusely illustrated catalog. Havdalah spice box collectors will marvel at the many intriguing reproductions of old pieces that are offered. Grand Sterling accepts commissions for special items as well as mail orders.

Jewish Folklore and Ethnology Newsletter
YIVO Institute for Jewish Research
1048 Fifth Avenue • New York, N.Y. 10028

For as long as they last, vintage Jewish New Year greeting cards from the early twentieth century are being offered by the Jewish Folklore and Ethnology Newsletter. All proceeds go to support the newsletter (see *Learning: Periodicals*). As with the artifacts offered by Degen Enterprises, these are not proper "antiques," yet when one considers

the many changes in Jewish life since the beginning of this century, everything that is pre W.W. II feels like a relic from a very distant era. The greetings offered here are multicolored lithographs on paper. One is a 3" × 8⅜" "check for 365 days of health, wealth, and happiness," featuring the New York skyline, a zeppelin, a ship's anchor, and assorted traditional symbols, "payable to the Bank of Heaven" ($3). The second takes the form of a ship's ticket which is good for 120 years of round trips in the stream of life. The imagery includes the Statue of Liberty, ships at sea, a dock, and a shofar. In Yiddish and Hebrew, pink, blue, yellow, and brown; 11¾" × 8¾" ($10). Both prints are as decorative as they are nostalgically fascinating.

The Jewish Museum Shop
1109 Fifth Ave. • New York, N.Y. 10028

The Jewish Museum Shop has a wide variety of interesting items for sale (see *Buying: Gifts*), and has reproduced some objects from the Museum's Judaica collection. These and other beautiful items make the shop an intriguing place to visit, but if you can't make it there in person a well-illustrated catalog (50¢) with price list is available. Mail orders are accepted and processed promptly, and fundraising organizations and sisterhoods are offered special discounts on purchases.

Bette Levin, Appraiser
930 Noriega St. • San Francisco, Calif. 94122

Bette Levin is associated with an appraisal firm with specialists in gems, jewelry, residential contents, machinery, antiques, and real estate. Bette's own specialty is fine arts and Judaica. She is a member of the American Society of Appraisers and of the Appraisers Association of America. Most of her work is done for insurance purposes and for estates. She works on an hourly basis (which in my

THE JEWISH MUSEUM SHOP, amulet, reproduction of a 17th-century good luck charm. Hebrew blessing and the names of angels were the source of its strength. 4" × 1¾", pewter.

opinion is preferable to a percentage of the appraised value system used by some appraisers) and will travel anywhere to appraise a collection. She must see the objects, which she examines and photographs. This is followed up with research for identification and valuation. The client receives two copies of the appraisal and mounted photographs. Her flat hourly rate ($100 for the first hour, then $60 per hour, plus travel time) includes photography and examination in the client's home; the research is on her own time. An average appraisal will take 3–5 hours.

Moriah Antique Judaica
699 Madison Ave. • New York, N.Y. 10021

Genuine love for the material is what makes Moriah Antique Judaica a very special place. Run by father and son, Peter and Michael Ehrenthal, this is the leading gallery of authentic Jewish antiques. The seasoned collector with thousands to spend for rare and magnificent early pieces is no doubt aware of how helpful and knowledgeable the Ehrenthals can be. I'd like novice collectors of moderate means to know that they too can find satisfying objects at Moriah. Turn-of-the-century Kiddush cups, spice boxes, and Torah pointers, for

BETTE LEVIN, examples of Judaica she is called upon to evaluate.

MORIAH, spice box, Polish, 17th-century, very rare.

example, can be found with price tags in the low hundreds. They also have old prints as well as ceremonial objects. Despite their Madison Avenue address the Ehrenthals make a point of having affordable quality items available. They also handle work by several contemporary artists (such as Moss and Muchnik, see *Creating: Pictures*) whose work they feel will be the antique heirlooms of the future. Moriah will send photographs on request and will help you find specific antique Judaica objects; they are also expert appraisers. A word of advice from Michael Ehrenthal: "Be careful and cautious at auctions!"

Alexander Oland, reproduction of antique amulets and a 17th century ceremonial wedding ring in 14K gold.

MORIAH, Havdalah candle holder with drawer for spices, 11", German, 17th century; silver Hanukkah lamp, Vienna, 1845.

The Museum Store
Spertus Museum of Judaica
618 S. Michigan Ave. • Chicago, Ill. 60605

The Spertus Museum store sells antiques (at least one hundred years old) and antiquities (objects from archaeological diggings) along with its large and diverse selection of Israeli arts and crafts. If you are looking for a specific item, write to the manager, Jeffrey Kraft. You can be assured of a considered reply and help in your search if at all possible.

Alexander Oland
120 W. 44th St. • New York, N.Y. 10036

Alex Oland was a manufacturing jeweler for over 30 years. Now his business interests are almost

entirely in real estate but his "hobby" (which for less energetic people would be a full-time business in itself) is the creation of replicas of antique gold ornaments. Among his reproductions of artifacts from many cultures are some of Jewish interest. He has a number of different amulet designs and several copies of 17th-century ceremonial wedding rings. Write for color brochure and price list. (See also *Buying: Gifts*.)

Charles Sessler, Inc.
1308 Walnut St. • Philadelphia, Pa. 19107

Lewis A. Shepard
2 Congress St. • Worcester, Mass. 01609

Both Charles Sessler and Lewis Shepard are purveyors of antique, old and rare prints, and maps. Sessler has a $4 catalog available, Shepard sends slides and photographs of work on request; both accept mail orders. At Shepard's I have seen interesting 18th- and 19th-century prints and drawings with Biblical subjects such as William Blake's Job Illustrations and Rembrandt's "Mordecai's Triumph". Shepard also has Chagall illustrations from the Bible. The prices begin at about $150–200 going much higher for 16th-century rarities.

Emanuel Weisberg Antique Judaica
45 Essex St. • New York, N.Y. 10002

This second-story shop on New York's Lower East Side sells antiques and antique reproductions alongside its stock of religious items. Antiques are, of course, one-of-a-kind, but the replicas are made in number. In particular, Weisberg features a reproduction of an antique amulet.

Art Dealers

BEZALEL JEWISH ART GALLERY, from left to right, M.D. and Olga Weinstock, proprietors; Zhanna and Emmanuil Snitkovsky, artists, and their work.

While many artists prefer to sell their works exclusively from their studios, most find that having at least one gallery or dealer who displays and sells their work is a great help. Not only does it free them to produce more art but gallery representation also introduces their work to more and different people than they might otherwise reach. Most dealers represent many artists, though perhaps specialize in a particular type of work, thus giving the collector-consumer the opportunity to become familiar with different styles. Some of the dealers in this section handle Israeli and

Jewish work exclusively, while others have non-Jewish work as well. If your organization is planning an art exhibit or craft fair for educational or fundraising purposes several of the galleries listed here can be very helpful. Ideally an art dealer of Judaica is equally knowledgeable about aesthetics, the iconographic and functional meaning of each piece, and the techniques and processes displayed in every work he/she sells. In that way the patron of the arts receives an education and becomes a more sophisticated and demanding consumer and encourages artists to reach for their highest levels.

Bezalel Jewish Art Gallery
11 Essex St. • New York, N.Y. 10002

Bezalel sells oil paintings, lithographs, and rare prints of Jewish interest. Since Bezalel does not have a catalog (because its stock is continuously changing), it helps if you know what you are looking for and can write with a specific request. They do, however, have illustrated brochures about the different artists they handle. Bezalel will accept collector's items or signed lithographs for resale on consignment. An art show or auction can be arranged in conjunction with a specific institutional event or as a separate fund-raising affair. In any case, this dealer will supply invitations, posters, and catalogs of the art to be sold. Between 20% and 50% of the gross income from such auctions or shows is given to the sponsoring organization.

The Chassidic Art Institute (CHAI)
375 Kingston Ave. • Brooklyn, N.Y. 11213

The Chassidic Art Institute exhibits and sells paintings and prints by Hasidic artists such as Zalman Kleinman (see *Creating: Pictures*) and also work by Israeli and Russian Jewish artists. They will help find you a calligrapher to do a ketubah and put you in touch with artists who can handle any Jewish design or art work. The gallery sponsors art auctions and the directors are available for lectures. The institute was founded with the express purpose of providing a permanent showcase for Hasidic art breaking the stereotype that the traditional Jewish lifestyle was rigid and devoid of creativity. Hasidic artists express their vision in every medium and on every subject. Brochure available.

Rachel Davis Gallery
2402 Addison • Houston, Texas 77030

Rachel Davis handles the work of California artist David Moss among others (see *Creating: Pictures*).

The Jewish Development Co.
18331-C Irvine Blvd. • Tustin, Calif. 92680

"Everything Jewish you've ever wanted and didn't know where to find" is the motto of this shop, the first (independent) all-Jewish bookstore and gallery to open in Southern California's rapidly growing Orange County. The store's owner, Anne Rolbin, feels that her merchandise offers buyers opportunities for intellectual and spiritual growth—thus the name Jewish Development Company. Artists and craftspeople take note: the store is seeking established and developing artists with unusual Jewish items and is interested in serving as a retail outlet for them. Inquiries and special orders are handled promptly.

Jay Johnson America's Folk Heritage Gallery
72 E. 56th Street • New York, N.Y. 10022

Jay Johnson's stock in trade is obvious from the name of his gallery. He has many works with Biblical themes and represents Malcah Zeldis exclusively (see *Creating: Pictures*). The gallery recently showed a collection of works depicting animals in the Bible. Brochures are available and Mr. Johnson lectures widely on Folk Art.

JAY JOHNSON GALLERY, "Jonah in the Whale" by Virgil Norberg. Weather vane sheet metal sculpture, 67" long × 67" high.

The Judaic Heritage Society
866 United Nations Plaza • Suite 4011
New York, N.Y. 10017

The Judaic Heritage Society commissions individual artists to design limited-edition artworks of an enduring nature such as sculptures and graphics. Write for more information.

Keresh Gallery
1223 Noyes Drive • Silver Spring, Md. 20910

The Keresh Gallery specializes in Israeli prints and provides a number of services for Jewish organizations such as illustrated talks and special showings. Contact Henry Einhorn for more information.

Kolbo
435 Harvard St. • Brookline, Mass. 02146

In the fall of 1978 Billy Mencow came to my studio and said, "I'm going to open a Hanukkah store, what do you have for me and who else do you know?" And with a high degree of energy and *hutzpah* Billy's shop "Kolbo" opened in November of that year in Cambridge, around the corner from Harvard University. He has since moved to Brookline, taking over what had once been a kosher butchershop. The atmosphere at Kolbo is lively; folks come in as much to visit as to see and buy the variety of contemporary craft and art objects on display. Kolbo has more Jewish ceramics by different ceramists from all over the country than any place I've yet visited. Billy is always eager to hear from artists specializing in Judaica—any medium—who would like him to represent them. An interesting collection of posters and greeting cards is available through the mail and Billy will make every effort to fill special requests for craft items. In the fall of 1980 Kolbo will be opening another shop on the Upper West Side of New York City. While not an artist himself, Billy has a flair for merchandising which one might call inspired; look out for Billy!

KOLBO, Billy Mencow: "One sensible pursuit and location for someone with a lifelong sense of strong family, Jewish community, and Jewish nationhood is as proprietor of a contemporary Judaica shop in the heart of Jewish Boston." (photo: Mae Rockland)

Marcus Fine Arts
5816 S. Blackstone Ave.
Chicago, Ill. 60637

Cilla and Joseph Marcus have recently started to officially represent the Association of Artists and Sculptors of the three kibbutz movements in Israel and work with the Kibbutz Gallery in Tel Aviv. Write for brochure and more information.

Pucker/Safrai Gallery
171 Newbury St. • Boston, Mass. 02116

The Pucker/Safrai Gallery has an outstanding collection of artwork by some of the finest Israeli artists. Among others, it represents Bak, Basson, Bezem, Katz, Moreh, Rothman, Rubin, Sharir, Stern, and Weil. As well as paintings, it has an extraordinary collection of graphics. A selection of these are shown in the gallery's "Graphics of Israel" catalog. All of the Pucker/Safrai catalogs are in themselves beautiful enough to keep with your art books. Mail orders are accepted, and if you write for catalogs ask for an order form and

PUCKER/SAFRAI GALLERY, "Virgin's Garden," color lithograph by David Sharir.

sample pack of notepaper, which comes in sixteen different designs, twelve cards and envelopes of one design to a box. An illustrated booklet explaining how to organize an exhibition of Israeli art is available upon request, and Bernie and Sue Pucker, who run the gallery, are as eager to be helpful as they are well informed. Bernie gives outstanding lectures on art—with special emphasis on Jewish artists and themes (the fee goes to charity). The Puckers are especially concerned with the careful handling and preservation of artwork, particularly that on paper which is so often damaged by improper matting and framing. Anyone buying a paper work of art from the Pucker/Safrai Gallery which they plan to have framed elsewhere receives a flyer discussing the proper way to care for art on paper. This flyer is available to readers of this book free of charge. When I thanked Bernie for providing this service, he said, ''If we save just ten pieces in the next twenty years, it's worth it.'' The gallery offers several other excellent services as well, such as traveling exhibits and appraisals. If you want to receive the gallery newsletter 3–4 times a year, just send your name and address. Should you want to receive their handsome color catalogues, the fee is $20.

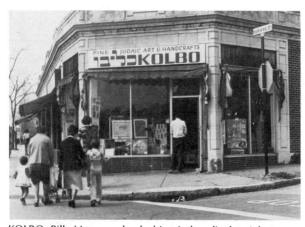

KOLBO, Billy Mencow checks his window display. (photo: Mae Rockland)

Russian Images Ltd.
The Bank Tower
307 Fourth Avenue • Pittsburgh, Pa. 15222

Russian Images is the exclusive gallery, dealer, and publisher for contemporary art from the USSR. They represent several Russian Jewish artists, among them Anatolii Kaplan. A handsome set of illustrated brochures representing several republics of the USSR is available for $1 to cover postage and handling. Mail orders are accepted. Russian Images offers a lecture program/slide presentation which is free in the Pittsburgh area; there is a fee for non-local presentations.

RUSSIAN IMAGES LTD., Lithograph from Sholom Aleichem's ''Tevia the Milkman'' by Anatolii Kaplan.

Cards, Gifts, and Collectibles

"Happy Birthday Zaydeh", from Keren and Shoshanah.
(photo: Jim McDonald)

I have so many collections, that my collections have collections. I fancy myself a fancier of Jewish art and antiques and bemoan the thin pocketbook that limits my manias. More accessible are artifacts from the popular culture, so I've started to collect them. *"Tchatchkes"* my mother used to call them, but nevertheless I am fond of my accumulation of Jewish trivia. I tell myself that future historians will document our era by its bumper-stickers, place mats, buttons, and T-shirts. Often when we look for a meaningful gift—even for a Jewish occasion—we overlook the possibility of getting something with Jewish content. Whether due to embarrassment or a certain (but inaccurate)

knowledge that there is "Nothing Jewish that's interesting", we tend to overlook the possibility of enriching our own as well as the recipient's Jewish cultural life. In this chapter I've grouped together those sources which identify themselves as purveyors of "gifts"—meaning something we wouldn't treat ourselves to but will buy for someone else. Goodies—tokens of affections and esteem. To this group I've added sources for additions to our collections which of course are also potential "gifts." Make certain to check listings in the other sections as well when you are looking for that specially important present.

CARDS

All through the year when holidays and special events come around, we look for unique greeting cards to convey personal messages. Until recently commercial Jewish cards by the major card companies were very dreary. Perhaps they have improved considerably because so many small card manufacturers and distributors have sprung up with innovative designs. This seems to be an example of healthy competition when more is more! Write to all of the addresses here for specific ordering directions and quantity discounts.

Adelantre!
The Judezmo Society
4594 Bedford Avenue
Brooklyn, N.Y. 11235

Ladino poetry and Purim cards.

American Jewish Historical Society
2 Thornton Road • Waltham, Mass. 02154

Full-color notecards reproducing six paintings in the Society's collections.

Artforms Card Corp.
1207 Glencoe Ave.
Highland Park, Ill. 60035

Outstanding full-color cards for all holidays, life cycle events, and get-well, sympathy, and new home; gift tags and wrap also.

ART FORMS CARD CORP.

Binah Bindell
"Silent Stories Art Creations"
19 Oakwood St. • Albany, N.Y. 12208

Blank note cards and occasion cards; commissions accepted for personalized cards for holidays and family events.

Rose Ann Chasman
6147 North Richmond • Chicago, Ill. 60659

Calligrapher, papercutter, and needlework artist Rose Ann Chasman also produces a folkloric and charming line of greeting cards. These are well printed on quality stock.

ROSE ANN CHASMAN.

Degi Designs
2201 Grand Ave. So.
Minneapolis, Minn. 55405

Peggy Davis is the designer for Degi Designs (see *Creating: Calligraphy*) which produces greeting cards and postcards for Rosh Hashanah and Hanukkah, $1.50 for a package of ten. Think of the postage you'll save!

Kadish Gaibel
Herzog 55 • Jerusalem, Israel

A variety of calligraphic New Year cards.

Jeff Graber
Yofi Stationery
92 Randolph St. • Springfield, Mass. 01108

An amusing all-occasion line. Personalized cards and notepaper can be arranged.

Hanucraft
8271 N.W. 56th Street • Miami, Fla. 33166

Nancy Greenberg the calligrapher and watercolor painter has created a series of greeting cards including designs for weddings, engagement, new baby, sympathy, confirmation, bar mitzvah, bat mitzvah, and general mazel tov. Each card is in full-color on white vellum stock. The inside is blank. They cost 60¢ per card plus postage. Write for details. (See also *Creating: Calligraphy.*)

King David Publishers Inc.
109-05 72nd Ave. • Forest Hills, N.Y. 11375

After receiving many requests to create Jewish greeting cards, Mark Podwal formed King David Publishers with his brother David who now runs the firm. The black-and-white drawings are exquisite and the blank cards are special for any occasion and holiday. (See also *Creating: Pictures.*)

KING DAVID PUBLISHERS INC.

Jonathan Kremer
124 Oxford Street #5
Cambridge, Mass. 02140

Jonathan Kremer's attractive brochure describes his interesting and illustrated line of greeting cards which are available in packages of 10, 20, 30, 40 or 50. There is an additional price break for orders of more than 50 cards. (See also *Creating: Calligraphy.*)

JONATHAN KREMER.

Pucker / Safrai Gallery
171 Newbury St. • Boston, Mass. 02116

This gallery, which handles some of the best Israeli artwork, reproduces some of the pictures in its collection on a series of sixteen different note cards. (See *Buying: Art Dealers.*)

Ruttenberg and Everette Yiddish Film Library
Lown Building
415 South St. • Waltham, Mass. 02154

Notecards containing memorable scenes from the following Yiddish films: *American Shadchan, Mirele Efros, The Singing Blacksmith, Tevye,* and *Where Is My Child.*

SDI Association Denmark-Israel
Kingosgade 13 • 1818 Copenhagen V

On December 4, 1975, in Copenhagen, the Association Denmark-Israel issued this press release:

SDI ASSOCIATION DENMARK-ISRAEL.

"Danes Combat Anti-Zionism Through Greeting Card Campaign." More recently, a small group of Danes, without political affiliations but with pro-Israel sympathies, launched a greeting-card campaign "For Israel's Right to Exist," in protest of discrimination against Israel in forums of international cooperation. This ongoing program grew out of a less formal effort the year before demanding the equality of Israel with other member countries of UNESCO. Sixteen well-known international artists have contributed their works to be used as greeting-card motifs. Sets of six of the designs (those by Sam Francis, Jasper Johns, Henry Moore, Robert Motherwell, Carl-Henning Pedersen, and Jacob Weidman) are available from the above address. (See *Posters.*)

Workmen's Circle
Education Department
45 E. 33rd St. • New York, N.Y. 10016

Seven different Yiddish greeting-card designs are available from Workmen's Circle.

YIVO Institute for Jewish Research
1048 Fifth Ave. • New York, N.Y. 10028

Photographs of Jewish life in Poland before World War II have been printed as postcards by the YIVO Institute. Sets of seventeen of these poignant images (4″ × 6″) are available.

YIVO, "Miss Judea" beauty contest winner, Warsaw 1929, postcard.

COINS, MEDALS, AND STAMPS

American Israel Numismatic Association
91-31 Queens Blvd. • Elmhurst, N.Y. 11373

This American organization of collectors of Israeli coins and medals was founded in 1967 and has grown to include thousands of members from all over the world. It sponsors seminars, conventions, traveling exhibits, and audio-visual shows as well as an annual spring study tour to Israel. It publishes an informative quarterly journal called "The Shekel" with the purpose of establishing an authoritative source of information pertaining to numismatics of both modern and ancient Israel. As well as selling and distributing Israeli coins and medals to its members, the Association provides information about medals of interest minted in the United States. Write for a descriptive flyer and membership application form.

Hy Goldberg
Calhoun Collector's Society
Calhoun Center • Minneapolis, Minn. 55435

Send for his lively brochure describing "The Holy Land Philatelic Cover Collection".

Ibeco Enterprises
53 Balfour St. • Tel Aviv, Israel

Along with many other things (see *Gifts*) Ibeco offers packets of Israeli stamps for collectors.

IBECO ENTERPRISES has this and other packets for stamp collectors.

Israel Government Coins and Medals Corp.
350 Fifth Avenue, 19th Floor
New York, N.Y. 10001

The Israel Government Coins and Medals Corporation is fully owned by the government of Israel. Its major undertaking is to commemorate national and historical events, as well as cultural, scientific, and other achievements of the State of Israel. Anyone in Israel or abroad can become a subscriber by completing an application form available by mail. Subscribers can buy numismatic items from official order forms, which are sent by registered mail prior to the issue of any new coin or medal. Older issues, which begin in 1958, can be ordered from a beautiful catalog, which contains full-color photos, both front and back, of all the coins and medals issued by this organization, as well as all the minting particulars. In addition, each coin or medal is accompanied by a brochure giving full historical background of the event or institution being commemorated.

The Israel Historical Society
1 S. Wacker Dr. • Chicago, Ill. 60606

This organization has a set of thirty commemorative medals based on important events in Israeli history. Write for details and prices.

Jewish-American Hall of Fame
Judah L. Magnes Memorial Museum
2911 Russell St. • Berkeley, Calif. 94705

Mel Wacks, the numismatic consultant to the Judah Magnes Museum's project of commemorative medals honoring important figures in American Jewish History, says that he "would like to believe that most, if not all, of the Jewish-American Hall of Fame medals will be included among the memorable commemoratives produced in America in these times." That is an ambitious statement, but after seeing the collection of medals at the Museum, I would have to agree with the many critics who found these mini-sculptures to be of surpassing beauty, even as they are fascinating from a historical point of view. The Hall of Fame has issued limited-edition medals in bronze and silver honoring Brandeis, Einstein, Gershwin, Lehman, Magnes, and Salomon. It also has a handsome descriptive flyer with photographs of the medals and an order form.

The Lincoln Mint
1 S. Wacker Dr. • Chicago, Ill. 60606

The Lincoln Mint has issued a set of thirty medals entitled "A Prophecy Fulfilled: The Birth of Israel." The medals depict thirty of the most significant events in the shaping of Israel's history, from the Balfour Declaration in 1917 to the Six-Day War. Upon subscribing you receive one medal a month for thirty months until your set is complete. Write for subscription form with prices.

Vidport, Inc.
Commemorative Medals Division
711 Third Ave. • New York, N.Y. 10017

Vidport, Inc., has issued a limited-edition medal to commemorate the liberation of the Nazi concentration camps. Write for information on prices since the medals come in various weights.

GIFTS

Jacob Ben-Ezer Ltd.
440 Park Ave. South • New York, N.Y. 10016

Jaffa oranges are the leading export products of Israel. The Ben-Ezer groves have a delightful gift-carton plan that makes buying Jaffa oranges for your own use or sending them as gifts to friends and family almost anywhere in the world simple and satisfying. Payment can be made by check, money order, or various charge plans. Write for the postage-paid order form.

B'nai B'rith Museum Shop and Bookstore
1640 Rhode Island Avenue, N.W.
Washington, D.C. 20036

The Museum Shop and Bookstore carries the widest selection of Jewish books, crafts, and gift items in the metropolitan Washington area. The stock includes imported ceremonial objects from Israel and Europe as well as handcrafted works by U.S. crafts people. There is also a wide variety of posters, cards, antiquities, and gift items. Write for their book catalog which offers Jewish books at a moderate discount. The catalog is updated twice a year, with additions made monthly.

Engraving Unlimited
1533 Carrol St. • Brooklyn, N.Y. 11213

This company carries a complete line of Jewish engraved or personalized lucite giftware. They also engrave plastic door and wall signs for synagogues, offices, and apartment buildings.

ENGRAVING UNLIMITED. (photo: Lee Photo Co.)

Wholesale and retail; write for full-color illustrated pricelists.

David A. Fishman
12 Cameo Ridge Rd. • Monsey, N.Y. 10952

David Fishman's interest in calligraphy led him to the handpiercing of Hebrew lettering in precious metals, and subsequently to the production of personalized jewelry, such as name necklaces, bracelets, and rings which are fashioned by hand in sterling silver or 14k gold. Family trees are made to order in any lettering desired including Torah Scroll characters, which is also used in creating ketubot in precious metals. The items are well-crafted and specialization enables prompt delivery at a reasonable price.

CHARLES GELLES AND SON, "Chai Tai" available in navy, brown, and maroon.

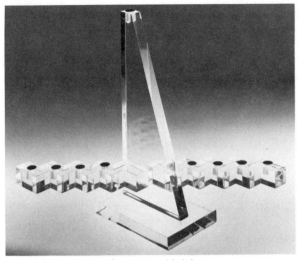

NORMAN GORDON, lucite Hanukkah lamp.

Charles Gelles and Son
68 Essex St. • Boston, Mass. 02111

This third generation manufacturer of men's neckware produces the "Chai Tai" which is the exclusive design of the firm's president, Sidney S. Gelles. Write for ordering information.

The Gift of Education
10 Rockefeller Plaza
New York, N.Y. 10020

The Gift of Education is a savings plan which offers a free tuition bonus for study in Israel. Funds deposited with the program are returned at the end of the savings period having earned 5% interest plus free tuition at one of Israel's finest universities, colleges, yeshivot or technical schools. An interesting way of combining savings, education, and philanthropy, since the plan is geared to help the Israel economy. Send for complete information and sample agreement.

Norman Gordon
2 Tamarack Way • Sharon, Mass. 02067

A physicist by profession, Norman Gordon sculpts for a hobby. He has come up with and is marketing three Judaica designs in lucite. He says that his "physics background has been very useful in helping me to develop the unique optical properties of lucite." Available: Hanukkah lamp, mezuzah, and spice box.

Ibeco Enterprises
53 Balfour St. • Tel Aviv, Israel

David Katz and David Zwiebel are Americans who moved to Israel in 1969 and established Ibeco to supply a popular priced line of gifts, crafts, and toys to the tourist industry in Israel and for the American market. Ibeco also provides the mail order buyer and individual tourist with a reliable source for giftware at manufacturer's prices. Of special interest is their full line of quality wooden recorders for musical education and enjoyment and their beautifully produced paper construction model of the Second Temple. Wholesale and retail inquiries invited; send for full-color illustrated brochures.

Israflower
116 E. 27th St. • New York, N.Y. 10016

Israflower will supply your organization with fresh cut Israeli flowers hours after they are picked. Your organization can then resell the flowers at a substantial profit to your membership. Deliveries begin the last week of November and end in May. During those months fifteen deliveries are made including those which coincide with Hanukkah, Purim, Tu B'Shevat, and Passover. Write for full price list and ordering information.

Israeli Gifts
575 Seventh Ave. • New York, N.Y. 10018

This shop imports and sells (retail only) Israeli manufactured menorot, candlesticks, plates, mezuzot, and tallitot as well as Israeli-handcrafted jewelry and plaques. It has several versions of Hebrew clocks, that is, clocks with the numbers represented by Hebrew letters. A brochure is available.

Jerusalem Products Corp.
P.O. Box 76, Dept. CC
Waitsfield, Vt. 05673

Mitchell Kontoff of Jerusalem Products is very proud of this unique mail-order item offered by his firm. For $25.95, including handling and shipping, you can have a bar mitzvah scroll sent to a bar or bat mitzvah person as an enduring memento of this important occasion. The scroll consists of the confirmant's Haftorah portion in Hebrew and English printed on parchment-like paper, inscribed with his/her name and the date of the event, scrolled into a 14½″ high carved-hardwood case. A protective cloth bag is included, and a lucite display stand is available. To avoid duplication of gifts only the first order received for any person's name is filled.

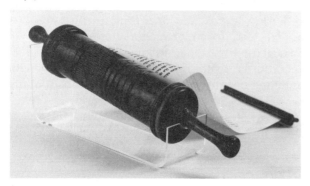

JERUSALEM PRODUCTS CORP., the bar mitzvah scroll.

The Jewish Museum Shop
1109 Fifth Ave. • New York, N.Y. 10028

The Museum Shop has a very large selection of hardcover and paperback books for both adults and children. It sells handsome holiday greeting cards, post cards, and an exclusive group of limited-edition lithographs and silkscreens by artists such as Leonard Baskin, Will Barnet, and Adja Yunkers as well. Posters and catalogs from its exhibitions are also on sale. Attractive versions of seasonal toys such as wooden dreidels and Purim graggers are available, and the Museum Shop also

imports a number of interesting items from Israel, including jewelry, and handmade felt Biblical puppets as well as the popular ceramic tiles designed by Shalom of Safed. Portfolios of photographs, maps, and slide packets showing objects from the Museum's collection of Judaica are some of the educational materials offered. A brochure is available and the Shop accepts mail orders. The most interesting group of items is a unique line of Judaica reproductions. (See *Buying: Antiques and Reproductions.*)

Jewish National Fund
42 E. 69th St. • New York, N.Y. 10021

To celebrate anniversaries or birthdays; to commemorate births, bar and bat mitzvahs, or weddings; to express sympathy for an illness or death—planting trees in Israel means you care. Look for JNF offices in your local telephone directory or consult your local synagogue. $3 per tree.

Judaic Heritage
719 Montgomery St. • Brooklyn, N.Y. 11213

From the heart of Lubavitch country, Crown Heights, Brooklyn, comes a personalized "Bracha mug" for children (adults will like it too). Basically a double-walled thermal plastic mug, decorated with the name ordered, the blessing for drinks other than wine, and a little house. Dishwasher safe and shatterproof it can be ordered at $2.50 each, $2 each for quantity orders. Write for a flyer describing this cup and ask about Judaic Heritage's original and inexpensive Kiddush cup too.

The Judaica House Ltd.
435 Cedar Ln. • Teaneck, N.J. 07666

The Judaica House Ltd. carries a wide variety of secular Judaica as well as religious items. It imports Israeli posters, tee shirts, placemats, silver, and general giftware. Brochures of various Israeli manufacturers' merchandise are available from Judaica House upon request. Try to specify what you're looking for. Mail orders accepted from institutions.

Judaica U.S.A.
P.O. Box 513 • Brookline, Mass. 02146

Mail order Judaica, catalog $1 refunded with first order. Judaica House has customers in 30 states, Okinawa, Guam, and Mexico.

Janet Kaplan
105 Taconic Ave.
Great Barrington, Mass. 01230

If a custom-made, hand-drawn ketubah is out of your price range, but you would like to have an elegant and antique-looking wedding document, consider the five designs produced by Janet Kaplan. The ketubot are original works of Israeli art based on old styles. They are reproduced on heavy vellum paper and range in price from $25 for a black-and-white contemporary design to $40 for an elegantly shaped, multi-colored document. The appropriate spaces have been left blank for names

JANET KAPLAN, ketubah printed on vellum, full-color, 13" × 20", $40.

and dates to be inserted, and each ketubah is accompanied by a descriptive flyer explaining the significance of the contract and providing an English translation of the Aramaic text. Write for a brochure.

Kar-Ben Copies
11713 Auth Lane • Silver Spring, Md. 20902

Kar-Ben copies makes the "I found it!" T-shirt, pictured here, for the afikomen finder(s) at your seder; $5. See *Learning: Books* for more about this growing firm.

KAR-BEN COPIES.

Carol Lebeaux
15 Monadnock Drive
Shrewsbury, Mass. 01545

Carol Lebeaux designs and screen prints on leather and linen. Among her novelty items is the Hebrew "Attack Cat" leather banner. (Literally it says "Warning! Cat that bites.") It is screen printed by hand on genuine cowhide. $8.50 includes postage and brings it to you packaged in a sturdy white mailing tube. Quantity discounts available.

CAROL LEBEAUX, "Attack Cat!" 12" × 16", hand screened on leather.

J. Levine Co.
58 Eldridge St. • New York, N.Y. 10002

In its seven floor department store of Judaica, J. Levine stocks an amazing assortment of giftware. Among the more unusual items are handblocked Iranian tablecloths with luscious intricate designs and Hebrew inscriptions. Write for catalog. See *Observing: Book and Religious Supply Stores.*

Judah L. Magnes Memorial Museum
The Jewish Museum of the West
2911 Russell St. • Berkeley, Calif. 94705

The gift shop at the Magnes Museum is considerably smaller than either the museum shop at the Jewish Museum in New York or that in the Spertus Museum in Chicago. Nevertheless, it has certain items of unique interest, and it is well worth the effort to write a letter of inquiry about its publications, which include *Pioneer Jews of the California Mother Lode, 1849–1880,* by Sara G. Cogan, *Ghetto of Warsaw,* sixteen woodcuts by Stefan Mrozewski, and *Proverbs and People: A Midrash on the Hebrew Alphabet,* with woodcuts by Nikos Stravroulakis. The gift shop has ceremonial objects and jewlery by Bay Area artists and craftspeople.

Ohio Poster Company
14077 Cedar Road • Cleveland, Ohio 44118

Along with a large selection of Israeli posters the Ohio Poster Company imports and distributes Israeli items of interest. Send for a brochure and order form. Orders of less than $25 are shipped C.O.D.

Alexander Oland
120 W. 44th St. • New York, N.Y. 10036

If you are as addicted to quotations as I am, this jewelry firm will delight you with its number and variety of inspirational and romantic quotations worked in silver or gold in the form of pendants and key chains. Without exaggeration it has more than a hundred different phrases available in a variety of jewelry styles. Most of the quotations are in Hebrew, some in Yiddish, and for non-Jewish friends there are quotations from the Bible and other sources in Latin, English, and Spanish. As well as the Hebrew and Yiddish quotations it also has several interesting sterling silver antique amulet reproductions with Hebrew kabbalistic inscriptions. It is exclusively mail order. Several well-illustrated brochures with price lists are available. (Since the price of gold and silver fluctuates I suggest you make a specific inquiry about prices at the time you order.)

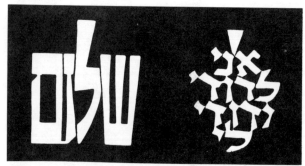

ALEXANDER OLAND, "Shalom" and "I am my beloved's and my beloved is mine" pendants.

Originals Only
15 W. 44th St. • New York, N.Y. 10036

Brochures available of a variety of jewelry designs, the most interesting a Magen David in jade.

S.E.M. Arts
P.O. Box 63 • Swampscott, Mass. 01907

Completely mail order business, specializing in jewelry from Israel, with several interesting filigree designs, and necklaces of Hebron glass and olive wood beads.

Skirball Museum Gift Gallery
3077 University Ave.
Los Angeles, Calif. 90007

Available at the Skirball Museum Gift Gallery are ceremonial and ritual objects, museum catalogs, records, jewelry, antiquities, posters, cards, books, glassware, and replicas. Mail orders accepted.

SKIRBALL MUSEUM GIFT GALLERY.

The Museum Store
Spertus Museum of Judaica
618 S. Michigan Ave. • Chicago, Ill. 60605

If you are in the Chicago area, the Museum Store at the Spertus Museum of Judaica is well worth a visit. It fills two rooms, including a pleasant gallery space, on the main floor of the museum and overflows with Israeli arts, crafts, books, religious articles, jewelry (they have some of the most handsome Elat stones I've seen anywhere), posters, and antiques. You can expect prices from $2 to $1,000, and if they help you find an extraordinary antique object consider spending more. The turnover is so quick that the store has no catalog. It does, however, accept mail orders. So if you know what you want write to them. Even if you are not certain of exactly what you are looking for they can

probably help you find it. Profits from the shop's sales benefit Spertus College. See also *Buying: Antiques and Reproductions.*

Things
P.O. Box 411 • Mercer Island, Wa. 98040

"Things" is a full-color mail order catalog-shop of "better" Judaica. Included in its pages are works by artists Eva Schonfield, Katya Miller-Wallin, Michoel Muchnik, and Fern Amper (see *Creating*). Also shown are some interesting Israeli items such as a folding set of traveling Shabbat candlesticks. Although Carol Gallant, who put the catalog together, had people living far from urban areas in mind, it will be of interest to urban dwellers as well.

Union of Orthodox Jewish Congregations of America
116 E. 27th St. • New York, N.Y. 10016

Demonstrate your commitment to the Prisoners of Conscience in the USSR. Send $3 each for bracelets engraved with the name of one of the P.O.C.'s along with their pleas "Let My People Go!" and the Soviet Jewry emblem.

Unique Judaica Ltd.
601 W. 67th St. • Kansas City, Mo. 64114

This mail order business was started by two past presidents of sisterhoods and a rabbi's wife "who know only too well how difficult it is to find unusual items of Judaica." Their goal is to offer gift shops unusual and beautiful pieces to "enrich the accessorizing of Jewish homes." They are prepared to be very helpful in the merchandising aspect of tending a temple gift store. Wholesale only. Send for catalogs and price lists.

Yugentruf
3328 Bainbridge Ave. • Bronx, N.Y. 10467

Yugentruf's tee shirt is white with the word "Yiddish" in Hebrew letters silkscreened across the chest in either red or blue. Adult sizes: S, M, L, XL cost $3.50 each, plus 35¢ postage and handling;

children's sizes: 6, 8, 10, 12, 14 cost $3 plus 30¢ for handling and postage. Yugentruf also has two buttons that I enjoy. Both say *"Redt mit Mir Yiddish"* (Speak Yiddish to me) in Hebrew letters.

One button is orange with a picture of a smiling sun, the other has a blue dove on a white button. The buttons cost 50¢ each, 4 for $1.50. Add 10% for postage and handling.

POSTERS

Central Conference of American Rabbis
790 Madison Ave. • New York, N.Y. 10021

The publications catalog of the Central Conference of American Rabbis devotes a page to the full-size, full-color posters made from Leonard Baskin's superb watercolor illustrations for its best-selling Passover Haggadah. These have understandably been very popular as gifts and as an inexpensive way of bringing contemporary Jewish art to the home.

The Exhumation
P.O. Box 2057 • Princeton, N.J. 08540

The Exhumation specializes in posters and graphics dating from 1890–1950. They offer Israeli travel posters and others of Jewish interest from time to time. I bought two World War I Jewish Welfare Board posters there. They currently have a fairly large stock of the "Civilians" poster. Catalogs issued every 8 months, $3.

CENTRAL CONFERENCE OF AMERICAN RABBIS, "David The King" poster by Leonard Baskin, from his illustrations for *A Passover Haggadah*.

THE EXHUMATION, a 1918 poster for the United War Work Campaign by Sidney Riesenberg; printed in brown, black, and blue, $30.

Heinle and Heinle Enterprises
29 Lexington Rd. • Concord, Mass. 01742

Heinle and Heinle specializes in educational materials but offers some of the most attractive and colorful posters I've seen anywhere. Notably "After The Flood" and Tower of Babel." Write for ordering information about these and the charming alef-bet poster they distribute.

Jewish Community Center
633 Salisbury St. • Worcester, Mass. 01609

One of the nicest posters in my collection is a reproduction of a National Jewish Welfare Board, United War Work Campaign poster originally printed in 1918. It is available only from the Jewish Community Center in Worcester, Mass. We have the creativity of Josh B. Malks, the former director of that center, to thank for its existence. He saw the original, which someone had found in a junk shop, hanging in the lobby of the Providence Jewish Community Center. He thought it was a great bit of Jewish nostalgia and decided to make it available to more people. He borrowed the print and, working with a local Massachusetts printer had a limited number of reproductions made in the original size, closely duplicating the old lithographic inks, paper color, and weight. The poster shows a J.W.B. chaplain reassuring the concerned parents of a W.W. I serviceman with the Yiddish phrase *Nit gezorgt, Er is all right* ("Don't worry, he's all right"). The poster can be ordered from the Worcester J.C.C. for $4.50, including shipping in a heavy mailing tube. Checks can be sent to the supervisor of cultural programming, but should be made payable to the Worcester J.C.C. I would love to see other Jewish centers doing things like this.

National Conference on Soviet Jewry
10 E. 40th St. • New York, N.Y. 10016

The plight of Soviet Jews has spawned a great deal of protest activity. Almost every Jewish organization has a committee or subgroup dedicated in some way to helping our Russian brethren. The National Conference on Soviet Jewry functions as an umbrella agency coordinating the efforts of various member groups in behalf of the Jews of the Soviet Union. It has a catalog of posters and other materials that are available at nominal costs or for free.

Ohio Poster Co.
14077 Cedar Road • Cleveland, Ohio 44118

The Ohio Poster Company offers a large variety of posters imported from Israel. One series consists of reproductions of thirteen different Israeli highway signs. It also offers a series of eight posters for children printed in bright colors on plastic, and a miscellany of fluorescent and other contemporary-style decorative posters, including my favorite—the Hebrew Coca-Cola sign, which is available from several other sources, attesting to its popularity. Flyers and price lists describing all of the varied line of posters and graphics are available on request.

SDI Association Denmark-Israel
Kingosgade 13
1818 Copenhagen V, Denmark

This Danish organization sprung up spontaneously a few years ago in response to international pressures against Israel in the United Nations (see

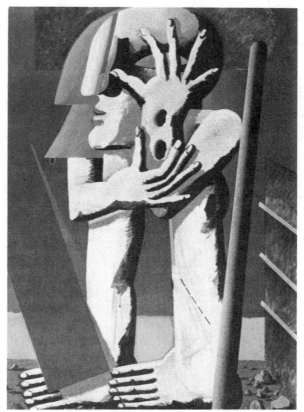

SDI ASSOCIATION DENMARK-ISRAEL, full-color poster reproduction of a painting by Horst Antes, entitled "Grosse Figur Mit Doppelstigma", 24" × 33".

Cards for more details). It publishes beautifully reproduced posters and greeting cards as well as attention-getting bumperstickers. The goal is two-fold: first, to gain public humanitarian support for Israel, and then to donate whatever profits there might be from the sale of these campaign materials to worthy organizations in Israel. Write for a brochure with information for ordering.

YIVO, kheyder (traditional Jewish primary school), Lublin 1920's. Poster 18" × 24", $4.50.

YIVO Institute for Jewish Research
1048 Fifth Ave. • New York, N.Y. 10028

The popularity of the photographic exhibit and book *Image Before My Eyes* prompted YIVO to produce 3 of the photographs in an 18" × 24" poster format; $4.50 each, set of three $11. YIVO has also reproduced a rare 1920's Yiddish theater poster for the New York production of Abraham

Goldfaden's *Tzvei Kuni Lemls*. Produced on ivory stock in red and black, the 22" × 35" poster is $7.50 plus 50¢ postage per poster.

Needlework

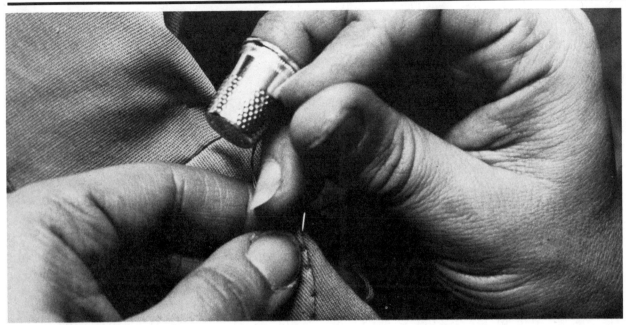

(photo: Richard Speedy)

"And let the graciousness of the Lord our God be upon us; Establish Thou also upon us the work of our hands; Yea, the work of our hands establish Thou it."　　Psalm 90:17

A few years ago, just as I finished giving a talk at the Jewish Community Center in Rochester, N.Y., two friendly people, mother and son, approached me and introduced themselves as my distant cousins. It seems that the patriarch of our family, my Great Uncle Layzer who keeps track of everyone, had told them that I was to be in town and wanted them to take me to visit his sister, my Great Aunt Tova at the Rochester Home for the Aged. When I walked into her room she said, "Ah, you're Chaiya Feigel's granddaughter. They tell me that you too have the family *goldeneh hendt.* Tell me, do any of your children?" She then pulled from her dresser drawer two exquisite aprons she had made years ago to show me the level of proficiency with a needle she had achieved. "Now," she said ruefully, "they take me to the third floor for 'occupational therapy' and we color paper plates to look like pumpkins for Halloween. My hands may be a little slippery now, but I can do more than that."

Not too long after that visit, I had occasion to visit Glenhaven, the nursing home where my husband's Great Aunt Mary spent the last years of her long life—she died at 101. There in Glencoe, Minnesota, the occupational therapy program has the home's residents making Scandinavian-style rag rugs, stuffed toys, and assorted pieces of "fancy work" which are sold in the home's "store" for money to buy those materials which are not donated. Craft shop dealers from Minneapolis often find their way to Glenhaven looking for stock and whenever we visit Glencoe, we always go to see what the new rugs are like.

It seems to me that with fabric and needlework of all sorts such a favorite pastime, Jewish nursing homes could almost be turned into "heirloom factories," thereby providing us with handmade ritual and decorative articles and returning self-respect to those of us who live there. When, as a bride of 17, living in Japan, I made my first hallah cover, there were no kits or patterns to follow—not that I really wanted any. Over the years as I turned my needle more and more to the production of Jewish ceremonial pieces, I have seen, participated in, and marveled at the growth and increasing liveliness of contemporary Judaic needlecraft in America. The people in this section are committed to promulgating quality Judaic needlecraft. Here you will find kits, designers, teachers, and colleagues. (Also see *Creating: Textiles; Playing: Toys; Observing: Holidays and Ceremonies* and *Mitzvot.*)

Jane Bearman
30 Spier Dr. • Livingston, N.J. 07039

Ms. Bearman creates Shalom designs on canvas, mizrahim, and other wall hangings. She will also accept commissions for Torah covers. Send for her attractive brochure, see *Creating: Pictures.*

Elissa Designs
613 Chestnut • Stroudsbury, Pa. 18360

Imitation, they say, is the sincerest form of flattery. So I can't deny being pleased when Elissa Westman asked permission to reproduce one of the designs from my book *The Work of Our Hands* as a kit. She has adapted one of my alef-bet designs and screened it on to #12 needlepoint canvas. Other designs available too; send for flyer and pricelist.

ELISSA DESIGNS.

MADELINE GLUCK, needlepoint rug to be read coming and going.

Madeline Gluck
4233 N.E. 74th St. • Seattle, Wa. 98115

Madeline Gluck designs needlework and does custom weaving. She can be commissioned to do needlepoint for both home and synagogue and weaves ark curtains, Torah binders and covers, and tallitot and bags. Her designs can also be purchased painted on canvas for you to work. Brochure available free, catalog $1, refundable upon first purchase.

Minnah Halpern
996 Richard Court • Teaneck, N.J. 07666

Minna Halpern is the distributor for Rimkah by Elazar contemporary and colorful printed needlepoint canvases from Israel.

Dorothy Lotstein
26 Berwyn Rd.
West Hartford, Conn. 06107

Dorothy Lotstein sells her own needlepoint designs for hangings, Torah covers, yarmulkes, and tallit bags. She has a workbook with simple line drawings of her canvasses.

Netzach Designs
1 Hamlin Drive
West Hartford, Conn. 06117

This new company offers personalized custom-designed needlepoint canvases to "eternalize your simcha." Projects offered include yarmulkes, tallit bags, engagement and wedding gifts, and baby plaques. The designers, Dorothy Lotstein and Riva Ruran, provide a research document which explains the historical background and cultural significance of canvas. Write for more information.

Alice Nussbaum
2835 Salem Ave. S.
Minneapolis, Minn. 55416

Alice Nussbaum has developed a full line of specially designed canvases for all occasions of the Jewish life cycle. She will also accept custom design orders and will execute commissions in needlepoint for synagogues. For a small extra fee she will also find the appropriate yarn for those who purchase her painted canvases. No brochure, but she does have photos available.

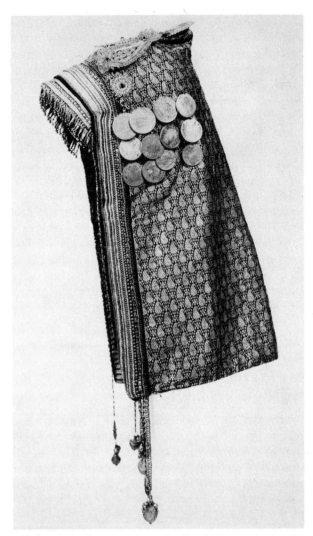

THE PAPER POMEGRANATE recently had an article on Yemenite embroidery. Woman's ceremonial headcovering (Gargush), brocade, gilded silver, filigree, Yemen 19th century, from the collection of the Spertus Museum, Chicago.

ALICE NUSSBAUM, doll which can be customized with name of your choice.

The Pomegranate Guild of Judaic Needlework
Sharon Moskow, President
289 Linden Place
Yorktown Heights, N.Y. 10598
and
Gilda Hecht, Membership Vice-President
12 Bayview Ave. • Great Neck, N.Y. 11021

One of the most exciting things to happen in the world of Jewish needlework these last few years is the formation of The Pomegranate Guild. The purpose of the Guild is "to disseminate information on Judaic embroidery, to provide a bulletin of information, to train teachers, to make archives available, to arrange field trips to make contact with people of similar interests in other countries, to provide, if possible, a showcase for members' work and to have lists of these members available for those seeking to grant commissions." The Guild also publishes *The Paper Pomegranate* four times a year. This very lively newsletter describes upcoming workshops and activities and is chock-full of valuable information on many areas of interest to embroiderers. There are designs to copy (not for resale but for personal work) and articles on technique. There are two ways to join the Guild: as a Friend ($10 annually), those who are interested in the work of the Guild and wish to support it and receive *The Paper Pomegranate*, and as a Member ($18 a year), who has his/her work judged for membership. Write to Sharon Moskow or Gilda Hecht for more information.

Betty Winter Samuels
390 W. Hudson Ave.
Englewood, N.J. 07631

Betty Samuel does needlepoint, crewel, and blackwork all with only Jewish themes. She will accept commissions and has a few styles of mezuzot "on hand." A flyer describing her and her slide show-lecture is available. She will also teach workshops.

The Sourcehouse
20410 Chapter Drive
Woodland Hills, Calif. 91364

The Sourcehouse has a new catalog of Judaic needlepoint kits. Send 50¢ and an SASE.

Bonnie Yales
23 Dane Rd. • Lexington, Mass. 02173

Bonnie Yales is a talented and proficient designer of large needlepoint tapestries, Torah covers, and ark curtains. She designs and coordinates the stitchery for these projects which are then exe-

BONNIE YALES (left) with Merry Gerber who helped with the design of this 6' × 10' tapestry for Temple Isaiah, Lexington, Mass.

cuted by the women of the congregation, often under her tutelage. She likes her pieces to include many different types of stitches. If the tapestry is worked in panels, she will assemble the pieces when the embroidery is completed. On large commissions she often works with a local artist, Merry Gerber. Bonnie is also able to supply the yarn for the projects at a moderate discount. The tapestry she designed for Temple Isaiah, in Lexington, Massachusetts, was worked in ten panels by 92 women, (all taught by Bonnie) and then assembled by her. A project such as this will cost anywhere from $1100 to $4000. She will also accept commissions from individuals for worked as well as unworked canvases.

PLAYING

Playing is such an ambiguous term that I had planned to begin this chapter with a definition from Webster's, but when I opened my dictionary and found almost two columns defining "play", I quickly changed my mind. The photo opening this chapter shows two people "playing" musical instruments—one definition—and they seem to be having a good time—another definition. Yet we know how much *work* goes into *learning* to *play* with abandon. This chapter restates what we all knew intuitively as children; that play in all its forms is essential to our well-being. Do not be surprised that many of the items and activities in this chapter overlap with entries in *Learning* and *Observing*. Jewish life is an intricate weave of serious, thoughtful, and playful elements. Even our most profound series of holidays which begins majestically with Rosh Hashanah and reaches its most sober moment on Yom Kippur, culminates with the lighthearted joy of Sukkot and Simhat Torah. Many of us will never "seriously" pursue a course of Jewish studies yet we might become quite well-informed Jewishly through popular historical novels and spy thrillers. We may find ourselves in the synagogue only rarely and uncomfortably; nevertheless we feel the desire for valid forms of Jewish expression and identification. It is through our leisure activities that we may discover a satisfying niche for our Jewish souls. Just as one can pray with tears and trembling, the Baal Shem Tov has taught that there is holiness in song, story, and dance. In this chapter you will find sections dealing with *Camping, Dance, Music, Theater, Toys and Games*, and *Travel*—cultural activities which broaden and enrich our lives especially when infused with the rich complexity of our Jewish heritage.

"When we face our Maker, we will have to account for those pleasures of life which we failed to enjoy."

Jerusalem Talmud: Kiddushin, end

Camping

(photo: John Waite)

The August 1979 issue of *Life* magazine had a two-page color spread entitled "A Long White Summer for KKK Kids," describing 12 day camps in six states run by the Invisible Kingdom. Photos of activities at a camp site in Alabama showed children playing badminton under the supervision of fully-robed, hooded, pistol-wearing "counselors." As well as the usual camp activities, there were also sessions in firearms training and lectures on the inferiority of certain races. *Life* went on to report that seven of the campers participated in burning a school bus to protest school desegregation.

This frightening story makes one sick at heart. I'm not about to advocate adding firearms instruction or hate lessons to the programs of the camps discussed here. I do think it is very important, however, to use the summer productively by choosing a camp which is committed to providing positive Jewish living experiences. There are Jewish camps reflecting almost every nuance of Jewish philosophy, from ultra-Orthodox to secular-Yiddishist to Labor-Zionist. For children who are deeply immersed in Jewish life the rest of the year, one of these camps is a natural extension of his or her activities. For the child who has little or no contact with a Jewish peer group in fun situations, Jewish camping can be an overwhelmingly important experience.

NOTE TO PROSPECTIVE COUNSELORS

Applicants seeking general counselor positions with the camps listed here should be at least eighteen years of age and have completed high school; some college experience is preferred. Application should be made to the Federation Employment and Guidance Service, 215 Park Avenue South, New York, N.Y. 10003.

Persons seeking supervisory positions in these camps or specialist jobs (waterfront, music, arts, and crafts) should apply to the National Jewish Welfare Board Camping Services, 15 E. 26th St., New York, N.Y. 10010.

The American Jewish Society for Service
15 E. 26th St. • Rm. 1302
New York, N.Y. 10010

The A.J.S.S. has a seven-week program for teen-agers who are entering their junior and senior year in high school. The tuition for the seven weeks of summer services is $450, plus traveling expenses to and from the project. In the thirty years since this program began, teenage work-campers have participated in such diverse projects as building a home for a legless black war veteran and his family, laying water lines, building bridges, and demolishing deteriorated buildings. This program is a once-in-a-lifetime experience that will really affect young adults' maturing processes.

American Zionist Youth Foundation
515 Park Ave. • New York, N.Y. 10022

The American Zionist Youth Foundation offers many different summer program possibilities in Israel for teenagers and young adults. Some are work-play programs on kibbutzim or moshavim, others include high-school and college-level courses. All three of my children spent the summer after their thirteenth birthdays in Israel with A.Z.Y.F.'s program called "Bar Mitzvah Pilgrimage." There is even a six-week program in Israel for folk-dance enthusiasts. Write for brochures and application forms; describe specifically what you are interested in.

Association of Jewish Sponsored Camps, Inc.
130 E. 59th St. • New York, N.Y. 10022

The Association of Jewish Sponsored Camps has a brochure available giving basic information about its forty-five eastern seaboard member camps. One of the many services provided by the Association is that of helping find the camp most suitable for the individual needs of the prospective camper. The camps serve many age groups including senior citizens. The brochure also lists Yiddish-oriented camps, such as Camp Kinderland (where all my lucky friends went when I was a child), Orthodox, Zionist, and "cultural" camps.

B'nai B'rith Camps
1640 Rhode Island Ave., NW
Washington, N.C. 20036

The B'nai B'rith Camps are listed in the National Jewish Welfare Board publication described below with several camps in Canada and one in Pennsylvania. A new American camp was inaugurated in the summer of 1976. Called B'nai B'rith Beber Camp, it is located in Mukwonago, Wisconsin, about seventy-five miles from Chicago's O'Hare Airport and thirty-five miles from the Milwaukee air terminal. Full information on all B'nai B'rith camps can be had from the above office.

Boy Scouts of America
National Director of Jewish Relationships
North Brunswick, N.J. 08902

The Boy Scouts of America offers a full scouting program combined with Jewish educational ideals. Just as in the rest of scouting, medals and awards are given for various accomplishments in Jewish scouting. Honors are achieved by fulfilling or mastering various Jewish activities and precepts. A Cub Scout, for example, can earn the "Aleph" medal for keeping an accurate notebook describing specific requirements he has fulfilled in the areas of Torah study, prayer, holiday understanding, synagogue attendance, Bible heroes, Jewish-American Heritage, and the Land of Israel. B.S.A., of course, has an active camping program. Write for further information and ask for brochures on "Kosher Food at Scout Camp" and "Keeping the Sabbath While Camping."

The Brandeis Camp Institute
Brandeis, Calif. 93064

The Brandeis Camp Institute offers a unique camp experience for college students. The camp is located on 3200 acres of secluded Southern California countryside and offers two intense month-long programs incorporating art, dance, music, drama, food, and philosophy. Write for additional information and brochure.

INTERNATIONAL TORAH CORPS., Littleton, N.H.

International Torah Corps
Rabbi Dov Taylor at Temple Ohabei Shalom
1187 Beacon St. • Brookline, Mass. 02146
or
Rabbi Gerald Brieger at Temple Emanuel
150 Derby Ave. • Orange, Conn. 06477

The International Torah Corps in Littleton, New Hampshire, brings together Reform teenagers and scholars for six weeks of study, worship, song, dance, play, and living by Jewish time. Study is concentrated on primary Jewish texts, from the Bible through modern Hebrew literature, emphasizing Hebrew as the key to our classics and as the language of modern Israel. Recreational activities include climbing, hiking, swimming, tennis, and canoeing. Registration is limited to keep classes small and to strengthen the sense of close community. ITC's descriptive brochure is available from either of the two addresses given. It makes me wish I were a teenager again.

National Jewish Welfare Board
Director Camping Services
15 E. 26th St. • New York, N.Y. 10010

The Directory of Jewish Resident Summer Camps Under the Auspices of Jewish Communal Organi-

zations, published by the National Jewish Welfare Board, is a great help to communal agencies, parents, and young people looking for camp counseling jobs. The information it provides about close to two hundred camps all over the United States and Canada includes the location of campsite and distance from the city office, age groups, whether co-ed or not, capacity, length of sessions, fees, registration requirements for campers, dietary practices, and requirements for general counselors. Once you have selected the camps you are interested in, you should write to the offices of the specific camps for more detailed information. In compiling this book I received so many different camp brochures that they all began to look alike. Unless you are going on a friend's recommendation, I suggest you send for the J.W.B. publication and proceed from there. Listing in the Directory does not necessarily imply endorsement by the J.W.B.

Olin-Sang-Ruby Union Institute Camp Oconomowoc, Wis.

OSRUI camp serves Jewish campers from all over the Midwest with a program of "working, playing, studying, and praying." For the small Jewish communities in the Midwest which have no daycamp experience available for their six to ten year olds, OSRUI offers its Camp Shalom program. A staff of five or so college students set up camps for two-week periods in suburban midwestern communities such as Grand Rapids, Mich.; Champaign, Ill.; and Green Bay, Wis. For more information contact Ruth Silverman, Spertus College of Judaica, 618 S. Michigan Ave., Chicago, Ill. 60605

Dance

JEFFREY ROCKLAND in "Coppelia". (photo: courtesy, Ballet Department, Virginia Intermont College)

Dance, which has been called the "mother of the arts", is certainly the oldest art form. Dancing was part of every important aspect of life for people in the ancient world. Not only was it used for storytelling, but it formed the basis of much early religious expression. The Bible records numerous instances of spontaneous dance expression at significant moments and dancing was considered to be essential at all life cycle events and seasonal festivals. Even among today's least traditional Jews a wedding seems flavorless and bland without some uncle or cousin encouraging everyone to join in circles and weaving linear dances. Jewish dance does not only mean Israeli folk dancing, though its popularity and influence cannot be denied. The vigor of Israeli dances reflect the newness of the country. But for the most part these dances are choreographed and, even though there are hundreds of them, only a few are done by the "folk". Even the Hora is a transplant of the Romanian Horo (said to have been brought to Israel by an immigrant and changed to move from right to left rather than left to right). In a few hundred years the choreographed dances utilizing movements from the diverse backgrounds of different groups of immigrants will have softened and been mellowed by time and Israeli "folk" dancing will belong to the folk. Even now that is happening and at the same time dance professionals and performers are exploring ways of expressing Jewish themes in the medium of traditional ballet and through modern and jazz movements. My son Jeffrey, shown here in *Coppelia*, represents the new generation of dancers. He writes: "I wish there was a ballet with a Jewish theme. Instead of the 'Nutcracker Suite' It could be the 'Latka Suite'."

Shlomo Bachar
5770 Ostrom Avenue • Encino, Calif. 91316

Shlomo Bachar is a choreographer and dance instructor who can be contacted for workshops and also for performances either alone or with his dance group "Hadarim", an Israeli dance and song ensemble. "Hadarim" will provide different size performing groups to suit all occasions. Bachar's dances range from the gentle Ladino-inspired "Erev Shel Shoshanim" to the vigorous "Hallelujah". He is also the producer of 10 albums of Israeli music. Write for his well-illustrated and informative booklet about "Hadarim" Israeli Dance Theatre.

SHLOMO AND DINA BACHAR.

Moshe Eskayo
99 Hillside Avenue • New York, N.Y. 10040

A seventh-generation Sabra, Eskayo has been a folk dance teacher and choreographer for more than twenty years. Some of his better known dances include "Ma Avarech" and "Sapari". For those lucky enough to live in the New York area you can visit his cafe for classes or parties. Write asking to be put on his mailing list. Eskayo will travel to teach workshops and classes. He has a small performing group and performances can also be arranged. For the last few years he has run a folk dance camp at the end of each summer. Studying there is intense, exhausting, and exhilarating. Eskayo has produced three records, which are available directly through him or from the Record Loft (see the Worldtone Music entry this section).

Felix Fibich
50 W. 97th St. • New York, N.Y. 10025

Felix Fibich began working in the field of Jewish dance in Poland where with his wife, Judith Berg, who is also a dancer and choreographer, he worked to develop a specifically Jewish form of dance. He writes: "Concerned with the preservation of Eastern European Jewish motifs, I have sought to develop this movement material into artistic form suitable for the concert stage and theater. In addition to using Jewish movement, I have sought to incorporate in my work a sense of Jewish tradition, literature, poetry, and liturgy. I have choreographed dances to works of Sholom Aleichem, Mendele Mocher Sforim, Peretz, Itzik Manger, and others." Since his arrival in the United States in 1950 he has choreographed for, and performed on, the concert stage, Broadway, and T.V. He is available for lecture demonstrations and dance recitals on themes ranging from Biblical to contemporary. He can also be contacted through the B'nai Brith Lecture Bureau.

FELIX FIBICH.

Evelyn Halper
38 Eastwood Lane
Valley Stream, N.Y. 11581

Evelyn Halper presents a lecture demonstration entitled: "Are Jews a Dancing People?" in which she discusses such questions as: "Did Jews dance before Biblical times?", "Were Jews ever too embarrassed to dance?", and "What role did dance assume in unifying the tattered remnants of the Holocaust?".

"Moshiko" Halevy
250 W. 15th St., Apt. H.
New York, N.Y. 10011

Known as "Moshiko" to his followers, Moshe Itzhak Halevy was born in Jaffa to a Yemenite family. He danced with Inbal, the famous Israeli dance group, for six years as one of their principal dancers. He is available for workshops and master classes. His teaching fee is based on the type of session, the size of the class, and the traveling costs. He has produced a double record with twenty of his dances and he teaches from them. It may be ordered from the Record Loft International. See the listing in this section under Worldtone Music, Inc.

Hamakor Israeli Folk Dance Troupe
P. O. Box 65 • Cambridge, Mass. 02140

Since it was founded in 1969 Hamakor has attracted some of the best non-professional dancers and musicians in the Boston area and has performed extensively in New England. Hamakor is available for costumed performances which range in length from 45 minutes to two hours, and for participatory workshops. For their illustrated brochure and more information about arrangements for performances throughout the New England–N.Y.–N.J.–eastern Pa. area, write Hamakor, which is a non-profit, tax exempt organization.

Israel Folk Dance Institute
American Zionist Youth Foundation
515 Park Ave. • New York, N.Y. 10022

The Israel Folk Dance Institute has an interesting and well-rounded program. They have a catalog

HAMAKOR ISRAELI FOLK DANCE TROUPE, INC. "Yemenite Suite"—traditional Yemenite style dance is performed in authentic costume.

offering a large selection of Israeli folk dance records with instruction booklets. The Institute publishes "Hora, a Review of Israel Folk Dance News" three times a year and sells Fred Berk's two books on Jewish dance, *The Chasidic Dance*, and *Ha-Rikud, The Jewish Dance*, both in paper. Ya'akov Eden conducts a leaders' training program at Camp Blue Star in North Carolina every June, two sessions of one week each. And there is a six-week folk dance workshop program in Israel every summer. If you are interested in either of these programs, write for brochures giving full details and prices.

Gerry Kaplan
73 Moran Ave. • Princeton, N.J. 08540

Gerry Kaplan is a folk dance teacher who can tailor programs and workshops including dances with Yemenite, Arabic, Hasidic, and Sabra elements for any size or age of group. He has worked with performing groups and so can arrange for performances as well as participatory workshops. Programs will be designed to meet your group's needs. Write or call for more details and fees.

Adina Kaufman
64 Elderwood Drive
Toronto, Ontario M5P 1X4
or
3755 Henry Hudson Parkway
New York, N.Y. 10463

Because she is trained as a dance therapist, it is vital to Adina Kaufman that her audience, whether passive or participatory, be relaxed and enjoying themselves. Her programs are as varied as her talents and will be tailored to suit your group. She sings in Yiddish, Hebrew, and English, and teaches Israeli, Yemenite, and Arabic dances. Definitely available for travel.

Keren Shemesh Israeli Dance Group
℅ MIT Hillel
312 Memorial Drive
Cambridge, Mass. 02139

Keren Shemesh is an Israeli dance group composed of twelve young men and women. Their repertoire consists of modern Israeli folk dances, Yemenite and Arabic dances, kibbutz dances, and an Eastern European suite. They are available for performances and will teach Israeli folk dances after the performance if desired. Their $100 fee allows them to cover the cost of costumes and equipment. Write for more information.

Natalie Ladin
157 Pembroke St. • Brooklyn, N.Y. 11235

Natalie Ladin teaches Israeli and international dances in the New York—New Jersey—Connecticut area and is available for one-day or one-night workshops. I've known her for a while and her enthusiasm and humor are contagious.

National Jewish Welfare Board
15 E. 26th St. • New York, N.Y. 10010

N.J.W.B.'s directory of artists and theater has two listings for dance leaders. The Moshe Ariel Dance Company presents a program of interpretive Israeli folk dances. Ariel and his cast will also teach classes for any group interested. Ed Jaffe sings and entertains as well as demonstrates and teaches Israeli and international dances. Contact both of these parties through the N.J.W.B. and also ask for information about performers listed with them.

Rakdaneem
Roberta Caplan
110 East End Ave. #7E
New York, N.Y. 10028
or 552 N. Neville St.
Pittsburgh, Pa. 15213

Rakdaneem is a group of three dancers coordinated by Roberta Caplan. Drawing on modern and folk dance idioms, their original contemporary dances are devoted to the expression of Jewish identity. The three dancers, one man and two women, all have extensive professional dance experience. The group is available for performances and workshops; write for more information.

RAKDANEEM, Roberta Kaplan. (photo: Otto M. Berk)

Jeffrey Marc Rockland
P.O. Box 488
Virginia Intermont College
Bristol, Va. 24201
or
106 Francis Street
Brookline, Mass. 02146

Jeffrey is a ballet dancer in training. He is available to teach ballet workshops at summer camps or

Jewish centers and is very interested in hearing from others interested in ballet with Jewish themes.

Miriam Rosenblum
14 Alton Place • Brookline, Mass. 02146

Miriam Rosenblum will teach Israeli folk dance at all types of events, from parties and weddings to one-night or weekend programs. Until recently Miriam lived in Ohio where she was the director and choreographer of the Sabra Dancers. She provided me with the addresses of the following performing groups in Ohio:

Ruah Hadasha
451 Loveman • Worthington, Ohio 43068
Eileen Nemzer, Director

Sabra Dancers
320 Straight St. • Cincinnati, Ohio 45219

Shelhevet
% Jewish Community Center
3505 Mayfield Road • Cleveland, Ohio 44105
Paul and Carole Kantor, Directors

Shomrei Tarbut Dancers
% Shalom Concert Bureau
P.O. Box 35092
Los Angeles, Calif. 90035

The Shomrei Tarbut Dancers are available for performances in the Los Angeles area. Contact Baruch Cohen at the Shalom Concert Bureau.

Danny Uziel
910 E. 21st St. • Brooklyn, N.Y. 11210

Danny Uziel is a choreographer who performs and teaches. Contact him directly for further details.

Worldtone Music, Inc.
Record Loft International
230 Seventh Ave. • New York, N.Y. 10011

The Record Loft recently moved to the above address from Flushing, N.Y., where it was known as Folk Music International. Kenneth Spears still runs the shop, which does more than simply sell records. If you or your group are looking for a teacher or performer, Ken Spears is a good person to write to, since he acts as a booking agent for a number of Israeli dance choreographers and teachers, such as Shlomo Bachar and Moshiko Halevy. Many of Bachar's dances are based on his Ladino background, those of Moshiko's on his Yemenite ancestry. Ken Spears also organizes folk dance weekends from time to time during the year with instruction by a top-level dancer. These usually take place at a hotel in the New York State area. When you write for his *Israeli Folk Dance Catalog,* ask to be put on the mailing list for information about classes and dance weekends. The Record Loft's catalog lists Tikva, Hed Arzi, Hadarim, Hataklit, Elektra, and Worldtone Music records among others. Most of the records come with instructions. Mail orders are shipped by parcel post. Delivery time is normally seven to twelve days, depending on the distance from New York.

Israel Yakovee
P.O. Box 3194 • Van Nuys, Calif. 91407

Israel Yakovee is a dance teacher and choreographer. An Israeli of Yemenite background, he was a member of Inbal, the Bat-Sheva Institute, and the Karmon dance group. He is available for Master Class workshops and performances with his group "Finjan". The fee is determined by the type of workshop or length of show. His record *Boi Teiman* is available from him (make check for $6.50 payable to Lyron Records) and includes a dance notation booklet. With Shlomo Bachar he co-directs the Shalom Israeli Dance Institute which sponsors Cafe Shalom three evenings a week (classes start at 8:30) and Camp Shalom which offers three weekends of Israeli dance annually. In 1980 the Shalom Israeli Dance Institute also organized a three-week folk dance tour of Israel. Write for further information.

(photo: Mae Rockland)

Music

DIASPORA YESHIVA BAND. (photo: courtesy The Jewish Star; see *Learning: Media*)

One of my best friends is a Greek Cypriot who left Cyprus to go to high school in Athens. There his brilliance was recognized and he was given a full scholarship to Yale. He has since become an internationally recognized astro-physicist but he continues to long for his home and to support his elderly refugee parents and other relatives in Cyprus. I asked him once how he gets through the low and lonely places. "My music," he said. "I put on my records and tapes and let myself go and just dance around the house; then it's not so bad." I've been through some pretty low places too and I've taken a clue from Telemachos and put on my favorite music and danced around the house. It helps! My record collection, like my taste in general, is very eclectic, but those records which most lift my spirits and work therapeutically for me seem to fall into the broad

category of *"freilach"* music, such as "Music for the Traditional Jewish Wedding" by Dave Tarras, "American Chai" by the Fabrangen Fiddlers, and Giora Feidman's "Soul Music". Buying information for these and other records follows. This section also has sources for Jewish music publications and for performers who are available for concerts and simchas. You will note that the word "klezmer" keeps recurring. This Yiddish word is derived from the Hebrew for "musical instruments"— *klei zemer*. Klezmer music, played by itinerant Jewish musicians who went from town to town playing at festive gatherings, was, like the Yiddish language, destined to die out. But, like Yiddish, it is tenacious and there is a new crop of musicians in their 20s and 30s picking up and carrying on the klezmer sound and traditions.

American Jewish Congress
15 E. 84th St. • New York, N.Y. 10028

The record: *Silent No More*. Jewish Underground songs from Soviet Russia. Based on tapes smuggled out by "Ben Tsion". Sung and narrated by Theodore Bikel; arranged and conducted by Issachar Miron. Also ask for information about the American Jewish Congress-CETA Artists Project which has as its goal bringing "Jewish Music in all its forms to the public—free".

Ramie and Merri Arian
Etz Chaim Creative Jewish Music
736 Forest Avenue
Larchmont, N.Y. 10538

Ramie and Merri Arian bring to their performances experience as Jewish educators and youth workers as well as musical background. They have both been very active in NFTY, the Reform Jewish youth movement, and can be heard on the "Songs NFTY Sings" record albums. For their programs they use the guitar primarily but also the piano, chalil, and dumbek (Arab drum). They are available for programs featuring Israeli and American Hebrew music, for organizations and family events; $175 plus expenses minimum, depending on the program.

Joseph Bach
1431 N. 40th St. • Allentown, Pa. 18104

Joseph Bach, cantor at Allentown's Temple Beth El, has put together several presentations which include slides as well as songs. One of his most popular programs is entitled "World of Our Fathers" and uses slides of New York's Lower East Side from around the turn of the century. Write for flyers and fees.

Balkan Arts Center
514 W. 110th St. #33
New York, N.Y. 10025

The Balkan Arts Center, a non-profit organization dedicated to the "research, documentation, and presentation of traditional ethnic expressive culture in the United States", has put out a jewel of a record. *Dave Tarras, Master of the Jewish Clarinet,*

Music for the Traditional Jewish Wedding is the epitome of klezmer music. It is no wonder that Giora Feidman, the great Argentine-Israeli clarinetist, in acknowledgment of how much he has learned from Tarras, has called him the "King of the Klezmers". On this record Tarras is very ably accompanied by Samuel Beckerman and Irving Graetz. Through their artistry wonderful images come alive and melodies such as *Opshpiel far di Makhatonim* (A Prelude for the In-Laws) and *Fun der Khupeh* (From the Wedding Canopy) make one truly grateful that Andrew Statman and Walter Zev Feldman (who are also klezmorim) have produced this record and that the Balkan Arts Center distributes it for $7 plus .75¢ postage. The Balkan Arts Center produces concerts of traditional Jewish instrumental and vocal music from time to time. Call or write for information.

Board of Jewish Education of Greater New York
426 W. 58th St. • New York, N.Y. 10019

Holiday melody cassettes, music of Israel, songbooks. Write for brochure.

Baruch Cohon
Shalom Concert Bureau
P.O. Box 35092
Los Angeles, Calif. 90035

Have you seen "The Frisco Kid" with Gene Wilder, one of my very favorite movies? Baruch Cohon did the special musical material for Gene Wilder—the davening, the Yiddish song he sang while skating, and the chant he did while tied to the stake in the Indian camp. He also does quite a few other things. A cantor and composer, he gives lecture-performances which unabashedly celebrate the joy of being Jewish. He is alternately funny and profound, *and* he's a consummate musician. He also operates the Shalom Concert Bureau and in this capacity is a program consultant to universities, organizations, congregations, private parties, folk night clubs, resorts, and community centers. His fees range from $250 for an afternoon or evening program to $1800 for a concert with supporting artists and orchestra. Weekend retreat or scholar-musician in residence is $500. Write for more details and flyers.

Diaspora Yeshiva Band
B'nai Brith Lecture Bureau
823 U.N. Plaza • New York, N.Y. 10017

The Diaspora Yeshiva Band (see photo opening this section) is the number one "religious rock" band in Israel. It is made up of five Americans who went to Israel to study Torah at the Diaspora Yeshiva. Their first American tour in the spring of 1979 met with a lot of acclaim as have their two records. Contact the B'nai Brith Lecture Bureau for future bookings.

Bruce Fagen
5225 Bay Rd. N. • Bensalem, Pa. 19020

Bruce Fagan is an exciting interpreter of Israeli and Jewish popular and folk music. He styles himself as an "entertainer" as well as a musician, since he intersperses the music of Eastern Europe and the Middle East with light commentary and stories. He accompanies himself on acoustic guitar, and sometimes appears with an ensemble of anywhere from three to ten musicians. As well as performing himself, he acts as a booking agent for other Israeli music resources and will help organizations and synagogues plan programs and find performing artists.

Fabrangen Fiddlers
2307 Forest Glen Rd.
Silver Spring, Md. 20910

I wish I could clone the Fabrangen Fiddlers. These five extremely gifted individuals—David Shneyer, vocals, guitar, and harmonica; Sue Roemer, vocals, piano, and guitar; Alan Oresky, fiddle and mandolin; Frank Sparber, clarinet; and Theo Stone, bass fiddle—have combined their talents and efforts to produce an authentic Jewish-American folk music. The Fiddlers, vaguely annoyed with the extent to which Israeli music dominates Jewish music in America, feel—as I do—that the time is ripe for a flowering of a hyphenated Jewish-American culture, of course including Jewish-American music. Throughout our long history, in every cultural environment where Jews have lived, we have borrowed cultural forms from the surrounding majority culture and have infused them with Jewish themes, messages, and motifs. The Fiddlers, acting in this tradition,

have produced some remarkable music, some of which (because it came dressed in bluegrass rhythms) has been affectionately called "Jewgrass". The Fabrangen Fiddlers play for simchas and do concerts and programs of Yiddish, Hasidic, Ladino, and new Jewish-American folk music. They also lead workshops in song and instrumentation. (Maybe that's the way we can have clones.) If you can't get to hear them in person there are two marvelous records available. *Country Klezmers,* traditional Jewish music with a bluegrass flavor performed by Shneyer, Stone, and Bruce Brill before the formation of the Fiddlers, has such melodies as the "Ufaratzta Blues" and "L'cha Dodi" set to "She'll be comin' round the mountain" (sounds silly but its fine!). *American Chai,* by the Fabrangen Fiddlers, is superbly recorded and has some lovely Yiddish vocals by Sue Roemer. Both records are available for $6 each from the above address. When I asked Ruth Rubin, the noted musicologist, what she thought of the Fiddlers, she replied, "They are the best there is . . . Alan is absolutely remarkable, the fiddle is part of his arm." I can't be more enthusiastic than to say: to hear them is to love them.

FABRANGEN FIDDLERS' fiddler, Alan Oresky. (photo: courtesy David Shneyer)

Giora Feidman
B'nai Brith Lecture Bureau
823 U.N. Plaza • New York, N.Y. 10017

If Israel was in the knighting business, Giora Feidman would have been knighted a long time ago. Originally from Argentina where he was affiliated with the Teatro Colon in Buenos Aires, he has played his magic clarinet with the Israel Philharmonic since his emigration to Israel in 1957. But the credential he announces with the most pride at just about every concert is that he is a fourth generation klezmer. His concerts are emotional experiences, but if you can't make it to one there is a wonderful record available: "Long live Giora, His Clarinet, and His Soul Music" produced by Star Record Co., 521 Fifth Avenue, New York, N.Y. 10017, record # ST AE 76A/B. The title of the record comes from the following testimonial letter:

Stephen Freedman
230 Walnut St. • Brookline, Mass. 02146

Stephen Freedman, folksinger and composer of Hebrew music, emphasizes the rich variety of Jewish music through his repertoire of traditional Hebrew ballads, Israeli hits, popular standards, and modern Hasidic songs. He is available for organizational programs, family festivities and religious school assemblies. Brochure available.

Debbie Friedman
JWB Lecture Bureau
15 E. 26th St. • New York, N.Y. 10010

I had heard Debbie Friedman's records but had not seen her in concert until the 1979 CAJE conference where I was caught up along with 1,000 other people by her vibrant presentation and infectious easy sing-along rhythms. While Debbie's music is contemporary and very American in feeling, she works in the best tradition of Hasidic music by taking a simple phrase such as "Am Yisroel Chai" and setting it to her own easy-to-pick-up melodies. The spirit and enthusiasm she generates comes about in part because you feel as though you've done it yourself. If you can't get to a concert you can still hear her songs and warm resonant voice on records: Not by Might, Not by Power; Sing Unto God; and Ani Ma-amin (I Believe) available from Behrman House, Inc., 1261 Broadway, New York, N.Y. 10001.

Sherwood Goffin
142 West End Ave.
New York, N.Y. 10023

In the 1960s and 1970s thousands of young people came to know and love Sherwood Goffin, his mellifluous voice, and his Hasidic "soul music" at Yeshiva University's Torah Leadership Seminars. For more than a dozen years he has been the chazan of New York's Lincoln Square Synagogue, contributing in no small way to that community's phenomenal growth and success. He has sung at more demonstrations and rallies on behalf of Soviet Jewry than perhaps any other artist. Contact him directly for details of his fees and availability for concerts, at which he accompanies himself on the guitar. His two wonderful records, Neshomo and Mimkomo (both also on cassette), are standard items at Jewish book and gift stores everywhere.

Hughes Dulcimer Company, Inc.
441 West Colfax Avenue
Denver, Colo. 80204

Ever since I was a little girl, I've been singing "tum-ba-la, tum-ba-la, tum-balalaika", hardly realizing that the Yiddish words referred to the Russian three-stringed folk instrument—the balalaika. I was delighted to find that the Hughes Dulcimer Company sells several kits for making different sizes of balalaikas. There is only one book in English on how to play the balalaika; Hughes sells it for $5. Write for an informative illustrated catalog that shows kits for a large variety of other instruments, including several types of the dulcimer, which is reputed to be of Biblical origin, mandolins, and lyres.

Jewish Music Council
National Jewish Welfare Board
15 E. 26th St. • New York, N.Y. 10010

The Jewish Music Council was founded in 1944. Every year it sponsors a Jewish Music Festival. It offers a free catalog of its publications about all aspects of Jewish Music. If you or your group are looking for a single performer or a full troupe for a single performance or a series of evenings, contact the N.J.W.B. and ask for its catalog entitled "The Jewish Arts; A Directory of Artists and Theatre." It gives listings and descriptions of vocalists, ensembles, bands, humorists, actors, children's entertainment, and dancers.

The Jewish Music Society
315 W. 36th St. • New York, N.Y. 10018

The Jewish Music Society operates in the manner of a book club. Your initial membership fee ($10) brings you a free selection then and a new selection to audition every two months which you either keep and pay for or return. There are no minimum purchase requirements and you can cancel whenever you wish. Their catalog of offerings is interesting and covers different areas of Jewish music—Yiddish, Ladino, Israeli, classical, and pop. There are selections especially for children. I was happy to see many records by Yehoram Gaon listed as well as one by the Diaspora Yeshiva Band. Write for more information about this relatively painless way to build a Jewish music collection.

Kadima
℅ Hal Katzman
34 Irving St.
Newton Centre, Mass. 02158

My daughter Keren came home from a friend's bar mitzvah party insisting that we hire the band she had just heard there for her forthcoming bat mitzvah celebration. I asked some adult friends who had also heard the group about them and they all heartily recommended Kadima. So, assured by my friends that it wouldn't be a disaster and of

course wanting to please Keren on her special day, I hired Kadima to play for our simcha. The three-piece band more than met my expectations. They sized up our mixture of family and friends and played a great variety of Jewish music, ranging from Hasidic to contemporary American-Israeli and threw in just enough standard pop selections to keep everyone happy. Their spacing, timing, and enthusiasm were perfect. Kadima is very willing to play in a variety of situations, ranging from coffee houses to meetings of Jewish organizations, to parties of all kinds. They will travel anywhere though there will generally be an additional charge for long distances from the Boston area.

Kapelye
℅ Henry Sapoznik
2018 Voorhies Ave, # B24
Brooklyn, N.Y. 11235

Kapelye, which means "band" in Yiddish, is a 6 member group (two fiddles, clarinet, accordion, tuba/bass with percussion, and mandolin) affiliated with the Martin Steinberg Center of the American Jewish Congress. Kapelye draws its material from klezmer tunes, the Yiddish theater, songs of the socialist movement, and folksongs; full translations of songs are provided. Kapelye is available for concert performances and family simchas. They specialize in traditional wedding music and in fact can "do" the whole wedding, ceremony included, since the father of one of the members is the cantor Zindel Sapoznik. They have a *badkhen* (Yiddish improvising poet, "M.C.") or can just provide dance music. Their basic fee is $600 but will vary depending on distance and employer's budget. Write for the brochure of this exciting young group of new wave klezmerim.

Kinneret
℅ Steve Reuben
3536 Cambridge Ave.
Riverdale, N.Y. 10463

Kinneret is an exciting concert group that offers a unique Jewish musical experience. Its interpretations of a diverse repertoire based on traditional and contemporary Jewish and Israeli music as well as original compositions features folk, rock, and jazz. The group performs and creates programs for community-based organizations, universities, and military bases. The group's co-director, Steve Reuben, is a Reform rabbi and so they will also do a folk-rock-jazz Friday evening service called "Shabbat a Celebration"; their fee is $75 plus expenses for 4. Steve and his wife Darleen Kummer Reuben are also available for a program entitled "Songs of Hope and Freedom" which is a multi-media concert presentation of their first secret Jewish musical tour of the Soviet Union. Through songs, slides, and stories, they bring the struggles of refuseniks and activists to their audience. Cost is $500, plus expenses. Steve Reuben has also written a book of simple, mostly English, holiday songs, *Especially Wonderful Days*, available from Alternatives in Religious Education, see *Learning*.

The Klezmorim
Directors: Lev Liberman
**1846 Spruce, 23 • Berkeley, Calif. 94709
and David Skuse
87 Edgecroft • Kensington, Calif. 94707**

The Klezmorim are five performers who specialize in Jewish music of Russia, Romania, Hungary, Israel, America, the Hasidim, and the Sephardim —with particular emphasis on music from the Yiddish theater. Members of the ensemble sing and are also accomplished instrumentalists on the violin (and its older cousin the gadulka), mandolin, flute, accordion, guitar, dumbek, tambourine, clarinet, oud, pennywhistle, saxophone, string bass, and contrabass balalaika. This creative group utilizes costume, dance, and theater to evoke the flavor of life in a variety of turn-of-the-century Jewish communities. Their presentations are based on years of research in Jewish folkways. Co-director Lev Liberman, as music archivist of the Judah L. Magnes Memorial Museum, makes a substantial collection of rare recordings and manuscripts available to the group. In addition to concert appearances, the ensemble performs at festivals, bar mitzvahs, and weddings. The co-directors also lecture on Jewish music, accompanied by musical examples both live and taped. Write for information about prices and scheduling. Although based in the San Francisco Bay Area, they are available for engagements elsewhere.

Merkos L'Inyonei Chinuch, Inc.
770 Eastern Parkway • Brooklyn, N.Y. 11213

Seven long-playing authentic recordings of Chabad-Lubavitch melodies.

The Stanley Miller Simha Band
**102-20 67th Drive (Room 202)
Forest Hills, N.Y. 11375**

Stanley Miller describes his Simha Band as a "modern oriented Chassidic band." He writes: "We utilize modern rock styles and instrumentation (bass guitar, rock drums, three-part harmony vocals) and play Chassidic music. (We also play society if the customer insists.) We have developed a merge of the modern styles and the Chassidic to give it a very ancient and deep flavor. Mind you, the music is not rock, it comes out as totally Chassidic, full of intense energy. In as much as it is difficult to get a picture of sound through words, maybe you'd like to come to our concert [a benefit for the Student Struggle for Soviet Jewry]. We hope it'll be very 'heimish.' "

NAMA Orchestra
**% David H. Owens
2367 Glendon Ave.
Los Angeles, Calif. 90064**

NAMA is a small folk orchestra whose members play a large variety of traditional acoustic instruments such as the violin, flute, accordion, bass, piano, guitar, frula, kaval, and tamburica. The group specializes in Yiddish and Israeli songs and other East European folk music from Romania,

Yugoslavia, Russia, Hungary, Bulgaria, and Greece. NAMA is very well known among Balkan folk dancers and is also active at Jewish events. They are available for concerts, folk dances and special occasions. As well as two Balkan folk dance records (NAMA 1 and 2) the orchestra has recently released *Mazltov! Yiddish Folk Songs,* which besides being a high quality recording showing off the versatility of the group also has an accompanying 14-page booklet. This not only gives all the words to the songs in phonetic transcriptions and English translation, but also in the original (Yiddish, Hebrew, or Cyrillic) alphabets. The record is a jewel; the vocalist, Pearl Rottenberg who sings in a straightforward, natural manner, has just the right amount of Yiddishe melancholia, and the musicians are superb. To order NAMA 3, send $7 plus 75¢ for postage ($1.50 in Canada). Flyer available free.

National Federation of Temple Youth
Union of American Hebrew Congregations
838 Fifth Ave. • New York, N.Y. 10021

Record albums that have been made by N.F.T.Y. groups and which include some original songs by them. Inquire about discounts for bulk purchases of these records.

Professional Percussion Center
151 W. 46th St. • New York, N.Y. 10036

The Professional Percussion Center includes among its offerings drums from the Middle East, such as the timbale, the dumbek, and others of brass and clay. Many of these are made in Israel and the countries surrounding it. Write for additional information.

Ruth Rubin
45 Gramercy Park N. (16C)
New York, N.Y. 10010

Some people's greatness moves me so much that I see and hear everything they do with tears in my eyes. Ruth Rubin is one of those people. I had been a fan of hers for years admiring both her books and records, but neither had fully prepared me for the subtle intensity of her presence when giving a lecture-recital to hundreds of people. Unprepossessing, with her little note book in hand, she simultaneously teaches and entertains, literally moving her audience from laughter to tears. With no accompaniment and a style which might be called a non-style, she evokes all the images and emotions folk songs are meant to conjure up but seldom do when they have been cleaned up for a performance. Ruth seems to become the mother crooning a lullaby, the seamstress at her machine, the hesitant bride, the valiant partisan, and even the local *"shicker"* when she does a drinking song. The programs she presents are quite varied and include topics such as "The Story of Yiddish Folksong", "The Jewish Woman and Her Yiddish Song", and "Folksong: A Universal Language". Write or call for more information about her programs and fees.

RUTH RUBIN, lecture-recital. (photos: Mae Rockland)

SAFAM
c/o Dan Funk
36 Hamlin Rd.
Newton Centre, Mass. 02159

SAFAM is a musical group that performs contemporary and traditional Jewish music, much of which is original. SAFAM has recorded two albums, "Dreams of Safam" and "Encore"; each sells for $6. A third album is in progress. They are available for concert performances for Jewish groups of all kinds and will travel.

Cantor Zindel Sapoznik
2108 Voorhies Ave #B24
Brooklyn, N.Y. 11235

Born in the city of Rovno in the Ukraine, Cantor Sapoznik began singing at the age of ten and by 13 was a *chazan*. As the "last of the Rovno khazunim", Cantor Sapoznik retains the beautiful cantorial repertoire of his region (Volyn). He also performs folk and popular Yiddish songs learned in Europe. In addition to serving as *chazan* at the Marine Park Jewish Center in Brooklyn, Cantor Sapoznik officiates at hundreds of weddings, bar and bat mitzvahs, and Passover seders in the U.S., the Caribbean, and in Israel. Solo performance $150, with accompanist, $275, and with a klezmer band (six pieces) $700 (all plus expenses).

Shalom Concert Bureau
P.O. Box 35092
Los Angeles, Calif. 90035

The Shalom Concert Bureau represents a wide variety of actors and musicians, including Nehemiah Persoff, Rivka Rebebb, Jack Bernardi, Esther Lawrence, and the Oriana Singers. Write for descriptive flyers.

Shanachie Records Corp.
Dalebrook Park
Ho-ho-kus, N.J. 07423

Zev Feldman and Andy Statman's marvelous record, *Jewish Klezmer Music*, is so far the only Jewish album produced by Shanachie, and it is a jewel! An instrumental which uses the *cimbal*, East European dulcimer, with marvelous effect, this record by disciples of Dave Tarras is at once nostalgic and fresh.

David Shneyer
2307 Forest Glen Rd.
Silver Spring, Md. 20910

David Shneyer: Jewish music-man and folk-chazan, a founder of the Fabrangen community in Washington, D.C., member of the Fabrangen Fiddlers, and Havurah resource person. David will travel to do musical programs, work with singers and musicians in congregations and Havurot. He has published *Psalm Songs*, a collection of thirty original compositions for services and simchas, available for five dollars, including postage and handling.

Moshe Shur
Hillel Foundation
Student Services Corporation
P.O. Box 446 • Flushing N.Y. 11367

Moshe (Mickey) Shur, sometimes called "The Jewish Minstrel", is on his way to being another Shlomo Carlebach-style guru. A Rabbi as well as a folk singer and composer, Shur entertains and enlightens his audiences with a personal mixture of storytelling and *niggunim*. He is also available as a lecturer on such topics as "Kabbalah" and "Finding our Future: Abrams, Issacs, and Jacobson". Whether for concerts or lectures Mickey is willing to travel.

Tara Publications
29 Derby Ave. • Cedarhurst, N.Y. 11516

Tara Publications is run by Velvel Pasternak, the noted authority on Hasidic music. He has compiled an invaluable two-volume sourcebook, *Songs of the Chassidim*, which is available from Tara for $22, the set. Write for his brochure, which also lists his other books including a spiral-bound handbook for musicians entitled *Hassidic-Israeli Club Date, Musicians Edition of Hasidic Favorites*, with chord symbols. See *Learning: Programs* for more about Velvel Pasternak.

Transcontinental Music Publishing
Union of American Hebrew Congregations
838 Fifth Avenue • New York, N.Y. 10021

Josef Freudenthal, who founded this company in 1938, is, in large part, responsible for the availability of printed scores of Jewish classical music in this country. Transcontinental Music Publications publishes, sells, and distributes Jewish liturgical and secular music. Write for a catalog.

Voice of the Turtle
Judith Wachs, Manager
70 Manemet Rd. • Newton, Mass. 02159

Having spoken Yiddish before English and grown up in a Yiddish working-class environment, my first allegiance has usually been to Eastern European Jewish music. But after living in Spanish speaking countries for close to six years and immersing myself in that language and in the history of the Sephardic Jews, I now have a feeling for Ladino music akin to that of my *mama loshen*. It was therefore a thrill to hear the young, dedicated performers who make up Voice of the Turtle. The four musicians all have impressive backgrounds in classical and antique music. Using Biblical "pipe and timbrel, harp and psaltery", as well as instruments of the medieval and Renaissance periods, the group explores and recreates the rich musical heritage of the Sephardic Jews. The authentic

VOICE OF THE TURTLE, from left: Judith Wachs, Jay Rosenberg, Lisle Kulbach, Derek Burrows. (photo: Kevin Strauss)

instruments they use and the clarity of their voices give their performance a truly haunting quality. If their record, "The Time of Singing is Come—Songs of the Sephardim", is as good as they are in person, it will be a rare treat. To order send $6.75 to the group manager. Voice of the Turtle is available for concerts, lectures, and family celebrations. They have recently designed a special program for children which can be geared to elementary or high school ages. It is a survey of the Jews in exile and their return to the homeland with examples of Sephardi, Yiddish, and Israeli music. Write for booking information and brochure.

Workmen's Circle
Education Department
45 E. 33rd St. • New York, N.Y. 10016

For those interested in authentic Yiddish music and song, the Workmen's Circle has some fascinating material. Five 33⅓ rpm, 7" records by Jewish musicologist Ruth Rubin are a delight, a learning experience, and a bargain at $3 plus $.50 postage for the complete set. Each record contains six songs performed in a simple folkloric manner without accompaniment, and comes with a complete libretto in transliterated Yiddish and English translation. There are notes on the origins and background of each song as well. As well as these records, Workmen's Circle has a substantial list of publications dealing with music.

Worldtone Music, Inc.
Record Loft International
230 Seventh Ave. • New York, N.Y. 10011

Write for Worldtone's Israeli folk dance record catalog. Not only are there dance records (most with instructions included), but quite a few Israeli folk song albums are listed as well. The catalog is free and contains a handy order form. See also *Playing: Dance* for a listing of Worldtone's other services.

World Zionist Organization
Department of Education and Culture
515 Park Ave. • New York, N.Y. 10022

The World Zionist Organization publishes an interesting record album of songs about Jerusalem.

**Yugentruf
Youth for Yiddish
3328 Bainbridge Avenue
Bronx, N.Y. 10467**

Vaserl (Yiddish for "stream"), a recording of new Yiddish songs by young people, is available from Yugentruf for $6. The collection shows two distinct musical styles; side 1 is in a traditional vein and includes lyrics from past generations, side 2 demonstrates the influence of today's popular music. An interesting and very worthwhile effort.

**Zamir Chorale of Boston Inc.
P.O. Box 126
Newton Centre, Mass. 02159**

The Zamir Chorale is a choral ensemble specializing in the music of Israel, the Yiddish Theatre, and Jewish liturgy. Since its formation by conductor Joshua Jacobson in 1969, the Chorale has remained committed to perpetuating Jewish culture through song and to sharing music of the highest quality with its audiences. The Chorale has performed throughout New England and New York, toured Israel and Great Britain, and appeared with the Jerusalem Symphony and the Israel Philharmonic orchestras, conductors Daniel Barenboim and Zubin Mehta, and soloists Theodore Bikel and Herschel Bernardi. Concert fees range from $500 to $1,000, plus traveling expenses. Fees depend upon the number of singers and the length of the program. The conductor, Joshua Jacobson, is available for lectures. He can be reached through the music department of Northeastern University where he teaches.

ZAMIR CHORALE conducted by Joshua Jacobson. (photo: L. Michael Kaye)

Theater

SUZANNE BENTON and the "Birthstory Body Mask" from the
ritual tale "Mary Adeline and the Birthstory". See *Creating:
Metal* and *Learning: Programs*.

My father always wanted to be an actor. He never
made it though; from the time he arrived as a 14 year-
old immigrant he worked as a glazier. Whenever he
could put the money together for a ticket he went to the
Yiddish theater on Second Avenue in New York and
there, when he was 25, he met (today we would say
"picked up") my mother who came from Poland to work
in a paper box factory. As soon as I was old enough to sit
through a performance, my parents began taking me to
Yiddish matinees. By the time I was *really* old enough to
understand the plots and the jokes, there were far fewer

performances and my other interests began to lead me
away from my parents' world. Now that once again I am
fascinated with all aspects of Jewish creativity, I find it
thrilling to watch the development of new Jewish-
American theater which reflects the trends and techniques found in the general acting community while
drawing on Jewish traditions and themes. Puppets of
every ilk, for example, have come back in fashion and
captured the imagination of performers everywhere,
and so in this section you will find puppeteers as well as
theater groups and individual actors.

Tova Ackerman
The Buttonhole Players
658 E. 7th St. • Brooklyn, New York 11218

Tova Ackerman uses puppets to teach Jewish values and to "manufacture dreams with Jewish soul". The four shows she does include *The Purim Story; Batya's Wedding*, a documentary of a Hasidic wedding suitable for older children; *The Big Fish,* an adaptation of the well-loved folk tale in which a poor but righteous man finds a diamond in the fish on which he spent his last penny to honor the Sabbath; and *Chanale's Shabbat Dress*, a delightful Israeli fairy tale in which the stains Chanale got on her new dress by helping an injured stranger are magically transformed into sparkling stars because of the mitzvah she did. All of the music for the puppet performances is composed and created especially for The Buttonhole Players by Vladimir Grindberg. The price of the shows varies depending upon location. Tova gives workshops and lectures as well as performances. Brochure and flyers.

TOVA ACKERMAN'S "Buttonhole Players".

BARKING ROOSTER THEATER, "Daniel and Sarah and the End of the World".

Barking Rooster Theater, Inc.
c/o Avram Pratt
RD #2 • Plainfield, Vt. 05667

The Barking Rooster Theater is a group of actors organized and now directed by Avram Patt, who also writes much of the group's material. Several of the Barking Rooster players were with the Bread and Puppet Theatre previously and those who have seen both groups perform note similarities in style. The Barking Rooster Theater presents original plays using masks, music, and actors, concerning Jewish themes, sometimes based on Yiddish stories. Past productions have included two plays based on I.L. Peretz' stories: "Not Afraid of Falling" and "The Bass Fiddle", and a play by Avram Patt dealing with the legends surrounding the false Messiah Sabbatai Sevi entitled "Daniel and Sarah and The End of The World". The language used for the works is primarily English; mime is also employed. The group will travel; fees are negotiable.

Robert Binder
B'Yad HaYotzer
24 Warwick Avenue
Toronto, Ontario M6C 1T6

Along with the many other things B'Yad HaYotzer does, under the direction of Robert Binder, are

puppet shows for Jewish groups and schools. See
Learning: Media.

Norman J. Fedder
Theater Program
Speech Department
Kansas State University
Manhattan, Kansas 66506

Norman Fedder is a Professor of Theater at Kansas
State University. His major field of interest is
Jewish theater and he was active in founding the
Jewish Theater Association. He writes plays based
on Jewish themes and directs their production by
the group he founded called *The Jewish Heritage
Theater.* As well as writing and directing the plays
he also acts in them. Presentations of these plays
can be arranged through Professor Fedder who is
also interested in commissions to write plays about
particular aspects of Jewish experience and history.

Sally Fox
Jewish Involvement Theatre
PO Box 3309, OSU Station
Columbus, Ohio 43210

Jewish Involvement Theatre offers the opportunity
for a group of people to come together and focus
on the humorous and the serious questions of

SALLY FOX, Jewish Involvement Theatre. (photo: Al Rit-
toneyer)

being a Jew today. Sally Fox, who plays about 250
different Jewish characters, involves her audience
as they help the character deal with the situation
he/she is facing. The program is between 1½–2½
hours long and engages audience members (to the
degree that they are comfortable) "in intimate
dialogue without threat". Despite the audience
participation, this is *theater* not therapy. Write for
Sally's brochure which explains the seating setup
she likes to work with and lists the broad range of
subjects with which she is prepared to deal.

The Jewish Puppet Theatre
766 Montgomery St. • Brooklyn, N.Y. 11213

Employing audience participation, parades, live
music, story-telling, and prizes, this group of
young Orthodox Jews uses their lively puppet
shows to teach Torah, mitzvot, midrash, and tales
of tzadikim. There are specific shows for each of
the Jewish Holidays plus shows which highlight a
particular aspect of Jewish life or history. They will
perform anywhere and anytime they are needed
except Shabbat and Yom Tov. Rates are reasonable
and negotiable; write for brochure.

THE JEWISH PUPPET THEATRE:
"***THRILL* to the great moments in Jewish history!
  ***CHEER* as Good triumphs over Evil!
  ***LEARN* about Jewish ethics, holidays, and doing
mitzvahs!"

Jewish Repertory Theatre
344 E. 14th St. • New York, N.Y. 10003

Ran Avni, the artistic director of the Jewish Reper-
tory Theatre, writes that the group "presents plays
in English that relate to the Jewish experience".
Write for more information.

Susan Merson
400 W. 43rd St. (#12F)
New York, N.Y. 10036

Susan Merson is an actress-playwright whose work explores Jewish tradition. Thus far she has completed two plays which are available for touring. *Reflections of a China Doll* is a one-woman play about growing up Jewish in America. It runs for an hour and a half with one intermission and works in a simple theater space. *The Exile of Sarah K.* is a two-character exploration of a young Jewish woman who comes to America at the turn of the century and explores the issues of personal power, sexuality, and spirituality against the background of the *shtetl* and the new social framework of America. *Sarah K.* needs a real theater setting complete with adequate technical facilities. It is not suitable for luncheon events but would work well on college campuses or for synagogue discussion groups. As well as these two plays Susan is available for an informal theatrical "event" entitled *Inquiries* in which excerpts from her own and other writings are assembled and presented around a particular theme such as "family", "the artist", "wanting and getting" or whatever theme the group may be interested in.

Sasha Nanus
c/o Lecture Bureau
J.W.B.
15 E. 26th St. • New York, N.Y. 10010

Using the universal language of movement and expression which people of all ages can understand, Sasha Nanus is a mime who portrays characters as varied as Adam and Eve in the Garden of Eden, and a female Israeli soldier. Her pieces are funny and also moving; she is available for seminars and workshops as well as performances. Contact Steve Bayer at the Jewish Welfare Board for day or weekend arrangements.

The New Artef Players
P.O. Box 345
Los Angeles, Calif. 90048

The New Artef Players took their name from the Artef Players, a Yiddish workers theater ensemble of the 1920's and 30's. "And along with the name," they write, "we bring to life the spirit of the Yiddish theater; the spirit of a culture which was transplanted to this country and which lives on in our community today". Under the artistic direction of Armand Volkas, the group is dedicated to exploring Jewish themes through experimental theater. Formed in 1976, they have created more than nine original pieces, beginning with *Survivors*, their critically acclaimed piece on the Holocaust. Much of their work is developed through improvisation but they have also produced scripted pieces. Two of their plays *The Goat, The Chasid and the City: A Yom Kippur Dream* and *Memories, Dreams and Prophecies* were commissioned. Now housed in their own theater, the Orpheum, a 99-seat Equity-waiver theater, they are able to offer their patrons a subscription season which includes both established works dealing with Jewish identity and original pieces created through experimental techniques. They do, however, continue to tour and are interested in creating commissioned pieces in the future. Write for further information.

Red Rug Puppet Theatre
Beth Katz, Puppeteer
2232 Pembroke Road
Lansing, Mich. 48906

Beth Katz writes: "My career in puppetry began when I spent a summer in London with my two children going from one delightful Punch and Judy show to another. When I performed the *Three Billy*

RED RUG PUPPET THEATRE, Beth Katz, puppeteer.

Goats Gruff at home, no one would believe that I was the Troll! Success as a professional puppeteer, an unwillingness to perform the lucrative Christmas shows, and the need for my children to learn about the Jewish holidays in a creative and exciting way—these were, together, the factors which led me to explore Jewish puppetry". Beth's shows which are written, directed, and performed by her alone—with the help of over 100 puppets—are delightful. In the good old puppet show tradition, she involves the children in a dialogue with "Pop the Hanukkah Cop" in his pursuit of the Dragon Gonif who has stolen Mrs. Froglady's Hanukkah lamp. As "Pop" queries the audience, the children's responses are based on the Hanukkah lore Beth is teaching. As well as spirited performances, Beth also offers workshops which discuss how to produce a puppet show, how to teach with puppets in the classroom, and how to use puppets for play-therapy. The workshop includes a short performance, a demonstration, and a lot of exercise using the puppets. Write for Beth's brochure, fee schedule, and available dates.

© Stuart Copans (see *Creating: Pictures*).

Shalom Concert Bureau
Box 35092 • Los Angeles, Calif. 90035

Jack Bernardi and the comic performers Hilda Vincent and Leo Fuchs are among the actors represented by the Shalom Concert Bureau, which also represents musicians and dancers. Write for details of current programs.

A Traveling Jewish Theatre
7967 Woodrow Wilson Drive
Los Angeles, Calif. 90046

A Traveling Jewish Theatre draws on historical, oral, and literary sources as it works towards the creation of contemporary Jewish theatrical expression. The group is very concerned with the exploration of language "the shapes and sounds—that can transmit our experience and make it sharable". The actors perform with and without masks and especially made puppets by Corey Fischer. A Traveling Jewish Theatre is available for performances, workshops, and residencies. Write for information about the pieces they perform, fees, and scheduling.

© Stuart Copans (see *Creating: Pictures*).

Toys and Games

PLUS A SPECIAL SUPPLEMENT ON MINIATURES

(photo: Mae Rockland)

There is no lack of toys in every price range in America. If anything, our children suffer more from surfeit than from deprivation. Quality toys with Jewish content, however, are not that easy to come by. But, as they say, necessity is the mother of invention. Several of the sources in the following pages began producing Jewish toys and games to fill personal needs. I think we will soon be seeing even more well-made, attractive Jewish playthings for all age levels.

Alternatives in Religious Education, Inc.
3945 S. Oneida St. • Denver, Colo. 80237

Alternatives in Religious Education produces several games of interest to teenagers and adults, which are important Jewish variations of the currently popular simulation games. In one of the games, called "Gestapo", players pit values against actual events which occurred during the Nazi era. Only those who are wise, lucky, or clever will "survive". The object of another board game, "On the Move", is to escape safely from the Soviet Union. In a less serious vein, Alternatives carries two sets of holiday Lotto, one for Passover and one for Shabbat. Write for Alternatives' handsome brochure which describes minicourses, cassettes and other material as well. Also see *Learning* for more information.

B. Arbit
8050 N. Port Washington Rd.
Milwaukee, Wis. 53217

B. Arbit has Scrabble sets in Hebrew, $7.50 for one game, $6.75 each for two or more.

Bellerophon Books
36 Anacapa St. • Santa Barbara, Calif. 93101

This is not a Jewish book company, but it does publish two items of interest. Among its beautifully drawn coloring books is one titled *Old Testament*, $2.50. My favorite, however, is the charming cut-out book of *Great Women Paper Dolls*, from Cleopatra to Golda Meir, $2.50. The caption with the Golda Meir doll reads: "When my colleagues, men, look at me . . . I say: 'Don't worry. We will see to it, we women, that you have the right to vote and equal pay for equal work. And once in a while, we will even elect a man as Prime Minister!' "

Board of Jewish Education
426 W. 58th St. • New York, N.Y. 10019

"Road to Freedom; a Game of Escape From the Soviet Union" was created by Shoshana Ramm, a young Soviet Jewish girl who played the real-life version of the game and arrived in Israel in 1976. Basically a race-to-the-goal board game, it is both informative and attractively designed with childish drawings. Write for ordering information.

Contemporary Designs
1414 Glendale Ave. • Ames, Iowa 50010

Contemporary Designs has recently introduced its new puzzle line, *The New York Times Puzzle Series: Great Moments in Jewish History*. The series includes the front pages of the Times for the day Israel was declared a state (May 15, 1948), the day the Six Day War broke out (June 6, 1967), and two other historic days (which would you guess?). The puzzles are a nice addition to a growing line of games including *Aliyah*, which has become popular nationally, and *Mishpacha Madness*, a paper and pencil game similar to *Family Feud*. Fully descriptive wholesale and retail catalogs are available free of charge.

The Dreidel Factory
2445 Prince St. • Berkeley, Calif. 94705

Two California families with young children began making redwood dreidels in a garage workshop out of exasperation with the manufactured plastic

THE DREIDEL FACTORY, redwood dreidel from California.

variety. They showed some of their cottage-industry products around and met with such good response that they went to work for six months, cutting the wood with a table saw and hand-burning the letters to produce 10,000 tops. The first year they sold just enough to cover their costs, but fortunately were not discouraged. The dreidels are so attractive that one sells another and the second year they were flooded with repeat orders. They now produce a small brass dreidel in the old-fashioned winged style as well. The wooden dreidels come attractively packaged with game instructions and are about 2" from tip to the top of the handle. Mail orders are filled promptly. Write for discount prices on quantity orders. Since they began making wooden dreidels they have been imitated, but theirs are still the nicest. Send for their brochure which also describes their Hanukkah lamp (see *Creating: Wood*) and their Flying Hai Frizbee.

Eden Arts
Elayne Denker • 35 Weybridge Road Brookline, Mass. 02146

Elayne Denker has come up with another contemporary version of a traditional toy, the Purim gragger (noisemaker). $3.75 brings you, postage paid, a complete kit to make your own wooden gragger. All you need is a hammer to assemble the precut parts. After it is assembled, the gragger can be personalized with paint, felt tips or by glueing on fabric. All orders are filled within 24 hours. Discounts on orders of 50 or more.

PAMI FAGELSON, "Shtetl people", approx. 14" tall.

Pami Slatt Fagelson
18555 Split Rock Land
Germantown, Md. 20767

Pami Fagelson's soft sculpture caricatures are more to look at than to play with. The dolls are dressed in a variety of fabrics and the faces are made of quilted and tucked nylon. They're made in series but each one will be a little different since they are done individually. Priced at about $30 each. Write for more information.

Anita Freimark
7054 Roundelay Rd. North
Reynoldsburg, Ohio 43068

As well as hand-crocheted kippot (see *Observing: Mitzvot*), Anita makes cloth books of Jewish objects for babies, $2.50, and soft stuffed objects and people: dreidel $1, menorah and hallah $2, David and Megillah characters $4.50—dolls are about 10" tall. She stresses that she is "not a factory but a one-person craft lady" who works by individual order. She will not make 100 of anything, but can make up someone else's special desires. She is available for craft fairs in the Ohio area.

Ellen Greenfield
22 Canterbury Lane
Roslyn Heights, N.Y. 11577

For the bored executive who has "everything," consider a contemporary sterling silver dreidel by sculptor Ellen Greenfield. The design is unusual with a hole in the middle to hold Hanukkah *gelt* (dollar bills). It doesn't spin terribly well but it certainly is a "conversation piece." The dreidel is 1½" high, ⅝" wide and deep, the cost is $50 and it is not available as a pendant. (See *Creating: Metal.*)

ELLEN GREENFIELD, sterling silver dreidel. (photo: Edward Greenfield).

Judith Kalina
Fable Soft Sculpture, Inc.
Box K • Shenorock, N.Y. 10587

Fable is a small manufacturing company which produces sophisticated soft sculpture legendary animals. Judith Kalina's version of the lion, so long associated with Jewish lore, has a crown and wings making him even more royal and special. The 20" × 18" Daddy lion, screen printed on cream muslin, is available fully assembled and stuffed ($50) and in kit form ($14.95). Both come with felt tip pens in case you want to color the finished lion which can also be embellished with beads and/or embroidery. A fully constructed, crowned, and winged baby lion, 7" × 8" ($12.95) is adorable. Also available is a simply printed cream muslin stuffed shaped cushion of Mordechai on a horse, 8" tall, which can also be colored ($6.95). To order, enclose a check for the amount indicated plus $2 for shipping. Write for wholesale information.

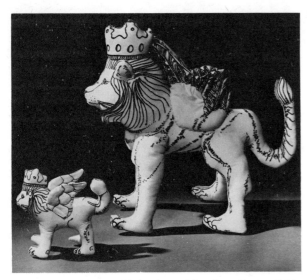

FABLE, winged Lion and baby, by Judith Kalina. Also available in kit form.

Ktav Publishing House, Inc.
75 Varick St. • New York, N.Y. 10013

Many of us may be familiar with the toys and holiday articles distributed by Ktav that are widely carried in synagogue and Jewish center giftshops. But until seeing Ktav's catalog, it seems I had missed some of their more interesting and novel offerings. I like wooden toys a lot and am happy to note that Ktav also stocks two attractive versions of the Hanukkah dreidel in wood. One is a pull toy for toddlers called "Dreidel Duck," a brightly painted duck on wheels with a dreidel on its back that turns as the duck is pulled along the floor. The other is the "Giant Spinner Dreidel." This dreidel fits into a separate handle; a string is wound around the dreidel stem then pulled and the dreidel spins like mad. Ktav sells to individuals as well as groups. Write for catalogs and ordering information.

Luckey Educational Publications
89 Abbottsford Road
Brookline, Mass. 02146

I lived in Spain for more than four years and have a love-hate relationship with that country. In the Middle Ages Jewish culture flourished to such an extent that our sojourn there is still considered to have been a golden age; and then came the expulsions and the Inquisition. Cherie Koller Fox, designer of the game "Expulsion," is the principal of the Harvard Hillel Children's School in Cam-

bridge, Massachusetts. She is a doctoral candidate in Jewish Education at Harvard University and a member of the national board of the Coalition for Alternatives in Jewish Education. Cherie produced *Expulsion* out of a desire to create a standard for the kind of materials used in Jewish schools. She wanted to demonstrate to educators and to publishers that such materials could be colorful, intelligent, sturdy, and well-researched. In her words, "Four-color printing isn't against Jewish Law!" Cherie, and her husband Everett Fox who teaches in the Judaic Studies department at Boston University and helped research material for the game, have succeeded admirably. The game combines solid content with attractive form. *Expulsion* is a quality educational experience which is also visually handsome. Especially suitable for the classroom it can also be played at home with 1 to 6 players by anyone over 9. No previous background is necessary to play; you learn about "Jewish Life in Spain from the Golden Age to 1492" as you travel around the game board. The brochure, which includes a full-color reproduction of the gameboard, fully explains the game. Individual orders are accepted; educators and retailers receive discounts.

LUCKEY EDUCATIONAL PUBLICATIONS, "Expulsion", available for $14.92 plus $2 postage and handling. (photo: Ken Bernstein)

Chaim Rosov
51 Seaton Place • Valley Stream, N.Y. 11580

After serving Jewish education for 25 years as a principal and educational director, Chaim Rosov has retired and is devoting his efforts to Jewish art and Judaica. He has done synagogue ritual pieces in wood and metal and is open to future commissions. His teaching and artistic skills have been cleverly combined in his *Hebrew Alef-Bet Coloring Book*. It's one of the nicest around. Available from him for $1.35. Write for brochure and quantity prices.

Judith Taylor
157 Babcock St. • Brookline, Mass. 02146

Judith Taylor makes soft cuddly dolls based on characters from Jewish history, Yiddish folklore, and literature. Her dolls are meticulously crafted in well-chosen fabrics; beads and fur are used where appropriate, yet the dolls are so sturdy and loveable that if you can relinquish one you might give it to a young child to love. As well as dolls of her own design, Judith will accept special orders for dolls depicting specific characters or individual portraits. Each doll is about 16" high and costs $25. That she loves the dolls is obvious in her careful attention to detail and in their joyful faces. Judith writes; "My dolls are my great-grandparents, Jews of the old world, the shtetl, Yiddish folk melodies and literature. They are sewn from scraps of memory and longing and love."

Tele-Total of Eastern Massachusetts
c/o Stephen Echlov
1682 Beacon St. • Brookline, Mass. 02146

Wooden Magen David kits made by assembling twelve precut pieces of pine and redwood are the specialty of this manufacturer. Wholesale only, write for illustrated pricelist.

Torah Toys
J. Levine Co.
58 Eldridge St. • New York, N.Y. 10002

Torah Toys was started by young Orthodox Jews in California and New York, and has recently made arrangements with J. Levine Company for dis-

TORAH TOYS, "Shabbos in a Sack". (photo: Richard Speedy)

tribution. Torah Toys is dedicated to the production of esthetically designed, well-made toys which embody and teach basic Torah concepts. Among several puzzles available, two contain variations of Shabbat themes—"Seven Days of Creation" and a daily blessings puzzle that illustrates the six basic blessings with pop-art-style drawings of bread, pastry, wine, fruit, vegetables, and "other foods" (nosherei). The puzzle gives the blessings in Hebrew and English. They are available in unbreakable ⅜"-thick wood fiberboard as well as in ¼" high-density cardboard. My favorite Torah Toy is the "Shabbos in a Sack" set. This consists of finely detailed natural birch miniatures of the basic Shabbat ceremonial objects: Kiddush cup, wine decanter with removable stopper, two hallahs, hallah plate, knife, and a pair of candlesticks with removable candles. These objects come packaged in a strong, unbleached muslin drawstring bag. The set, which is very attractive in its natural state, could also be painted. Write for Torah Toys' attractive brochure and order form.

Tucker Toys
431 Somerville St.
Manchester, N.H. 03103

For years I have been searching for a well-made, reasonably priced Noah's Ark and was absolutely delighted when I discovered the one made by Tucker Toys almost in my backyard. Tucker's ark is on wheels and has a lift-off roof and two gang planks so the wheeled, screen printed, simplified

TUCKER TOYS, "Noah's Ark". (photo: Mae Rockland)

animals can negotiate their passage easily. Noah and his wife, also simplified, complete the set. The very well-crafted and carefully finished ("look Ma, no splinters") toy was tested for "playability and interest" by my daughter (13) and some of the 3–6 year olds she babysits for; we all love it. Available for about $40; write for brochure describing this and other wooden pull toys and ordering information.

Rivkah Weil
888 Montgomery St. #E9
Brooklyn, N.Y. 11213

Rivkah Weil's dolls are simple, direct, and honest and, one is tempted to add, friendly and lively. They range in size from 4½" (my favorite in this series is the mini "super hero" with *tzitzit*, mask, and a Shin emblazoned on his chest (is that you, Sabraman?) to 4'. Rivka has also made puppets for a local Jewish puppet group and will accept commissions—depending on the project. Rivka writes that she "returned to Judaism 4 years ago" and is "presently learning and living in Crown Heights, Brooklyn, N.Y.—the center of the Lubavitch Hasidic movement." See her puppets in color on the cover and write for her brochure.

RIVKA WEIL, and friends.

JEWISH DOLL HOUSE THINGS

"The world of miniatures is getting bigger"
The New York Times, April 24, 1980

When the N.Y. Times finally said that collecting miniatures is the most popular hobby in the country after stamp and coin collecting, and that it was adults, not children, who spend more than $200 million each year on bits and pieces $^1/_{12}$ life size, I breathed a sigh of relief and knew that I could come out of the closet and confess to being a passionate doll house enthusiast. If I were a total purist, I would not even say "doll house," but would rather speak only of "miniatures." I can't quite make it that far, however, because not only do my daughter and I collect and decorate our houses (there are now three of them), we also play with them and the folks who live in them quite a bit. To the distress of all of us—there are now 24 inhabitants including babies, two sets of grandparents and a toothfairy—we've had a terrible time finding attractive miniature Judaica (sound familiar?). As we scouted the shops and fairs we would find lots of mini Christmas trees and decorations but rarely anything Jewish. So just as we solved the same problem in real life by making a lot of things ourselves, we did the same for our doll houses. Then we began to commission things by craftspeople with special skills who were willing to try their hands at a collaborative effort. I am so happy to be able to introduce you to some of our discoveries which I trust will serve to stimulate more. I hope anyone who knows of—or makes—doll house Judaica will let me know.

The Country Mouse Shop
River Road • Bucksport, Me. 04416

Whenever we can, we run away to Maine. Last summer, to our delight, just a few miles from our tiny cabin in the woods, we discovered The Country Mouse which specializes in miniatures. Bob Black, an ex-marine, and his wife took on the shop as a retirement project, Betty tending the store and Bob custom-making and repairing doll houses in the workshop attached to it. My daughter Keren and I had wanted a sukkah for our doll house people for a long time and the end of August in Maine was the perfect place to plan one. I approached Bob with the project and he was ready

and willing. Initially he knew nothing about Sukkot customs but said he would read anything I gave him and follow my directions. The sukkah I had fantasized was meant to suggest the kind of detailing found in the old Polish wooden synagogues. When I returned to Boston, I had left Bob with a book and some tentative sketches. Imagine our euphoria when a few weeks later the sukkah shown here arrived. Keren wrote Bob a letter and I also dashed off a delighted note which also asked if Bob would make similar sukkot for the readers of *The New Jewish Yellow Pages;* and he will!

The sukkah, scaled 1" to 1', measures 8" × 8½" and the four panels are hinged so that it can be opened flat for painting if desired. The lattice roof lifts off making it easy to tie on tiny hanging decorations before adding foliage to the top. There are three arched windows and one round one with a diamond shaped molding. Assembled the sukkah will cost around $30; the parts (including lattice) cut out and ready to assemble will be in the $15–$20 range . . . there are *a lot* of pieces. Betty Black will also help locate miniature Judaica through her extensive source catalogs. Write for more information and current prices.

THE COUNTRY MOUSE, wooden sukkah 8" × 8½" by Bob Black. (photo: Mae Rockland)

Sharon Frankel
812 W. 181 St. • New York, N.Y. 10033

A calligrapher and greeting card designer, Sharon Frankel also makes miniature braided hallah. Available through the mail individually (75¢); quantities available for craft fairs.

Leslie Jarige
c/o Kagan
370 Grandview Ave. • Bangor, Me. 04401

I met Leslie Jarige when she was delivering an order of her marvelous mini cherry pies to The Country Mouse Shop in Bucksport. After listening to Bob Black and me planning the sukkah, Leslie became enthused about trying her hand at tiny Jewish foods. Her miniature plants and foods are among the finest I'd seen anywhere and so I looked forward with great anticipation to what she would produce in the realm of *nosherei*. Her Jewish goodies turned out to be as delectable as her cherry pies. For Keren's bat mitzvah, Leslie made a 1" (the equivalent of a 12") pink party cake with "Mazal Tov Keren" in Hebrew and English on it. She also makes bagels: whole, cut, with and without lox (30¢–$1.50), hallah (70¢ a loaf), deli sandwiches: salami, lettuce, etc. on dark bread ($2.50), specify cut in half or whole. Her specialty however is cakes. For bar and bat mitzvahs and weddings, these will range from about $4 to $25 and up, depending on size and complexity. Leslie can work from a photo and

LESLIE JARIGE, platter of bagels, Keren's bat mitzvah cake, deli sandwich. The plants are by Leslie also.

would be able to duplicate the real cake you had at some occasion. She is willing to try anything as a custom order. These she says should be "VERY specific." But since she understandably likes everything she makes she will take back an order if the customer is not fully satisfied. She will do work for dealers, but small orders only since she simply doesn't have enough time and will only accept a 60%–40% arrangement, no consignments.

Manhattan Doll Hospital and Toy Shop
176 Ninth Avenue • New York, N.Y. 10011

This New York store has: hallah with Shabbat cover, $3.49; a Hanukkah lamp, $4.99; bagel stand with bagels, $4.99; mezuzah, 99¢; matzah cover with two matzot, $2.49; and a Seder plate, $4.99. Write for order form so you will know how much postage to add.

Miniature Homes and Furnishings, Inc.
P.O. Box 25 • Everette, Mass. 02149

Miniature Homes and Furnishings Inc. is a retail mail order business. Its well-illustrated color catalog shows high quality doll houses, furniture, kits, and accessories at competitive prices. When I came to the Christmas page showing a tree, gifts, and toys, I picked up the phone and called the

MINIATURE HOMES AND FURNISHINGS INC. (photo: courtesy Vincent Vassello)

company president Vincent Jo Vassallo to ask if he couldn't put together a Jewish page. At first, I imagine, he thought I was a bit eccentric, but after I had explained the kind of items which might exist and said that if he could find them and put them all together in one place it would really be a unique contribution, Vinny became quite enthusiastic. He did his homework and came up with the page shown here, which frankly exceeds what I thought he might find for the well provided Jewish home. His catalog ask for the new Jewish page is available for $2.50.

Carol-Lynn Rossel Waugh
5 Morrill St. • Winthrop, Me. 04364

When I called on doll artist Carol-Lynn Waugh, I had in mind encouraging her to make Jewish doll house dolls. But, as I explored my own feelings about what these dolls would be like I realized that I really don't like the idea of producing stereotypes. Jews, after all can look like anybody! I like Carol-Lynn's dolls so much because their porcelain heads are modeled after real people. The photos shown here have some of her dolls doing Jewish things. She will accept commissions for portrait dolls done in 1"–1' scale, when her busy schedule allows. She could make a Jewish doll that looks like you or a relative. She will need several photographic views to work from. Prices for portrait dolls are around $200, doll house dolls done from her original sculptures are approximately $50. Write for more information and send $1 and a business-sized SASE for her illustrated brochure and pricelist.

CAROL-LYNN WAUGH, father and son with tallitot and yarmulkas.

CAROL-LYNN WAUGH, doll house family Shabbat.

Travel

As Bill Aron's poetically humorous photograph shows us, Jewish "travel" means many things. For most of our history we have been a traveling people, pushed and pulled here and there by the forces of history. As we moved around, our most precious possessions have been our values and faith, which fortunately are portable and have sustained us through many a strange trip. Sensitized by our own background of wanderings, we can't help but feel compassion for others who are now caught up in events beyond their control and are struggling to find a place to live in the framework of human decency. American Jews are fortunate to live in a place and time when people are free to travel at their own whim, limited only for the most part by their pocketbooks, and when Israel the country of our dreams and prayers is accessible for visits or for "homecoming". Whenever I travel to a new country or city I make a point of contacting the local Jewish community in some way, enriching what otherwise might be just an ordinary business trip and making vacations truly memorable. But Bill's photo has another message. Some of the most interesting Jewish "sights" are nearby. So, especially with increasing prices, we might do well exploring and discovering places of Jewish significance in our own and neighboring communities. Anyone going to the Los Angeles area, for example, should pay a visit to Venice (see Barbara Meyerhoff's entry in *Learning: Media*).

This section provides addresses for some of the Jewish organizations offering tour opportunities, certain travel agencies which specialize in travel arrangements with Jewish religious and/or cultural features, and some ideas for lesser-known but interesting ways of traveling Jewishly.

The following organizations will send you brochures about the tours they offer.

American Jewish Congress
15 E. 84th St. ● New York, N.Y. 10028
(or, write the regional AJC office in your area)

B'nai B'rith Tours
1640 Rhode Island Ave. ● Washington, D.C. 20036
or in New York
B'nai B'rith Tour Office
823 U.N. Plaza ● New York, N.Y. 10017

Hadassah
Tour Department
50 W. 58th St. ● New York, N.Y. 10019

Union of American Hebrew Congregations Tour Committee
838 Fifth Avenue ● New York, N.Y. 10021

SO YOU LIKE TO TRAVEL ... VISIT THE U.S.S.R.

At my request, Rabbi Albert S. Axelrad, Hillel Director and Chaplain at Brandeis University who recently returned from a trip to the Soviet Union, has prepared a list of suggestions and tips for those of you who are thinking about or planning a visit to the U.S.S.R. If you want to continue the discussion, contact Rabbi Axelrad at the Hillel Office, Usdan, Brandeis University, Waltham, Mass. 02154.

I'd like to urge the would-be traveller, Jewish and non-Jewish alike, to visit the Soviet Union. Awaiting the tourist there are not only exciting points of interest such as the Kremlin, the celebrated ballets of Moscow, and the Hermitage in Leningrad, but historical sites of great interest, not the least of which is Babi Yar, near Kiev, scene of the Nazis' infamous massacre of Jews, and Vilna, home of the great Gaon. Visitors to the U.S.S.R. also serve as good will emissaries, fostering a measure of reciprocal friendship between two countries which share, otherwise, in an official relationship laden with mutual enmity and distrust. By visiting with Soviet Jews and conveying to them the love and loyalty of Jews everywhere, we are talking about a fundamentally life-changing experience. All this, apart from the enlarging experience of meeting a very different people and culture, makes the Soviet Union a "must".

BEFORE LEAVING FOR THE U.S.S.R.

1) Through your travel agent, learn the addresses of synagogues in the cities you plan to visit. Also acquire the addresses of Jewish points of interest with the help of your rabbi or a Hillel director in your vicinity. Have a Russian writing friend write these addresses for you on index cards so you can easily show them to taxi drivers.

2) Learn the Cyrillic alphabet, at the very least, if not basic conversational Russian, so as to be able to read Metro station and street signs.

3) Read, but do *not* take with you: *The Russians*, by Hedrick Smith and Fodor's *Guide to the Soviet Union*. They are seen as anti-Soviet and might be confiscated.

4) Purchase good street maps for the cities you

Saturday afternoon, outside the synagogue on Arkhipova Street, Moscow, July 1978. (photo: Richard Sobol, see *Creating: Pictures*)

intend to visit. The Falk maps are the best I have seen, showing not only the streets but the Metro systems as well.

5) Carry a photocopy of your passport and visa. The originals of these documents will have to be temporarily relinquished upon checking into your first hotel and may not be returned until your departure.

6) Additional items to take along include: a flashlight for the dark Soviet nighttime streets when it might be hard to find an address or apartment; a pair of lightweight folding rubbers or boots and a collapsible umbrella—the U.S.S.R. seems to have more than its share of mud; the maximal quantity of American cigarettes, which we all know are a health hazard and should be declared unkosher but which serve as an invaluable aid in flagging down taxicabs; and, if you eat only kosher food, you will have to take *everything* you need for *all* your meals.

7) Become familiar with Soviet nicknames and diminutives so as to avoid confusion over names in the U.S.S.R. Thus: Mikhail = Misha, Gregory = Grisha, Alexander = Sasha or Sanya, Pavel = Pasha, Valentina = Valya, Anatoly = Tolya, Yevgeny = Genia, Natasha = Natalya, etc. Not infrequently some of the Jews you will meet prefer to be known by their Hebrew names, according to which "Boris" becomes "Baruch", "Lyova" becomes "Arieh", etc.

ONCE IN THE U.S.S.R.

1) Anticipate, but do not fear questioning by customs officials upon arrival. In most countries, customs searches for drugs and jewels; in the U.S.S.R. they are on the lookout for Judaica and Hebrew books. Searches and interrogations happen only periodically. They waste time but do nothing else. Relax and don't be anxious; you are absolutely entitled to bring in Jewish objects for your own use. If you are mistreated by customs officials it would probably be comforting to visit the U.S. Embassy in Moscow or the consulate in Leningrad.

2) *Do not sign any document at the request of an official.* Insist that before you affix your signature to anything you must first have it translated into English *in writing* and that both a lawyer and American official must be present to advise you. If officials give you a hard time, ask to know the law you are presumed to be violating and the name and number of the official. Be firm but not overbearing or hostile.

3) Get thee to the synagogue. Attend services on Sabbath morning in every Soviet city. This suggestion is not just rabbinic propaganda—it is an excellent way to meet Soviet Jews. Greet the worshippers warmly and accept whatever honor is offered. Men would be well advised to bone up on the Torah blessings in advance so that they will be in a position to accept an *aliyah* and can acquit themselves well. It is after services that the most meaningful encounters take place. On the street, right in front of the synagogue, Jews from all over the city gather along with visiting Jews who happen to be in town. Here you will meet many people informally, learn their news, convey your own concerns and greetings, and perhaps be invited to a group meeting or to a home or two. Be prepared for an exhilarating experience. The times of these Sabbath gatherings vary from city to city and season to season.

4) If you visit a Soviet Jew at home, you may want to bring a treat with you, apart from any items from home. Accept hospitality graciously. True, financial resources are often limited, but they are extraordinary hosts, who love receiving visitors and sharing their food and their homes with guests. Your friendly visits do not jeapordize anyone. On the contrary, you are responding to their constantly articulated requests and are assisting them. Your presence points out that far from being anonymous, the people you visit are known outside the Soviet Union and are not to be trifled with imprudently. These visits constitute an invaluable link and lifeline. Whatever adventures and experiences befall you, a trip to the U.S.S.R. will alter your consciousness and remain an important part of you for the rest of your days.

Agudath Israel of America
Travel Department
5 Beekman St. • New York, N.Y. 10038

Agudath Israel of America was founded in 1922 for the perpetuation of traditional Orthodox Judaism. It offers a broad range of constructive projects including camping and travel. Write for information about general travel service around the world.

American Zionist Youth Foundation
515 Park Ave. • New York, N.Y. 10022

The American Zionist Youth Foundation sponsors a number of tours to Israel for high school and college students. Some are in conjunction with other institutions, such as Nassau Community College Summer Institute in Israel, which give college credit for courses taken during the summer. Even the work-study programs sponsored by A.Z.Y.F. include a good amount of traveling about Israel. Write for descriptive brochures. Many of these programs fill up before January, and some require personal interviews, so contact A.Z.Y.F. as early as possible.

Rose Ann Chasman
6147 North Richmond • Chicago, Ill. 60659

As well as creating Jewish art in a variety of media, Rose Ann Chasman talks about it. She gives tours of "The Chicago Art Institute-The Jewish Connection", touching on Jews and the Bible as subject matter, Jewish artists, and relations between art history, Jewish history, and history in general. (See also: *Creating; Calligraphy* and *Pictures;* and *Buying: Cards, Gifts and Collectibles*)

Crown Heights Jewish Community Council
387 Kingston Ave. • Brooklyn, N.Y. 11225

Rabbi Isser Smetana, with the assistance of the Crown Heights Community Council has published a delightful map of Crown Heights in Brooklyn, a neighborhood where the majority of the residents are Lubavitcher Chassidim. The Lubavitch are very hospitable and anxious for visitors to experience their community, and the charmingly drawn map by Michoel Muchnik is entitled "Welcome to Crown Heights." The reverse side is a guide of places to see, restaurants, shuls (indicating those that have a mikveh), and places to buy religious articles.

Eastours, Inc. and Eastours' Scholastic Journeys
1140 Avenue of the Americas
New York, N.Y. 10036

This company specializes in custom-designed travel programs for individuals or groups, with an emphasis on the client's special interests. For instance, Eastours will help you arrange to have your son's bar mitzvah in Israel, including everything from a service at the Western Wall to the planting of a tree in the name of the bar mitzvah boy at the Bnei Mitzvah Forest. Accommodations, and whatever social functions you may desire will be handled by Eastours, as will all travel arrangements. Check to see if your group may be eligible for discount package prices and write for Eastours' brochures on other trips to Israel, and Israel and Europe as well.

Harriet and Melvin Goldfarb
Receive-a-Guest of London
300 Pinehurst Ave. • New York, N.Y. 10033

Harriet and Melvin Goldfarb, the American representatives of "Receive-a-Guest" have had many years of scouting and camp experience. The tour they operate takes American-Jewish teenagers to London where they spend four or six weeks as guests in Anglo-Jewish homes. The itinerary includes a mixture of sightseeing, some with Jewish content, free-time, and events arranged with British teenagers at the Redbridge Jewish Youth Center (the largest in Britain). Write for a descrip-

tive brochure, itinerary, and prices (summer 1980 prices were $1,095 for four weeks, $1,775 for six weeks).

Greater Boston Jewish Community Center
Joint Israel Program
72 Franklin St. • Boston, Mass. 02110

This department of the Greater Boston Jewish Community Center provides a variety of summer and year-round programs in Israel. They can arrange temporary stays in Israeli high schools and universities, kibbutzim, and development towns for Boston area youth. They will also help direct people from outside the area to sponsoring agencies in their own regions or, if none are available, will help find appropriate places for people interested in the programs they offer.

Jewish Federation Council of Greater Los Angeles
Youth Department
6505 Wilshire Blvd.
Los Angeles, Calif. 90048

The Youth Department of the Los Angeles Jewish Federation has a fascinating booklet available describing programs in Israel for individuals of all ages from the Los Angeles area. Included in the booklet are descriptions of study, work, and kibbutz programs of varying durations, sponsored by groups from every segment of the Jewish community.

National Federation of Temple Youth
International Education Department,
Union of American Hebrew Congregations
838 Fifth Ave. • New York, N.Y. 10021

The National Federation of Temple Youth offers several different types of Israeli summer programs for Reform Jewish youth, as well as a number of longterm stays (half-year to full-year). Some of the programs incorporate study, while others stress service. All have built-in touring to spots of interest. Write for a brochure.

NEOT KEDUMIM, "The Gardens of Israel".

Neot Kedumim
770 Elder Court • Glencoe, Ill. 60022

Dozens of teenagers from England and the U.S. come to Neot Kedumim in Israel every summer. It is a network of Biblical and Talmudic gardens which is being created on 400 rocky acres on the Jerusalem side of Lod, not far from Modi'in. The intensive seven week program includes a special work project at Neot Kedumim and full tours of Israel. Other visitors to Israel are also welcome for tours of the gardens. Guided tours for individuals or groups may be arranged by writing to Mr. Nogah Hareuveni, Director General, Neot Kedumim, Box 299, Kiryat Ono, Israel. The $125 tour fee goes towards work on the gardens, which include the Dale (valley) of the Song of Songs, the Hill of the Menorah and the Myrtle Garden, the Garden of Wisdom Literature, and the Pool of Solomon. Write for attractive brochure.

The Rashi Association
c/o American Jewish Committee
165 E. 56th Street • New York, N.Y. 10022

The Rashi Association is a lobbying organization exclusively oriented towards the preservation of significant Jewish monuments in Europe. It also serves to furnish information for the Jewish public in America. In the words of Werner Cahnman, the chairman of the group who is Professor Emeritus of Sociology at Rutgers University, "A people should know its past, for sure. But there is an educational aspect. Jewish youth will not read about Worms and Venice, but they will go and look at these places. Christians are eager, and in increasing numbers, to acquaint themselves with Jewish life and institutions in their countries. The effect, especially on young people is immeasurable". This

dedicated organization is small but has accomplished an amazing amount. Our support is needed. If we want to have Jewish sights to visit in Europe it well behooves us to become members ($10 annual tax-deductible dues; contributor $35; sponsor, over $35). Write for their very informative reports which are well-illustrated and detail the work of the organization.

Society for the Protection of Nature in Israel
4 Hashfela St.
Tel-Aviv 66183

The S.P.N.I., which is also called *Keren Ha-Tzvi*, was founded in the early fifties as a public membership organization dedicated to the conservation and protection of landscapes, animal life, and relics of the past in Israel. The group is non-profit and non-political, being concerned solely with the environment and ecological issues in Israel. Since people all over the world are concerned about the universal aspects of Israel's landscapes and historical sites, international membership has been growing steadily. Membership is $10 per year and will bring you *Israel—Land and Nature*, their quarterly English magazine, as well as a variety of other periodical publications. Of interest to non-members as well are the "off-the-beaten-track" tours, hikes, and outings available through the organization with specially trained guides. Special tours can also be tailored to meet the requirements of any group. Write for their booklet: "Discover Israel with Israelis".

SUSAN FLEISCHMAN, "View of Jerusalem from the Petra Hotel". (see *Creating: Pictures*.)

Synagogue Rescue Project
Lillian Wald Recreation Rooms
12 Ave. D • New York, N.Y. 10009

Also dedicated to the preservation of Jewish culture is the Synagogue Rescue Project directed by Eric Byron. The group has acquired an abandoned synagogue on East 7th St. in New York City which will house a library and museum about the Lower East Side, and contain some of the 6,000 items which have been rescued from abandoned and vandalized Jewish buildings. There are about fifty synagogues left on the East Side, of which only 15 are now in use by Jews. The Synagogue Project sponsors tours to these fifty synagogues. Contact Eric Byron at the above address for tour and other information.

Tripmasters
1140 Broadway • New York, N.Y. 10001

Tripmasters specializes in Glatt Kosher tours to Israel, Spain, and Egypt. In Cairo tour members stay at The Vendome, Cairo's first Kosher hotel.

West Central Jewish Center
23 Hand Court (off High Holborn)
London WC1V 66JF
tel: (01) 405-3327

If you are on your own in London and looking for Jewish social activity, health advice, or plan a lengthy stay and want to find a "flat-mate," check in at the West Central Jewish Center. The Center is basically geared to the needs of the local community, but any Jewish-American person visiting or intending to live in London (especially if he or she is in the 17–30 age group) is welcome to contact the Center for specific or general help.

World Zionist Organization
Department of Education and Culture
515 Park Ave. • New York, N.Y. 10022

W.Z.O. sponsors summer seminars in Israel for youth and adults. Its offerings include a "bar mitzvah pilgrimage" for thirteen-year-old boys and girls, seminars for students fourteen and fifteen, and an eight-week Hebrew ulpan for adults. There are also winter siminars for educators. If you are interested in a long stay in Israel or are thinking of aliyah, write for W.Z.O.'s booklet, "A Guide to Israel Programs," which details many work and study programs of various durations at different academic levels.

BOOKS AND PAMPHLETS OF INTEREST TO THE JEWISH TRAVELER

AMERICAN JEWISH LANDMARKS: A TRAVEL GUIDE AND HISTORY, Bernard Postal and Lionel Koppman. Volume I (East Coast), Volume II (South and Southwest), Volume III (Middle West and West). Also by the same authors, *Jewish Landmarks of New York*. All from Fleet Press Corporation, 160 Fifth Ave. • New York, N.Y. 10010.

HOW TO FIND AND MEET RUSSIAN JEWS: A BRIEFING KIT FOR TRAVELERS TO THE U.S.S.R. American Jewish Congress 15 E. 84th St. • New York, N.Y. 10028

SEVEN TOURS OF JERUSALEM AND HER SURROUNDINGS. World Zionist Organization Department of Education and Culture 515 Park Ave. • New York, N.Y. 10022

THE TRAVELER'S GUIDE TO JEWISH LANDMARKS OF EUROPE, by Bernard Postal and Samuel Abramson. Fleet Press Corporation 160 Fifth Ave. • New York, N.Y. 10010

THE UNDERGROUND JERUSALEM GUIDE and THE UNDERGROUND TEL-AVIV GUIDE both by Janet Kaplan and Judy Stacy Goldman. Available throughout Israel in bookshops and hotels but in the U.S. only through:
The Jerusalem Post (single copies)
110 E. 59th St. • New York, N.Y. 10022
or wholesale from:
Keter Publishing House
440 Park Ave. South
New York, N.Y. 10016
Both are lively, personal guidebooks to interesting people and places. Lots of photographs.

OBSERVING

It is told that after the destruction of the Temple, the three pillars of Judaism, *Torah* (study), *Avodah* (prayer), and *Gemilut Hasadim* (kind deeds) came crying before the throne of the Holy One. They were very distraught, fearing that the Jewish people in Diaspora would forget them. "Don't worry," the Lord comforted them, "that won't happen. I will tell them to build synagogues and there the rabbis will teach them Torah and the cantors will lead them in prayer." Kind Deeds stepped forward, more worried than before. "How will they remember *me?*" he asked. "Well", replied the All-Knowing One, "in the synagogues during the services every Jew will turn to his neighbor and offer to share a pinch from his snuffbox."

This story can be taken in many different ways, not the least of which as a reminder to avoid the sanctimonious. There are 613 mitzvot (commandments) in the Torah, of which 248 are positive precepts and 365 are prohibitions. Centuries have been spent in discussion and volumes written on the way in which these mitzvot are observed. If we could have an overview of Jewish practices in both space and time we would probably be impressed as much with the diversity of religious expression as by the unity and continuity which has "kept us in life to this day". Judaism is as much an *orthopraxy* as an *orthodoxy;* that is, we are known as much by what we do as by what we philosophize. Though from time to time this book attempts to be inspirational, this is not the place to lecture on, or even describe at length our religious practices. Each one of us must find his/her own way. It is my hope that this book—and this section in particular—will give you some more ideas with which to enrich your religious life.

Charity

> "God has no riches of His own; it's what He takes from one that He gives to another."
>
> Yiddish saying

As I was clearing out my mother's apartment after her death I was terribly moved to find visible evidence everywhere of her continuous preoccupation with tzedakah. The English word "charity" is the closest we can come to tzedakah, which has its root in the Hebrew word for justice. All over my mother's apartment were little jars and boxes with accumulations of coins being saved for one cause or another. In the kitchen there was the Jewish National Fund pushka (charity box) and along with her household bills and receipts, a file of envelopes from an assortment of organizations waiting their turn for a check. Every time anything of any significance happened to any of us—from a baby's new tooth to completion of a course—my mother would "make a little donation". She saw the world as a system of weights and balances and if something good happened in the family's life, why it was only "fair" to make a small contribution to someone else's well-being. My family has not been Orthodox for generations, but giving tzedakah is the "mentschlach" thing to do. Traditional Jews have pushkas in their homes and give charity, even if just a few pennies, every day except Shabbat and holidays. An extra amount is usually given just before the beginning of Shabbat and holidays. In this way when the container is full one can buy a money order to give to a favorite charity. Even if major contributions are made by check, the presence of a simple pushka in a home is an excellent way both of raising our own tzedakah consciousness and teaching the concept of mutual responsibility to our children.

Those listed in the following pages are only a sampling of the many worthwhile institutions deserving support in our multi-faceted community. Some have appeared elsewhere in these pages because of the products they sell to raise funds or the educational services which they offer. Others make their appearance here for the first time. Danny Siegel, who is not an organization but a one-man unpaid tzedakah emissary (and

(photo: © 1980 Barbara Gingold, see *Creating: Pictures.*)

maven, if that word applies here), is also discussed in the hopes that many more people will join the Tzedakah Chevra and that other such collectives will be formed.

Maimonides defined eight degrees of giving charity, in ascending order:

One who gives reluctantly and grudgingly.
One who gives graciously, but less than he should.
One who gives what he should, but only after being asked.
One who gives before being asked.
One who gives without knowing to whom the charity goes, while the recipient knows the donor's identity.
One who gives anonymously.
One who gives anonymously to an unknown recipient.
One who helps another person with a gift, a loan, or by finding him employment to become self-supporting.

Yad ha-Hazakah, 10:7–12.

American Council for Judaism Philanthropic Fund
386 Park Ave. S. • New York, N.Y. 10016

The Council maintains programs for the relief and resettlement in Western Europe and the United States of Jewish refugees from the Soviet Union, Eastern Europe, and the Arab countries. It has offices in Austria, France, and Italy.

American Jewish Joint Distribution Committee
60 E. 42nd St. • New York, N.Y. 10017

The Joint Distribution Committee organizes and subsidizes rescue, relief, and rehabilitation programs for needy Jews overseas, as well as conducting a wide range of health, welfare, and educational-assistance programs for 400,000 needy Jews in twenty-five countries.

American ORT Federation (Organization for Rehabilitation through Training)
817 Broadway • New York, N.Y. 10003

ORT is an organization that teaches vocational skills in twenty-four countries around the world, particularly in Israel. Its women's division, located at 1250 Broadway, is particularly active. ORT is a unique organization, which is imbued with many of the best ideas of the old Labor Movement, of Jewish craftsmanship, and of Jewish solidarity.

Dorot
212 W. 93rd St. • New York, N.Y. 10025

On Manhattan's Upper West Side there are an estimated 15,000 elderly Jews who live alone, without family and friends to care for them. (In other cities many thousands more can be added to this number.) Ironically, these elderly New York Jews are alone, even though they exist amidst one of the largest Jewish communities in the world. Project Dorot (Hebrew for generations) is committed to building a community that fosters veneration of our elders while providing them with needed care and attention. The feeling at Dorot is that real help comes in the form of interchange.

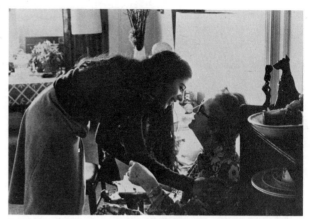

DOROT, a volunteer community project serving the Jewish elderly and homebound on Manhattan's Upper West Side.

Dorot's regular programs include: Friendly Visiting (ongoing visits once a week); Intergenerational Sunday Programs once a month (homebound people are escorted to the program); Holiday package deliveries and visits; Holiday services in apartment house lobbies; and Holiday meals in the homes of community members. Project Dorot also provides referral resources such as crisis intervention referrals to other agencies, and information about basic entitlements, home safety, home care, and services to the aged. Although their program is limited geographically, it is a model program for providing and caring for our senior citizens, a program which could be copied in many other areas of the country. The Dorot staff and board members are available to consult with other groups and individuals who provide similar services or who wish to.

Hadassah, The Women's Zionist Organization of America
50 W. 58th St. • New York, N.Y. 10019

Hadassah is a marvelous organization that is too often joked about by popular novelists. Its efforts, particularly in the medical field, have been instrumental in the survival of Israel. Hadassah Hospital in Jerusalem is one of the finest treatment and research hospitals in the world. Hadassah was founded by Henrietta Szold, known as the Jewish Florence Nightingale.

The Jewish Braille Institute of America, Inc.
110 E. 30th St. • New York, N.Y. 10018

It is estimated that in the United States there are 20,000 Jewish blind as well as more than 50,000 whose vision is severely impaired. The Jewish Braille Institute is dedicated to "equality of Jewish participation for the blind and partially sighted". Some of its services include: preparation for bar and bat mitzvah with the use of material in Hebrew and English braille or large type; a vast sound library of recorded materials in English, Hebrew, and Yiddish; daily and holiday prayerbooks both in braille and large type for Orthodox, Conservative, and Reform synagogue participation; and guidance for blind and partially sighted graduates and students making aliyah to Israel. As well as these specifically Jewish services the Institute also provides secular help such as career counseling. All services of the Jewish Braille Institute of America are available to anyone in need of them regardless of religious affiliation, providing "a window on Judaism for the Jewish and non-Jewish blind throughout the world."

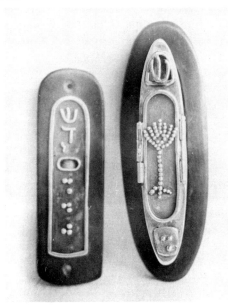

DANIEL BLUMBERG, silver and wood mezuzot with Shaddai and shin in Hebrew Braille (see *Creating: Metal* for more about Blumberg).

Jewish Peace Fellowship
Box 271 • Nyack, N.Y. 10960

Taking as their motto the words of Hillel, "Be of the disciples of Aaron—loving peace and pursuing peace, loving mankind and drawing them to the Torah", the Jewish Peace Fellowship is a pacifist organization offering the opportunity to express one's convictions through concerted action. As with other pacifist organizations, records are maintained of people who are opposed to conscription and draft counseling is made available when required. The fellowship will help groups locate lecturers on Jewish pacifism. Membership is $10 per year, $6 for students, and includes their newsletter.

Shlomo Lakein
Outreach Products
546 Montgomery St. • Brooklyn, N.Y. 11225

A few months ago I had a conversation with Danny Siegel (see below) in which his passionate dedication to teaching tzedakah and mine for Jewish crafts overlapped as we both decried the fact that nobody seemed to make attractive, inexpensive (non-specific) pushkas which could be distributed to children in schools and families at Jewish Centers. Well, Danny Siegel meet Shlomo Lakein! Through Outreach Products Shlomo Lakein produces and distributes simple pushkas which are available blank, imprinted with organizational information, or with loose labels on which you can put your own design and message. Michoel Muchnick, the talented Hasidic artist (see *Creating: Pictures*), has designed a series of labels for these pushkas which transforms them into works of art. These are also available from Outreach, personalized with your Hebrew name if desired. Call or write for more information.

National Conference on Soviet Jewry
10 E. 40th St. • New York, N.Y. 10016
Student Struggle for Soviet Jewry
200 W. 72nd St. • New York, N.Y. 10023

The Student Struggle for Soviet Jewry is an independent Jewish student organization, though it is a member of the National Conference on Soviet Jewry. Its activities parallel those of the Conference, but it concerns itself primarily with mobilizing youth. It has available materials such as buttons, posters, and bumper stickers. The National Conference coordinates all United States activities for Soviet Jews. Among the items it distributes is the "Matzoh of Hope," a prayer for Soviet Jews which has in recent years been added to Passover Seders.

"Solzhenitsyn After Solitary Confinement" (oil on masonite 32" × 32") by Malcah Zeldis. (photo: courtesy Jay Johnson, America's Folk Heritage Gallery)

Reform Jewish Appeal
838 Fifth Avenue • New York, N.Y. 10021

The R.J.A. seeks contributions in order to provide supplementary financing for the creative programs of the Union of American Hebrew Congregations and Hebrew Union College-Jewish Institute of Religion. The National Federation of Temple Youth (NFTY), one of its most outstanding programs, is now over forty years old having proudly directed many young people towards creative leadership in the Jewish community.

Danny Siegel
c/o Dr. and Mrs. Julius Siegel
1600 S. Eads St., 712-N
Arlington, Va. 22202

As Danny Siegel made his goodbyes in preparation for a trip to Israel in 1975, he said to each one of his friends and relatives: "Give me a buck for tzedakah". He knew he would pass it along to someone who needed it in Israel. Before he left he had collected $955 (quite a few gave more than the

Danny Siegel's U.S.Y.ers visiting Lifeline for the Old in Jerusalem.

requested "buck"). In Israel he distributed the money to groups of people outside the mainstream of Federation funding and when he returned he issued the first of his annual Tzedakah Reports—now eagerly awaited every fall by hundreds of people who make up his Tzedakah Chevra. Every year for the last six, Danny has returned to Israel taking groups of U.S.Y. young people with him to share in his role of "tzedakah shaliach" (emmisary). Each year the amount of money Danny has collected has grown, bringing the total to date to more than $30,000. Some of the places to which the Tzedakah Chevra has given money include Lifeline for the Old, Yad La-Kashish, directed by Myriam Medilow, whose "thirteen workshops produce beautiful products, toys, clothes, Shabbat tablecloths, wall hangings, whatever—often from the hands of people who had given up, wished to die in fragments, abandoned to loneliness and uselessness"; Yad Sara, an organization of volunteers that lends medical supplies—wheelchairs, hospital beds, vaporizers, at no cost to those who can't afford them; a nameless, small volunteer organization of paratroopers working to provide bar mitzvahs, summer camping, and other benefits to orphaned children—children of their chaverim who have died in the wars. From Danny's Tzedakah Report I learned about Daniel and Charlotte Kuttler who lend wedding dresses to needy brides. "If you wish to send one, label the package 'Used Clothes'. Long-sleeved dresses with a high neck are preferred, since most of the weddings take place in the Ashkenazi Orthodox community. Bridesmaids dresses are also of use to them." Send to:

The Daniel Kuttler Charity Fund
Keren HaYesod St. 7
Jerusalem, Israel.

In addition to being a tzedakah emmissary, Danny has become a "consultant", meaning that several people with sizable donations to make have turned to him for advice on how to give their money and to whom. He also has a packet of tzedakah material which he sends out upon request. (He didn't ask, but since I'm his friend I'll ask for him: please enclose a 9" × 12" SASE.) Danny's talent for being a mentsch is immeasurable; he concludes his most recent Tzedakah Report with "May we continue to do mitzvot together in the coming years". If you want to join with him and the Tzedakah Chevra do not hesitate to write. See also: *Learning: Programs.*

Union of Councils for Soviet Jews
24 Crescent St., Suite 3A,
Waltham, Mass. 02154

The UCSJ is the oldest national (non-student) organization working on behalf of the rights and interests of Soviet Jews. It is composed of twenty-four Soviet Jewry councils in major cities across the country, and is dedicated to education and action to further the continuing struggle for human rights and the freedom of emigration for all Soviet Jews. A $36 minimum contribution will bring you *Alert,* the only weekly newsletter on Soviet Jewry published in this country. Any contribution of course will be helpful in furthering the councils' work which is truly inspiring. Write for more information about activities and about councils near you in which you might become involved.

United Jewish Appeal
1290 Avenue of the Americas
New York, N.Y. 10019

There is very little that this book can say about the United Jewish Appeal that has not been said already. The initials U.J.A. are so familiar to Jews the world over that they have become permanently ingrained in our psyches. Perhaps more than any other organization, the U.J.A. has united American Jews on a local level and with fellow Jews around the world.

Simon Wiesenthal Center for Holocaust
Studies
9760 West Pico Blvd.
Los Angeles, Calif. 90035

The Simon Wiesenthal Center is establishing the largest museum of its kind in the U.S., doing research into every aspect of the Holocaust, building a permanent collection of documents of all kinds, and developing an educational program designed to teach people all over the country about the Holocaust so that it should never happen again. Support is very much needed. Your entire donation is tax-deductible. $15 Associate; $25 Sponsor; $50 Member; $100 Participant; $500 Builder. (See *Learning: Holocaust.*)

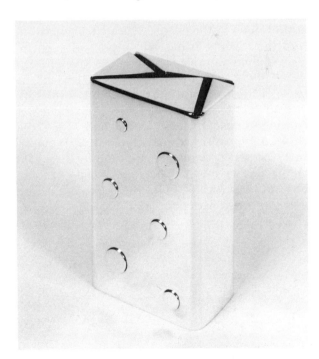

MOSHE ZABARI, charity box, silver, see *Creating: Metal.*
(photo: Eric Pollitzer)

Food

What makes Jewish food different from other ethnic foods is neither a special combination of spices nor the amount of love and attention lavished upon it by generations of mothers urging us to consume vast quantities because other children are starving in Europe (Asia, Africa). Rather it is the insistence on kashrut. It is ironic that many of the same people who eagerly try one diet after another in the hope of forthcoming spiritual or physical change are so ready to dismiss the concept of kashrut. They don't recognize that, at its very minimum, eating kosher food can be a continuous spiritual exercise in which every morsel of food consumed plays an important part. This is not the place for a full discussion of the philosophy and rules of kashrut. It is interesting to note that a growing number of Jews in America keep kosher and that non-Jews as well as Jews often buy kosher food as an insurance of quality without observing all the details of keeping a kosher kitchen. Others want "Jewish style" food, which raises yet another set of questions since Jewish cuisine has varied throughout the centuries and no matter where Jews have lived they have tailored local recipes to the rules of keeping kosher. Jews in the United States have americanized their eating habits and produced such interesting multi-ethnic hybrids as the Kosher Pizza Bagel (the bagel, so prototypically "Jewish", is really of Polish origin), and lasagna made with tofu instead of cheese. If you live away from the major concentrations of Jewish population it is often close to impossible to find certain Jewish delicacies. The small companies and catering establishments have as much as they can handle keeping up with local business and the larger outfits are only interested in big orders. Cooperative buying groups pose one possible solution to the prob-

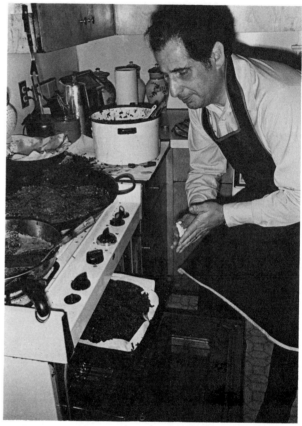

Latkes and more latkes. (photo: © Bill Aron, see *Creating: Pictures*)

lem; another is to make as many things as possible yourself—or for more enjoyment with a similarly inclined friend. This kind of effort has in a number of cases turned into profitable cottage industries. In this section you will find an annotated cookbook bibliography to help you get started, along with those sources I could find which are willing to be helpful to individuals and small groups outside their immediate area.

Jacob Ben-Ezer Ltd.
440 Park Ave. S. • New York, N.Y. 10016

See the listing under *Buying: Cards, Gifts, and Collectibles* for instructions for ordering cartons of Jaffa oranges from Israel, which are of course kosher. By ordering them we help support the Israeli economy.

⬛ Benita Cohen
60 Gramercy Park • New York, N.Y. 10010

Benita Cohen's specialty is translating fattening gourmet dishes into tasty dietetic kosher equivalents with as few steps as possible. She offers cooking lessons for individuals and groups, teaching the preparation of specific dishes as well as the concepts behind them. She also designs diets, menus, and recipes for special diet problems. Benita also offers a series of cooking lessons on traditional Jewish holiday cooking. All of her courses include information on how to organize your cooking time more efficiently. Individual classes are available mainly to people in the New York metropolitan area. She will travel to give courses for groups and she will design recipes and menus for those who write to her or phone. Benita creates recipes for a kosher winery and will also recommend appropriate kosher wines to serve with each of her menus and dishes. Here is her version of Salmon Mousse:

BENITA'S SALMON MOUSSE

½   tsp. onion powder
1   tsp. lemon juice
½   tsp. dill
1   envelope vegetable bouillon
½   cup boiling water
2   tsps. kosher gelatin
1   lb. canned salmon with liquid
1   cup milk, buttermilk or yogurt

1. Grease one quart mold with dietetic lowfat margarine or non-stick spray.
2. Place first six ingredients in blender. Blend 10–15 seconds.
3. Add half of salmon and half of milk. Blend 10–15 seconds.
4. Add remaining salmon and milk. Blend 20–30 seconds.
5. Pour into greased mold, chill until firm.
6. Unmold on lettuce-lined platter, garnish with colorful cut vegetables.

Serves 4–6 as main dish and 12–15 as appetizer or cocktail spread. Serve with a kosher dry white wine.

Crown Heights Health Foods
304 Kingston Ave.
Brooklyn, N.Y. 11213

This young firm, which supplies the local Lubavitch community with bakery products, knishes, grains, nuts, and snack foods, has just begun a mail-order business. The pleasantness of the Kaplans who run the shop and the stringency of their kashrut, which has been attested to by the local clientele, will surely be welcomed by customers far from Brooklyn. For their catalog describing kosher vitamins and health foods available through the mail write to:
Adama Health Foods Inc.
P.O. Box 2370
Brooklyn, N.Y. 11202

Freeda Kosher Vitamins
110 E. 41st St. • New York, N.Y. 10017

This firm manufactures and sells its own brand of vitamins for infants, children, and adults. Every vitamin product I've ever imagined seems to be listed in its enormous brochure. It also has a flyer describing twenty-one different kosher-for-Passover pharmaceuticals and cosmetics. Write for the catalog. Mail orders are accepted.

Gimme Seltzer
241 Mulberry St. #2
New York, N.Y. 10012

Seltzer is about as Jewish as bagels, adopted beloved children. But because my grandfather was a "seltzer man" in Poland, meaning he carted around some very heavy equipment and sold carbonated drinks in the street during the summer months, and because I foster a terrific nostalgia for the sounds and sight of the home delivered cases of seltzer bottles back in the Bronx where I grew up, I am happy to report that a new seltzer delivery service has been formed by Mike Ross. Gimme Seltzer will deliver cases of seltzer in the characteristic deposit bottles as well as 28 oz. and gallon containers of soda fountain syrups including

Coca-Cola, Sprite, Tab, and Lo-Cal flavors, and of course Chocolate. Send a business-size SASE for their seltzer recipe flyer (the REAL way to make an egg cream) which also provides the "history" of seltzer, information about their delivery service, and a description of their new Gimme Seltzer T-shirt.

Barney Greengrass Sturgeon
541 Amsterdam Ave.
New York, N.Y. 10024

Barney Greengrass will accept mail orders for whitefish, sturgeon, lox, and Nova Scotia salmon. Packages are sent air mail and special delivery. Write for specific details on prices and shipping.

The Jewish Homemaker
P.O. Box 324 • Brooklyn, N.Y. 11204

This magazine contains the kosher food guide compiled by the O.K. Laboratories, as well as articles of interest to the Jewish housewife and information on all matters pertaining to kashrut. The kosher food guide is brought up to date with each issue of the magazine. Write for subscription information.

The Jewish Vegetarian Society
American Secretariat
℅ Samuel Judah Grossberg
68-38 Yellowstone Blvd.
Forest Hills, N.Y. 11375

The Jewish Vegetarian Society, an international society with many members in the U.S., has its headquarters in London. It publishes and distributes a quarterly magazine called *The Jewish Vegetarian*. Membership, which includes subscription to the magazine, is $5 annually and may be applied for by sending directly to:
The Jewish Vegetarian Society
853-855 Finchley Road
London, England, NW11 8LX.
The American Secretariat will gladly answer questions regarding the society, but since it functions on a voluntary basis, please include an SASE.

Kedem Wines
420 Kent Ave. • Brooklyn, N.Y. 11211

The Kedem winery is located in the town of Milton, New York, and offers tours and winetasting every Sunday through Friday from May 1st through the fall. The tour begins with a film about wine making and the history of the Herzog family, Kedem's owners, tracing their 166 years in the wine business in the Austro-Hungarian Empire and in the United States. After the film there is an informative guided tour around the winery and then wine tasting in a 120 year-old railway station. Kedem produces more than 60 kosher wines, champagnes, and cordials. The winery is open from 10–5, Sunday through Friday and tours begin every hour on the hour until 4 P.M. Plan to bring your lunch and picnic on the grounds overlooking the Hudson river. Call or write the Brooklyn office to make an appointment and for travel directions to the winery.

Kineret Kosher • Row D, Office 434
NYC Terminal Market • Bronx, N.Y. 10474

This Bronx firm produces and distributes an expanding line of kosher frozen food, including fish, vegetables, dinners, and desserts. It is working hard to make kosher frozen food available to smaller buyers across the country at the lowest possible prices. The two items that interest me the most are its gefilte fish and hallah. The gefilte fish is packaged pre-formed into the characteristic patties, but they are raw when frozen. Therefore all the messy grinding and mixing of the fish has been done, but when you cook them, you can add

KINERET KOSHER, ready-to-bake hallah. Frozen ready-to-bake rye bread and round hallahs also available.

whatever seasonings you prefer to the cooking stock to make them sweet, oniony, or salty. The frozen ready-to-bake hallahs must be seen to be believed. In their raw, frozen state they are about eight inches long, white, and braided. To prepare, leave them at room temperature for about four hours until the dough has doubled its bulk. Then bake in a pre-heated oven at 325° for about half an hour. Kineret will accept mail orders from groups and stores. Write for further information.

Lekvar by the Barrel, Inc.
H. Roth & Son, Importers
1577 First Ave. • New York, N.Y. 10028

Mail-order suppliers of European cooking and baking utensils and items such as halvah, sesame tahini, strudel dough, and their house specialty, prune lekvar to be used as a spread or filling for cakes and pastries. Their well-illustrated catalog also shows six-pointed star cookie cutters in sizes ranging from 1" to 3¾".

Lox Box
P.O. Box 2489
Reston, Va. 22090

Invest $2 in a foolproof lox recipe which will save you more than that when you make the first pound of lox in your own kitchen. The recipe, which is printed appropriately on salmon colored paper, includes smoked salt, giving the lox a "nova" flavor. Evelyn Hollander, who is the lady behind the Lox Box, says that most of her requests have come from areas outside the "lox belt" but that she has also had an enthusiastic response from people wanting to save $$. "Once they try it," she says, "they love it!"

Michele's Deli
1225 State Rd. • Princeton, N.J. 08540

In keeping with Princeton's image, where everyone lives around the corner from where Einstein used to, Sidney Colodney calls his shop "the educated delicatessen for smart buyers". Colodney will send delicatessen, appetizing, and bakery items anywhere in the country. His *ruggelah* (pastries) are especially good. They come from a glatt kosher, Shomer Shabbat bakery and

will be sent in their original bakery containers. Everything from varieties of lox and other fishes to pastramis and corned beef and marvelous sour pickles are available. Write and ask for current prices and shipping details.

Murray's Sturgeon Shop
2429 Broadway • New York, N.Y. 10024

Like Barney Greengrass, Murray's Sturgeon Shop will send retail orders of a variety of smoked fish and other appetizing items almost any place in the United States. Mail orders are shipped Tuesday through Friday via express mail or air freight which just about guarantees next day delivery. All orders are packed in enough ice to last for forty-eight hours. There is a charge of $1 for the ice. Send for Murray's mail-order price list (prices are subject to change without notice), where you will find smoked Nova Scotia salmon, whitefish chubs, bagels, and bialys. There is also homemade pickled herring and smoked winter carp in season. A 50 percent deposit is required with initial order, the balance payable within seven days.

Jerry Rossman
1090 Carolan Ave.
Burlinghame, Calif. 94010

Keep your eye out for "Noches Noshes", packages of fortune cookies with humorous Yiddish "fortunes". Write for more information.

Sinai Kosher Sausage Corp.
1000 W. Pershing Rd. • Chicago, Ill. 60609

This firm sells a wide variety of delicatessen products. These are available through the mail, and gift packages will also be sent. Sinai also sells freezer-wrapped meats in consumer-sized packages for your home freezer. Mail orders are accepted from individuals and small groups as well as from shops. Write for details and price lists. You can even call them collect: (312) 927–2810.

Paprikas Weiss
1546 Second Ave. • New York, N.Y. 10028

If you long for kitchen utensils like those your grandmother or great-grandmother may have

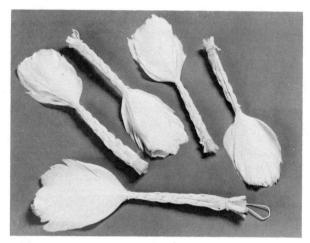

PAPRIKAS WEISS, feather brushes for glazing baked goods or basting meat.

used in Eastern Europe, or a copper Russian samovar, this is the place to contact. As well as the exciting array of kitchen utensils you will find the basic ingredients to make many Eastern European specialties. Note, however, that although this shop does import some kosher products from Israel, notably gefilte fish, it specializes in *ethnic* not necessarily kosher foods. Many of the products are parve and Mr. Weiss will send a list of them on request. For example, the canned chestnut puree is bought in huge quantities by the Hungarian Hasidim in Williamsburg. All spices (including of course the paprika) are kosher and parve. The shop's fantastic strudel dough is parve, as are the apricot, almond paste, poppy seed, and prune lekvar fillings. Hungarian acacia honey and freshly ground walnuts, almonds, poppy seeds, and hazelnuts, are all kosher and parve. (The chopped liver is *not* kosher.)

The annual catalog ($1) is so atmospheric that if you are planning to make strudel and you'd like to feel and look authentically ethnic too, you can order some Hungarian records to listen to and embroidered blouses and shawls or kerchiefs to wear while you cook.

Judith Taylor
157 Babcock St.
Brookline, Mass. 02146

Judith Taylor is a multi-talented artist (see also *Playing: Toys*), some of whose most charming creations are made in cookie dough. She will make jewelry, fine art reproductions, centerpieces, wall plaques, bas reliefs, and three-dimensional ob-

jects from gingerbread dough. Everything is edible unless you choose to have them plastic coated for permanence. Her prices begin at $5. She is interested in commissions and says that her most interesting pieces have been created in response to a person or an event requiring individualized detail. She is available for demonstrations and workshops and loves sharing her know-how with children and adults. Judith writes:

"Cookies are playful. I began modeling with gingersnap dough because I enjoyed doing it for myself and my family. Now I am ready to make my art available to a larger audience. I like gingersnap dough as a medium because it's possible to enjoy my art on many levels—as unique and delicious cookies, or as whimsical permanent art. I've done portraits, Jewish holiday themes and symbols: an edible sukkah with marzipan fruits and vegetables, spice-scented edible necklaces for Shabbat, plus old-fashioned gingerbread people with a *yiddishe tam* (Jewish flavor), and more. Write so we can explore possibilities and if you'd like to try making cookie sculpture on your own here is my recipe:

GINGERBREAD DOUGH FOR SCULPTED COOKIES

½ cup water
½ cup dark corn syrup
1 cup sugar
2 teaspoons cinnamon
2 teaspoons ground cloves
1 tablespoon ground ginger
1 cup butter or margarine
1½ teaspoons baking soda
4 cups all-purpose flour

JUDITH TAYLOR, "Hamsa amulet", cookie sculpture. (photo: Kenneth M. Bernstein)

Combine water, corn syrup, sugar, and spices in a saucepan and bring to a boil. Remove from heat. Add butter or margarine to hot mixture, stirring until cool. Pour into a large mixing bowl. Add flour and baking soda gradually and stir until thoroughly blended. Mixture will resemble soft caramel taffy. Cover and refrigerate overnight or longer. When ready to use, remove a small portion from the refrigerator, knead to soften, and shape on an ungreased cookie sheet. Make "cookies" of an approximately even thickness, ¼" maximum height. Bake in a preheated 375° oven, on the middle shelf, for about 6 to 12 minutes, depending on cookie thickness. Check to make certain that the cookies brown evenly. Cookies will be soft while warm, crisp when they cool. Allow to cool slightly before removing from the cookie sheet. When cool, the cookies will keep indefinitely, as long as they are stored carefully. They are relatively fragile. If they are not meant to be eaten they can be painted with a polyurethane vinyl coating and mounted on a stiff backing such as masonite or wood with plain white glue. Unbaked dough keeps for weeks in the refrigerator as long as it is well covered. I like having it handy for kids projects, or sudden inspirations. Besides, it makes terrific plain old round gingersnaps!"

Union of Orthodox Jewish Congregations of America • Kashrut Division
116 E. 27th St. • New York, N.Y. 10016

·The Ⓤ of the Kashrut Division of the U.O.J.C.A. is the most widely recognized symbol used to certify foods kosher. The organization, in addition to its inspecting and certifying duties, publishes a number of interesting pamphlets. The "Kashrut Handbook for Home and School" offers a detailed explanation of the various aspects of kashrut. Two directories of kosher food products are available—the "Kosher Products and Services Directory" and the "Institutional and Industrial Kosher Products Directory." An annual "Passover Products Directory" and the "Ⓤ News Reporter" may also be had for no charge, as may all of the publications mentioned.

COOKBOOKS

The number of Jewish cookbooks has proliferated incredibly in the last few years. The following list does not pretend to be definitive. It is, however, a fair sampling of the variety of approaches to Jewish cooking.

Bar-David, Molly. *The Israeli Cookbook: What's Cooking in Israel's Melting Pot.* New York, Crown Publishing. Delicious and varied recipes accompanied by fascinating historical anecdotes; my long-time favorite.

Fround, Nina, ed. *The International Jewish Cookbook.* New York, Stein & Day. An excellent collection by members of Women's International ORT of recipes from around the world. (Also available in paperback.)

Gether, Judith and Lefft, Elizabeth. *The World Famous Ratner's Meatless Cookbook,* New York, Bantam. The diary cookbook for anyone who has ever eaten at Ratner's or wished they had. Paperback.

Kasden, Sara. *Love and Knishes: An Irrepressible Guide to Jewish Cooking.* New York, Vanguard. The Louisville, Kentucky, author has assembled a classic collection of Jewish home cooking and spiced it with comfortable humor.

Kasden, Sara. *Mazel Tov Y'All.* New York, Vanguard. A book for bakers.

Leonard, Leah. *Jewish Cookery, in accordance with Jewish dietary laws.* New York, Crown. First published in the forties, this book has gone through about 24 editions. Classic tested recipes.

Lubavitch Women's Organization-Junior Division. *The Spice and Spirit of Kosher Jewish Cooking,* New York, Bloch. An excellent thorough coverage of the laws of Kashrut, keeping a Kosher home, and guide to holiday observance. The book is a labor of love from this vibrant community; charming illustrations by Michoel Muchnik.

Nathan, Joan. *The Jewish Holiday Kitchen.* New York, Schocken. An international assortment of recipes for special occasions, accompanied by anecdotes about Jewish customs and food lore.

Rodon, Claudia. *A Book of Middle Eastern Food.* New York, Knopf. An excellent selection of sephardic recipes.

Rose, Evelyn. *The Complete International Jewish Cookbook.* New York, St. Martin's Press. While non-ashkenazi recipes are underrepresented in what purports to be an international collection, the excellent recipes and presentation provide an interesting look at contemporary Jewish cooking customs in Great Britain where the author is a rabbi's wife.

Roth, June. *Healthier Jewish Cooking; the Unsaturated Fat Way*. New York, Arco. Modern methods of health and nutrition combined with traditional Jewish recipes from the author of more than 16 cookbooks including: *The Bagel Book* (Grosset and Dunlap) and *Low-Cholesterol Jewish Cooking* (Arco).

Seaman, Dorothy and Smith, Paula. *Not Chopped Liver! The Kosher Way to cook Gourmet*. Conn., Jetsand Publishers. A useful book for those who want to prepare classic international gourmet food in a kosher kitchen. Essentially a meat cookbook, everything in it can be eaten at a meat meal. Here you will find creamy lox canapes, lasagna, and veal parmesan all prepared with tofu instead of cheese, and dessert custards, tortes, and souffles made with non-dairy substitutes for butter, milk, and cream. A kosher Chinese section is included. The paperback is available for $10.75 plus $1 postage from Jetsand Publishers, P.O. Box 17052, West Hartford, Conn. 06117

Witty, Helen and Colche, Elizabeth Schneider. *Better Than Store-Bought*. New York, Harper and Row. While this is not a kosher or even Jewish cookbook, many of the amazing recipes are for delicacies we all think of as "Jewish" and also think are impossible to make at home. Here you will find recipes for corning your own beef in brine and for making pastrami. There are also recipes for making cottage and cream cheese at home, a variety of kosher pickles, and breads such as bagels, pita, and salty soft pretzels. With care and adjustments the sausage making section could have you making your own kosher knackwursts and hot dogs.

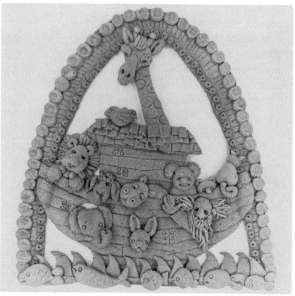

JUDITH TAYLOR, "Noah's Ark", cookie sculpture. (photo: Kenneth M. Bernstein)

(photo: © Laurence Salzmann, see *Creating: Pictures*)

Holidays and Ceremonies

Children called to the Torah on Simchat Torah. (photo: Bill Aron; see *Creating: Pictures*)

There was once a time when the only things that were bigger than trees were mountains and we could see the stars clearly at night. We were simultaneously more in tune with the natural world and more in awe of its power to affect our lives. Most of our holidays originated in those long-ago years as natural and seasonal celebrations. In time we added historical and mystical interpretations to our festivals, intellectualized them, and cleaned them up. Holidays change their meanings all the time as they wax and wane in the popular imagination. It is hard to imagine the time when Rosh Hodesh (the festival of the New Moon) was at least as important a celebration as the Sabbath. In our time we are witnessing the transformation of Hanukkah from a minor holiday into a significant one while Purim, which was much more important to our European ancestors a bare generation or two ago, has faded considerably. For American Jews living according to the patterns of the secular calendar, the Jewish holidays often seem to come at inconvenient times. Yet, precisely because we have maintained allegiance to the Hebrew calendar, it serves to unite Jews all over the world each time we celebrate a holiday and to unite us with generations which have gone before. The very "inconvenience" of holidays which come "early" or "late" serves to transport us to the realm of sacred time providing an insulated space in which to express some of our most profound feelings and to translate them into communal experiences. In the fall, just as we've finally gotten back into the swing of work and the children are finally back in school, the High Holiday cycle comes along invariably taking many of us by surprise. Yet the very thought of turning Rosh Hashanah-Yom Kippur into a convenient three-day weekend is ludicrous and the suggestion of forcing the 25th of Kislev (Hanukkah) to coincide regularly with the 25th of December belies the very meaning of the festival of rededication. Here you will find items of special interest for certain of the holidays, a representative listing of bookstores which, along with books and giftware, stock complete lines of holiday supplies, and descriptions of companies that specialize in synagogue appurtenances.

Ritual and ceremonial items can be found in other places in this book, particularly in the *Creating* and *Buying* sections.

SABBATH AND HOLIDAY OBSERVANCE

We often have the notion that holidays have to be a certain way or they are not "right". For me it is important to keep in mind that the Sabbath and festivals were made for *us* not vice-versa. The more we know about our celebrations the more we can personalize and own them. I am sure that our efforts to enhance the holy days will be greeted by the songs of angels rather than bolts of lightning. To begin with, it's a very good idea to have a Jewish calendar on hand. Two which I find invaluable are:

The Comprehensive Hebrew Calendar
Behrman House
1261 Broadway • New York, N.Y. 10001

This is a textbook-form calendar (228 pages) by Arthur Spier and is intriguing to have, because it covers the whole century from 1900–2000 (5660–5760). You can look up the Hebrew birthdays of family members and plan events far in the future. The manner in which the Jewish calendar is calculated is also explained, and Torah portions are given.

The Jewish Calendar
Universe Books
381 Park Ave. S. • New York, N.Y. 10016

Richard Siegel and Michael Strassfeld have been compiling this useful and informative calendar annually since 1975 and it is reissued every year with appropriate revisions. It is very attractively printed and presented in spiral book form with lots

Sukkot. (photo: © Bill Aron; see *Creating: Pictures*)

of room to write in appointments and events. The calendar provides information about holidays and festivals, candlelighting times, Torah portions, and prophetic readings for Sabbaths and High Holidays, and also many interesting historical facts and vignettes. Available at most bookstores or order it from the publisher.

For two different approaches to the holidays, write for holiday pamphlets and brochures from the organizations listed below. Both present the backgrounds of the holidays and suggestions for observation and enjoyment.

Education Department
American Zionist Youth Foundation
515 Park Ave. • New York, N.Y. 10022

Mitzvah Campaign
Lubavitch Youth Organization
770 Eastern Pkwy. • Brooklyn, N.Y. 11213

Four books which should be staples of every Jewish holiday library are listed below. The first one is for children, the third is my own effort to explain and enjoy the holidays and life cycle celebrations as a contemporary American Jew, and the other two are classics. The books are available from their publishers or through your bookseller.

Cashman, Greer F. *Jewish Days and Holidays*, illustrated by Alona Frankel, Englewood, N.J., SBS Publishing Inc.

Gaster, Theodor H. *Festivals of the Jewish Year: A Modern Interpretation and Guide*, N.Y., William Morrow Co.

Rockland, Mae Shafter. *The Jewish Party Book: A Contemporary Guide to Customs, Crafts, and Foods*, N.Y., Schocken Books Inc.

Schauss, Hayyim. *Guide to Jewish Holy Days, History and Observance*, N.Y., Schocken Books Inc.

B'nai Brith Hillel Foundation
Brandeis University
Waltham, Mass. 02154

Folklorists of the future will not need an Alan Lomax to go searching for the last survivors of the

Brandeis egalitarian minyan. Rabbi Albert Axelrad has saved them the trouble. The Hillel Foundation at Brandeis has produced two large sets of cassettes which in fact document the living folk art of the group while serving the very useful function of teaching the rest of us the prayers and nigunim for the Sabbath (including Havdalah), Torah cantillation, how to lead a group in prayer, officiate at a funeral, sing love ballads at a wedding, and table songs at all celebrations. When a Reform family finds their child having an Orthodox wedding and feeling as though they went to the wrong summer camp, these cassettes can bail them out. The tapes are an excellent help for those who haven't had a traditional background and want to immerse themselves in the sound of Jewish prayer and also for small communities. These cassettes are the next best thing to being there. The sometimes amateurish quality only adds to their charm because it invites one to sing along and Al Axelrad's explanations and lovely natural voice unifies the set. I especially appreciate all the words of encouragement for women to take leadership roles in worship. Write to the Hillel Foundation for information about the specific cassettes available and their prices.

Havdalah. (photo © Neil Folberg; see *Creating: Pictures*)

Andrea Hartman
9547 Saddlebag Row • Columbia, Md. 21045

Andrea Hartman specializes in traditional batik for contemporary designs. Her hallah covers, batiked on soft open weave fabric are available in combinations of blue and green, green and yellow, and orange and yellow; $28 includes postage and a ''Good Yontif'' gift box. She will also custom-make other ritual items and wall hangings.

Dona Rosenblatt
5623 Coolbrook
Montreal, Quebec, Canada H3X 2L8

Dona Rosenblatt has a line of handpainted placemats for Shabbat, Rosh Hashanah, Sukkot, Hanukkah, Tu B'Shevat, Passover, and Shavuot. She also makes a handpainted hallah cover and will custom-weave aleph bet and Jerusalem hangings and tallitot. Allow 3–6 months for the woven articles. Prices range from $6.25 each for the placemats to $150 for the tallit. Write for descriptive literature.

HANUKKAH

The Hanukkah Book
by Mae Shafter Rockland
Schocken Books Inc.
200 Madison Ave. • New York, N.Y. 10016

In recent years, Hanukkah has changed from a minor holiday to a major means of expressing

Hanukkah lamp, 18"w × 24" h, by Harry Green; see *Creating: Art for Architecture* and *Ceramics.*

Jewish identity. My book explores the reasons behind this change while encouraging Jews to look more deeply into Judaic source material to find ways of enriching Hanukkah in an authentically Jewish way. *Library Journal* said this about the book:

> Besides a detailed history of the origins of Hanukkah and the variety of observances throughout the world, over the centuries, (Rockland) includes recipes, ideas for homemade gifts party decorations and religious articles, children's games and music. Photographs and drawings illustrate many of the ideas described in the text. The total effect is one of a unique and joyous ethnic holiday celebration.

Available from your bookseller or by mail from the publisher.

PASSOVER

Passover is so important in the Jewish holiday cycle that even though I'm certain you can get Haggadahs through the book and Judaica shops listed below, I would like to present my favorite ones. If you don't find them at your bookstore you can always write directly to the publisher.

MESORAH PUBLICATIONS LTD., Art Scroll Series; see *Learning: Books*. (photo: Menachem Adelman)

**A Passover Haggadah
Drawings by Leonard Baskin
Central Conference of American Rabbis
790 Madison Ave.
New York, N.Y. 10021**

A careful combination of tradition and Reform Judaism, and beautifully illustrated. Write for a

Matzah platter by Lynn Rosen of Yetzirah Pottery; see Creating: Ceramics. (photo Russ Lake)

DEBORAH KELMAN, matzah cover, 14" × 14", and matching afikoman envelope.

complete publications list, which has quantity prices and describes the limited edition version as well.

**Let My People Go, A Haggadah
Illustrated by Mark Podwal
The Macmillan Company
866 Third Ave. • New York, N.Y. 10022**

Both the commentary and the powerfully sensitive drawings relate to the plight of the Soviet Jews. A very meaningful contemporary interpretation of our timeless festival. (See *Buying: Cards, Gifts and Collectibles*.)

My Very Own Haggadah
Kar-Ben Copies
11713 Auth Ln.
Silver Springs, Md. 20902

Two women publish this Seder service for very young children. The Passover story is simply told and the book has pictures to color, recipes, and craft ideas. Write for the brochure and order form; quantity discounts are available on large orders. See *Buying: Cards, Gifts and Collectibles* for their "I found it" T-shirt for the afikoman finder at your Seder, and *Learning: Books*.

San Diego Woman's Haggadah
Woman's Institute for Continuing Jewish Education
4079 54th St.
San Diego, Calif. 92105

A new version of the ancient story of the Exodus which includes the important role of women in the search for freedom. The San Diego Woman's Haggadah can be used independently or in conjunction with a traditional Haggadah at the Seder table and is a useful tool for discussion groups. Copies are available from the Woman's Institute for $3.50 plus 50¢ postage. Add 20¢ postage for each additional copy.

Isa Goldfarb
137 Norwood Ave.
Newtonville, Mass. 02160

Isa Goldfarb is a calligrapher turned batik artist. She will make custom-designed Seder pillows, some in unusual shapes. Slides available on request.

Deborah Kelman
5173 Coronado Ave.
Oakland, Calif. 94618

Available from this talented batik artist: matzah covers, 14″ × 14″ (white with one color), $16; afikoman envelopes to match, $6. These come in a marvelous assortment of subtle colors, earthtone range, yellow, red-orange, rust, brown; blues, greens and blues. Deborah also makes hallah

covers (depending on number of colors used), $15–$21. Write for color catalogue. (See *Creating: Textiles*.)

SUKKOT

Craftwood Lumber Co.
1590 Old Deerfield Road
Highland Park, Ill. 60035

The Craftwood Lumber Company offers a sukkah kit made completely of wood. The kit consists of rafters, uprights, horizontal and diagonal bars, corner blocks, screw shafts and round heads for construction of an 8′ × 12′ × 7′ high sukkah. The kit, which comes with illustrated directions, a brief history of the holiday, prayers and decorating suggestions, is packaged in sturdy cartons for storage. High density plastic walls are optional; replacement parts and extension kits are also available. Wooden sukkah kit, $129; optional set of plastic walls, $60. Illinois residents add 5% sales tax; Visa and MasterCard accepted. Write or call for more information and descriptive brochure.

Frank Supply Corp.
21-07 Cornaga Ave.
Far Rockaway, N.Y. 11691

Frank Supply Corp. is a wholesale plumbing supplier which has pre-fab sukkahs for family or congregational use made of galvanized pipes, slip

Paul Steinfeld of Gilead Tree Farm with *skhakh*.

fittings, and brightly colored nylon canvas. Mr. Frank, who is *shomer shabbat,* offers complete religious guidance to new sukkah owners. Write or call for prices and delivery information. In New England these sukkahs are distributed by R. Krochmal, 71 Monastery Rd., Brighton, Mass.

Paul B. Steinfeld
Gilead Tree Farm
Holcott Center, N.Y. 12437

Need *skhakh* for your sukkah? Paul B. Steinfeld operates a farm in Greene County, N.Y., to produce forest products. The farm supplies tons of evergreen boughs, mainly Scotch pine, red pine, and Austrian pine for *skhakh,* sukkah roofing. The boughs can be tied in 20 to 50 pound bales as desired, and shipped to individuals via United Parcel. Synagogues, community centers, or other organizations may order truckloads for resale. Individuals, families or groups may arrange to choose and cut their own boughs at the farm, and order custom-made sukkah decorations from natural materials. Additional information and driving directions may be obtained by writing or calling.

YOM HA-SHOAH

Yom Ha-Shoah (Day of Remembrance of the Holocaust) which is observed on the 28th of Nisan, thirteen days after Passover begins, is a new holiday and so far has very little fixed ritual about it. It has, however, begun to be customary to light a memorial candle which burns for 24 hours on that day. A number of the artists in the *Creating* section make lamps which will hold the standard *yahrzeit* candles available in many supermarkets and Jewish bookstores. Moshe Zabari, Ken Rosenfeld, and Kathy Goos in particular have made *yahrzeit* lamps which are simultaneously functional and symbolically meaningful. Shown here is a memorial light by Chava Wolpert Richard which has the phrase "The soul of man is the lamp of the Lord" screen printed on the glass container.

BOOKSTORES AND SYNAGOGUE SUPPLY HOUSES

Most of the bookstores listed here sell a wide variety of holiday and gift items, religious articles, toys, Israeli imports, and records and tapes, as well as books. Note that this is only a representative list; there are many more stores just as good as those mentioned here. You'll find a complete list of them in *Jewish Literary Marketplace* (see *Learning: Books*).

CALIFORNIA

Joseph Herskovitz Hebrew Book Store
428 N. Fairfax Ave. ● Los Angeles, Calif. 90036

Jewish American Book Shop
P.O. Box 36185 ● Los Angeles, Calif. 90036

The Jewish Development Company
18331-C Irvine Blvd.
Tustin, Calif. 92680
The slogan of this shop is: "Everything you've ever wanted, but didn't know where to find". Anne Rolbin, whose shop it is, works very hard to see that you are not disappointed. See *Buying: Art Dealers.*

Judaic Book Service ● Steven L. Maimes, Bookseller
3726 Virden Ave. ● Oakland, Calif. 94619

Noshing in the sukkah. (photo: E. Jan Kounitz, see *Creating: Pictures*)

Liber's Book Store
3240 Geary Blvd. ● San Francisco, Calif. 94121

The Merkaz
4600 El Camino Real ● Los Altos, Calif. 94022
and 244 Noriega St. ● San Francisco, Calif. 94122
As well as books and a large assortment of religious
supplies and gift items, The Merkaz also carries certain
Jewish food items and wine. Mail orders accepted.

J. Roth/Bookseller
9427 W. Pico Blvd. ● Los Angeles, Calif. 90035
(See *Learning: Books* for more on Jack Roth.)

The Shtetl (Used Books)
7603 Beverly Blvd. ● Los Angeles, Calif. 90048

FLORIDA

Ner Tamid Book Distributors
P.O. Box 10401 ● Riviera Beach, Fla. 33404

Shalom Judaica
1668 N.E. 205th Ter. ● North Miami Beach, Fla. 33179

ILLINOIS

Architectural Bronze and Aluminum Corp.
3638 W. Oakton St. ● Skokie, Ill. 60076
Manufacturer and distributor of bronze yahrzeit memorial
plaques and "trees of life".

Hamakor Judaica, Inc.
6112 N. Lincoln Ave. ● Chicago, Ill. 60659

Schwartz-Rosenblum Hebrew Book Store
2906 W. Devon Ave. ● Chicago, Ill. 60659

MARYLAND

Central Hebrew Book Store
228 Reisterstown Rd. ● Baltimore, Md. 21208

Goodman's Hebrew Books and Gifts
2305 University Blvd. West ● Wheaton, Md. 20902

Jewish Book Store of Greater Washington
11250 Georgia Ave. ● Wheaton, Md. 20902
The largest Judaica shop in the South, its slogan is "if it's
Jewish, we have it".

MASSACHUSETTS

Chai House
158 Pleasant St. ● Malden, Mass. 02148
Chai House attempts to be a center for Jewish living
providing "a real mishmash of marvelous material". They
buy and sell used goods, *especially* books, have a mini art
gallery and at Pesah time stock food for the holiday.

Israel Book Shop Inc.
410 Harvard St. ● Brookline, Mass. 02146
A pleasant place to spend a Sunday afternoon.

Melvin Drug Co.
197-99 Main St. ● Great Barrington, Mass. 01230

MICHIGAN

Borenstein's Book & Music Store
25242 Greenfield Rd. ● Oak Park, Mich. 48237

Spitzer's Hebrew Book and Gift Center
21770 Eleven Mile Rd. ● Southfield, Mich. 48076

MINNESOTA

Brochin's Book and Gift Shop
4813 Minnetonka Blvd. ● Minneapolis, Minn. 55416
Now owned by Sybil Wilensky, Brochin's calls itself "the
one-stop shop for all your personal,. religious, and social
needs" and the list of items available is indeed impressive.

MISSOURI

Midwest Merchandise Co.
8318 Olive St. Rd. ● St. Louis, Mo. 63132

NEW JERSEY

Judaica House Ltd.
435 Cedar Ln. ● Teaneck, N.J. 07666

NEW YORK

W. & E. Baum Bronze Tablet Corp.
524 W. 43rd St. ● New York, N.Y. 10036
Manufacturers of bronze and aluminum signs for
synagogues. An illustrated brochure of different styles of
honorary plaques is available.

J. Biegeleisen Co.
83 Division St. ● New York, N.Y. 10002

Behrman House Inc.
1261 Broadway ● New York, N.Y. 10001

Bloch Publishing Co., Inc.
915 Broadway ● New York, N.Y. 10010

C & S Skull Cap Co.
1265 Coney Island Ave. ● Brooklyn, N.Y. 11230

Center of Jewish Books
1660 Ocean Pkwy. ● Brooklyn, N.Y. 11223

ISRAEL BOOK SHOP, Brookline, Mass. (photo: © Bill Aron;
see *Creating: Pictures*)

Theo S. Cinnamon Ltd.
420 Jerusalem Ave. ● Hicksville, N.Y. 11801

Eagle Regalia Co., Inc.
305 Broadway ● New York, N.Y. 10007
Eagle Regalia manufactures buttons, badges, ribbons, emblem pins, flags, banners, pennants, and awards of all types. It has catalogs showing its ready-made things and will custom-make banners and buttons for your group. Israeli flags are available in a variety of sizes and qualities.

Philipp Feldheim Inc.
96 East Broadway ● New York, N.Y. 10002

Hebrew Book and Gift World
72-20 Main St. ● Kew Gardens Hills, N.Y. 11367

Judea Importers Co.
60 Canal St. ● New York, N.Y. 10002
Judea Importers has a brochure of imported Israeli holiday items, including a profusion of Hanukkah lamps and an assortment of Shabbat and decorative objects. Write for brochure with prices.

J. Levine Co.
58 Eldridge St. ● New York, N.Y. 10002
In the late 1880s a scribe named Hirsch Landy, the great-grandfather of Dan Levine, the present assistant V.P. in charge of public relations and sales, supplied Torahs and religious articles to communities throughout Europe from his firm in Vilkameer, Lithuania. In 1905, because of the deterioration of Jewish communities in the area, Hirsch Landy and his family moved to America and settled on the Lower East Side of New York where he developed a distribution center for European Torahs, tefillin, and tallitot. In 1920, his son-in-law, Joseph Levine, took over and expanded the business to include embroidering and sewing religious materials. J. Levine Co. became the major manufacturer of ark covers, Torah covers, and embroideries, and also began selling religious books. The next generation of Levines expanded the company into a complete department store of supplies and services for the synagogue, school, and home. Today, still on the Lower East Side in a seven story building filled to the brim with an amazing assortment of goods to fill every Jewish need from *Sabraman* comics to tallitot in a variety of styles and fabrics, the family business has given the fourth generation Dan Levine the responsibility of bringing the firm into the 80's and 90's. Twenty-four year old Dan, who coined J. Levine's slogan, "A Modern Tradition Since 1890", personifies the mixture of traditional merchandise and contemporary merchandising which characterizes the company. Yeshiva trained, Dan is, like his great-grandfather, an Orthodox scribe—certified by the Chief Rabbinate in Jerusalem—and has a master's degree in public relations from Boston University. He writes: "One of the most meaningful experiences of the past year was a trip to Reno, Nevada, where I sold a new Sefer Torah and performed the *siyyum* ceremony, completing the last few letters. When I arrived at the airport the entire Jewish community was there to meet me together with the local T.V. stations. I had brought along a *huppah* which matched perfectly the form-fitted *atarah* I had designed for the Rabbi of Reno. The Rabbi, the tallit, the huppah, the Torah and me (they were

J. LEVINE CO., "A Modern Tradition Since 1890".

probably expecting someone who looked more like my great-grandfather did)—it was a real scene and the T.V. stations loved it. After I returned to N.Y. I received letters saying how I 'touched the hearts of the people in the community'. It was very gratifying."

Write for their new catalog, "Gallery of Judaica" ($5) compiled by Dan in honor of J. Levine Company's 90th year, which should give you a fair idea of the diverse items and services offered by this energetic firm which "is embarking on a major campaign to let world Jewry know what we have to offer".

Miriam Manufacturing Corp.
48 Canal St. ● New York, N.Y. 10002
This is a general supply house specializing in embroidered items. A large illustrated catalog is available.

Solomon Rabinowitz Hebrew Book Store
30 Canal St. ● New York, N.Y. 10002

Source Gift Shop, Inc.
307 Central Ave. ● Lawrence, N.Y. 11559

Louis Stavsky Co., Inc.
147 Essex St. ● New York, N.Y. 10002

United States Bronze Sign Co., Inc.
101 W. 31st St. ● New York, N.Y. 10001
The catalog has a very large selection of memorial plaques and donor wall plaques and tablets. The company also sells large bronze Hebrew and English letters for exterior use on synagogue walls.

OHIO

Frank's Hebrew Book Store
1647 Lee Rd. ● Cleveland Heights, Ohio 44118
This is the largest and oldest Jewish book and gift center in the Ohio and western Pennsylvania area. Established in 1916, it is a family business and has become an integral part of the Jewish community. Mail orders are speedily filled.

Hebrew Union College Bookstore
3101 Clifton Ave. ● Cincinnati, Ohio 45220

PENNSYLVANIA

Jas. H. Matthews & Co., Bronze Division
1315 W. Liberty Ave. ● Pittsburgh, Pa. 15222
Brochure available showing many different Jewish
emblems in bronze.

Pinsker's
2028 Murray Ave. ● Pittsburgh, Pa. 15207

Rabbi Piotrkowski's Judaica Center
289 Montgomery Ave. ● Bala Cynwyd, Pa. 19004
Avram Piotrkowski calls his stores and warehouse "the
most complete Judaica center in the United States of
America." The shop has everything from tefillin to tee
shirts, and a lot in between.

Rosenberg's Hebrew Bookstore
413 York Rd. ● Jenkintown, Pa. 19046

RHODE ISLAND

Melzer's Hebrew & Religious Goods
742 Hope St. ● Providence, R.I. 02906

CANADA

Book Center, Inc.
1140 Beaulac St. ● Montreal, Quebec

Rodal's Hebrew Book Store and Gift Shop
4685 Van Horne St. ● Montreal, Quebec

Zucker's Jewish Books and Art
3453 Bathurst St. ● Toronto, Ontario

ARCHITECTURAL BRONZE & ALUMINUM CORP., "Tree of
Life".

MAXWELL M. CHAYAT, Torah breastplate and yad; see
Creating: Metal.

HANA GEBER, Kiddush cup, 7″ high, silver bronze, one-of-a-
kind, $450; see *Creating: Metal.* (photo: Walter Geber)

Life Cycle

"Artist's Family" by Harry Green; see *Creating: Art for Architecture* and *Ceramics*.

The Talmud teaches that God created Adam as a solitary human being so that no one person could claim "My father is better than your father", and so that no one could say that vice and virtue are inherited. The Talmud also points out that when a craftsman uses a die to stamp out coins, they are all alike; yet when God stamps all men with the die of Adam each one is different; therefore everyone has the right to say, "The world was created for *my* sake" (Talmud, *Sanhedrin*). The life cycle is the same for people everywhere. But the way in which the major rites of passage are marked varies considerably and subtly from culture to culture. These variations reflect the relationship between the individual and his/her community and demonstrate the way in which we perceive our obligations to those generations who have gone before. Other sections of this book will provide you with sources for many of the accouterments with which to celebrate the Jewish life cycle rites. I have concentrated here on certain specific services which I hope you will find useful. Some of the organizations listed in this section serve limited geographic areas; they are listed with the hope that they will be imitated in other areas where they are needed.

BABIES

National Foundation for Jewish Genetic Diseases
609 Fifth Ave. • New York, N.Y. 10017

Every parent's primary desire is for a healthy baby. Recent medical attention has focused on diseases which are hereditary among Jews, particularly those whose families come from certain areas of Europe. The National Foundation for Jewish Genetic Diseases has an audio-visual filmstrip entitled *The Tragic Legacy* on this important subject.

CIRCUMCISION

Brit Milah, Brooklyn. (photo: © Neil Folberg; see *Creating: Pictures*)

Brit milah, the covenant of circumcision performed on the eighth day after a male child's birth, is one of the cornerstones of the Jewish faith: "Every male among you shall be circumcised. And ye shall be circumcised in the flesh of your foreskin, and it shall be a token of a covenant betwixt Me and you" (Genesis 17:11-12). Once performed primarily in the synagogue, the ceremony of circumcision now takes place more often in the home or hospital. And while the traditional mohel still conducts the ritual in Orthodox circles, for many Reform and some Conservative Jews the actual circumcision is often done by a doctor with a rabbi in attendance to recite the prayers. Your rabbi is the best person to contact for arranging a brit milah. If you live in a sizable Jewish community, chances are that a certified mohel can be located easily either through him or the nearest board of rabbis. In the New York area, you may write to the Brit Milah Board of New York, a division of the New York Board of Rabbis, 10 E. 73rd St., New York, N.Y. 10021.

Alternatives in Religious Education
3945 S. Oneida St.
Denver, Colo. 80237

A.R.E. offers manuals for a special four-to-six-hour mini-course exploring the meaning of covenant in daily life. The course, which is designed for fifth graders through high school students, discusses the history of circumcision among Jews and non-Jews, the ritual, symbols, superstitions, and folklore attending the ceremony. A teacher guide is included plus twenty student manuals.

Jewish Women's Resource Center
92nd St. YM/YWHA Library
1395 Lexington Ave.
New York, N.Y. 10028

The Jewish Women's Resource Center, which among its other activities provides a showcase for Jewish women artists, runs Rosh Hodesh groups and publishes a quarterly newsletter, has produced a ceremonial guide toward celebrating the birth of a daughter. Write for more information.

Toby Fishbein Reifman
231 Sunset Ave. • Englewood, N.J. 07631

Jewish law and custom provide for the formal induction of every boy baby into the Jewish people. Traditionally little ceremonial fuss is made over a girl infant. In recent years parents wanting to mark the birth of their daughters in special ways have come up with a number of meaningful ceremonies. Toby Reifman has gathered seven of them together in a booklet entitled *Blessing the Birth of a Daughter: Jewish Naming Ceremonies for Girls*. Also included is a discussion of a mother's participation in the male child ceremony of brit milah by Shoshana and Mel Silberman. Copies may be ordered from Toby for $3.

(photo: Richard Sobol)

ADOPTION AND CHILD CARE

Because of the easy availability of contraceptives and liberalized abortion laws in many states, it has become increasingly difficult in recent years to adopt a newborn baby. Jewish babies are even more difficult to find. The few babies and older children from homes broken by death, disease, or divorce, who are not available for adoption but who need foster care, are helped by a number of agencies. If you want to adopt a child or look after a foster child, remember that in the human services, state laws often make a considerable difference in the availability of services and in eligibility requirements. Consult with your local rabbi, who should be familiar with the closest agency, or write one of the agencies listed below.

(photo: Mae Rockland)

Jewish Child Care Association of New York
345 Madison Ave.
New York, N.Y. 10017

The Association cares for 2,000 children ranging in age from infancy to twenty-one. A variety of services are provided for children whose families cannot give them the care they need. Some of the children are placed in special residence schools, others in foster or permanent homes. A well-written illustrated booklet defines and explains the Association's various services.

Lubavitch Nursery School
3109 North Lake Drive
Milwaukee, Wis. 53211

The nursery school's brochure recounts the story of a woman asking a prominent psychiatrist how early she could begin educating her child. "When will your child be born?" the psychiatrist asked. "Born?" she exclaimed, "why, he is already five years old!". "Hurry home," said the psychiatrist, "don't stand here talking to me. You have already wasted the five best years!". While this particular school can only service children in its immediate area, I've listed it to encourage people to in the words of their brochure: "Take advantage of your child's best years and send him/her to a maximum Jewish educational nursery school". With more and more children spending their earliest and most formative years in day-care centers of one sort or another, it well behooves us to seek out those with Jewish programming and if there aren't any in our areas to work towards creating them.

Ohel Children's Home
4907 16th Ave. • Brooklyn, N.Y. 11204

Ohel is a nonprofit agency sponsored by the Orthodox community to meet the urgent needs of Jewish children from disintegrated families. It has two residence homes for boys—one for young boys, the other for teenagers—a home for teenaged girls, a foster-care division, and an adoption service. Most of Ohel's work is based in the metropolitan area but it makes every effort to help people from other states as well. Ohel is constantly searching for suitable Orthodox foster families. It only accepts about 25 percent of those who apply.

If a foster child is placed in your home, Ohel provides medical care, yeshiva tuition, summer camp, clothing, and a room-and-board allowance. And its professional counseling staff is available to assist you.

Louise Waterman Wise Services
12 E. 94th St. • New York, N.Y. 10028

This small agency has helped countless families adopt babies. The Jewish Unmarried Mothers Service is at the same address.

SERVICES FOR YOUNG PEOPLE

Emanuel Press
306 Rumsey Rd. • Yonkers, N.Y. 10705

Rabbi Abraham Lausner has designed a Sabbath Bar Mitzvah Service which is printed and illustrated in color and represents a combined learning and prayer service. A help for families planning an independent bar mitzvah. (Also see Burt Jacobson entry under *Other Services.*)

Yavneh
25 W. 26th St. • New York, N.Y. 10010

Yavneh has published a handy directory to Jewish facilities on various college campuses entitled *A Guide to Jewish Life on the College Campus.* While not all-inclusive, it gives the Jewish student a good background for evaluating schools he or she may be thinking of applying to.

Encounter with Chabad
Lubavitch Youth Organization
770 Eastern Pkwy. • Brooklyn, N.Y. 11213

Chabad is an acronym formed from the initial letters of the Hebrew words *chochmah, binah,* and *daas,* which mean wisdom, understanding, and knowledge. The Lubavitch Youth Organization sponsors a variety of programs designed to introduce Jewish college students to the meaning of Torah Judaism. For more information on their campus visitation programs, Hasidic Shabbatons, and annual conclaves, write to the above address. There are active Chabad houses all over the country, some have residence facilities, all offer at the very least an introduction to the Hasidic way of life. A complete list of these centers is available by writing to the Brooklyn headquarters.

B'nai B'rith Career and Counseling Services
1640 Rhode Island Ave., NW
Washington, D.C. 20036

Brochures are available discussing career opportunities for young people in fields as diverse as city management and the rabbinate, engineering and community relations. A catalog of publications is also available.

Personnel Services
National Jewish Welfare Board
15 E. 26th St. • New York, N.Y. 10010

The National Jewish Welfare Board, which offers so many services, also has information available regarding careers in Jewish service institutions. One of its brochures provides information regarding scholarships and loans in preparation for community-center work.

CONVERSION

National Jewish Information Service
for the Propagation of Judaism
5174 W. 8th St.
Los Angeles, Calif. 90036

In our long history, Jews have very rarely sought converts. And most of us are most comfortable in that position, although we welcome the gentile who converts out of his/her own inclination and motivation as one of our own, perhaps even with a touch of awe that he should take on our historic burden of his own free will. Therefore, it came as rather a surprise to find flourishing in California a group that styles itself as a Jewish missionary organization. Its founder and president, Rabbi Moshe M. Maggal, is available to speak at temple or secular meetings on subjects such as: "Should Judaism again become a missionary religion?" and "The new trend: Conversion to Judaism". His nonprofit organization has a Correspondence Academy of Judaism offering instruction to Jew

(Photo: courtesy Sarina Goidich)

and non-Jew alike. Its goal is to "help propagate Judaism throughout the world; train Jewish ambassadors (missionaries); convert non-Jews to Judaism". Although I must admit to my own skepticism, the basic question of Jewish proselytizing is worth considering. Anyone interested should write for brochures.

DATING—MARRIAGE—DIVORCE

A suitable match may seem easy to make, yet God considers it as difficult a task as dividing the Red Sea.

Genesis Rabbah

American Jewish Committee
National Jewish Family Center
165 E. 56th St. • New York, N.Y. 10022

We can no longer pretend that the time-honored strength and sanctity of the Jewish family has remained untouched by the 20th-century currents disrupting all of family life in America. Rather than moaning about the increased divorce rate, intermarriage, couples living together without benefit of ceremony, childlessness by choice, and other manifestations of changing (some say disintegrating) family structure, we could better devote our energies to creatively tackling the problems of how to have a Jewish family life if one is single, divorced, or married to a non-Jew. The National Jewish Family Center serves as a clearing house for information and research on the Jewish family. The

Center develops policies and programs, offers training seminars for professional and lay leaders, and initiates and sponsors needed research. It hopes to facilitate coordinated approaches to meet the needs of the changing American Jewish family.

Chutzpah Unlimited
c/o Eleanor H. Siegel
P.O. Box 2400 • Chicago, Ill. 60690

Chutzpah Unlimited is a social club designed to provide a warm supportive atmosphere of fellowship and friendship for single Jewish adults, 25–45. Events such as game nights, theater parties, and Sunday brunches are held in central areas of Chicago. Even though at the moment the activities of Chutzpah Unlimited are primarily Chicago-based, Eleanor Siegel (29, single, and an employee of Uncle Sam), who directs the program along with a small cadre of fellow singles, says that she is eagerly interested in sharing her ideas with single Jews all over the country and encourages them to contact her.

(photo: Robert Leverant)

Federation of Jewish Philanthropies
130 E. 59th St. • New York, N.Y. 10022
Attn: Jewish Singles Task Force.

The Task Force on Jewish Singles was formed in response to the fact that one of the most difficult problems faced by the single Jewish adult in the fluid American social environment at a time of an escalating rate of intermarriage and divorce is that of meeting new people. The Task Force offers guidance to institutions which want to start programs for singles from eighteen-years-old up. It also publishes a newsletter eleven times a year (one issue for July–August), listing social, cultural, and service opportunities for Jewish singles in the greater New York area. It is useful to out-of-towners as well, since many of the events listed are an indication of useful kinds of programs that other institutions might emulate.

Jewish Singles Introduction Service
United Synagogue of America
155 Fifth Ave. • New York, N.Y. 10010

The New York Metropolitan Region of the United Synagogue of America has a nonprofit introduction service for Jewish adults over the age of eighteen. If you or your synagogue is interested, write for the descriptive brochure and questionnaire. The introduction service uses computers and serves only the New York metropolitan area, but the regional offices of the United Synagogue of America in Chicago and Los Angeles may be starting similar programs. Check with offices in those cities.

Tzemed-Helena, Inc.
400 Madison Ave. • New York, N.Y. 10017

Tzemed-Helena, Inc. is a service which provides singles who are serious about matrimony with an opportunity to meet like-minded people. In response to my querying letter, Tzemed-Helena replied: "Helena's singles consultation service is not computerized, video-taped, nor is it a dating service. The members here are pre-screened by Helena in an interview and are then further screened by a graphologist, a psychologist, and a private investigator. This procedure is to assure all prospective members that they will be introduced

to people who are single, honest, attractive, financially stable, and free of outstanding problems." The initial interview with Helena is free of charge and without obligation to register. Write for their free snazzy brochure entitled: "Come and join the First International Jewish-Israeli to Happiness Shuttle". Mrs. Helena Am-Ram, the founder, is available for lectures and will travel.

Alternatives in Religious Education
3945 South Oneida St.
Denver, Colo. 80237

At my daughter's bat mitzvah celebration, a full 50% of the invited children came from divided families. This painful issue can no longer be ignored by our religious schools. A.R.E. offers an excellent mini-course as part of its life cycle series of courses entitled "Divorce in Jewish Life and Tradition". It is designed for grades 7–12 and aimed at all students, regardless of their family situation. The course material can be covered in a few hours or extended to a full semester. It covers such subjects as the rising divorce rate, separation, and the Jewish view of divorce, and concludes with students sharing ways in which they can be supportive to youngsters—and adults—going through the traumas of family crisis. Leader guide included with 20 student manuals, $22; additional manuals, $1.10.

Richard J. Kurtz
445 Park Ave. • New York, N.Y. 10022

Richard Kurtz is a trial lawyer who does substantial matrimonial trial work for other members of the bar as well as for his own clients. He is a graduate of Yeshiva University and has lectured and taught extensively on Jewish law vis-à-vis its similarities and differences with other codes and with American law, and on the subject of Jewish divorce. He recently won a landmark ruling by a Brooklyn Supreme Court justice which said that a man must grant his wife a *get* (Jewish divorce decree) in addition to a civil divorce. Since according to Jewish tradition only the husband can initiate divorce proceedings, it is not uncommon for a *get* to be withheld for emotional or financial (extortion) reasons. Richard Kurtz will lecture on questions related to Jewish divorce and is available for consultations on obtaining a *get*.

OTHER SERVICES

Agudath Israel of America
5 Beekman St. • New York, N.Y. 10038

Agudath Israel is a movement every bit as much as a service organization. It is dedicated to the perpetuation of traditional Judaism. It has projects and services for every age group and many activities all over the world. Its social services include a burial society, a free loan fund, blood bank, and senior citizen programs. If you are interested, send for their detailed brochure.

Burt Jacobson
Kehilla
2619 Regent • Berkeley, Calif. 94704

Burt Jacobson, a rabbi since 1966, founded Kehilla as an alternative to synagogue affiliation for families living in the Bay Area. Kehilla will help you create weddings, study programs and celebrations for bar/bat mitzvah and other rites of passage, facilitate the formation of alternative forms of Jewish community and extended family, give counsel at difficult times, and teach individuals how to discover spiritual and practical guidance from within. Jacobson calls Kehilla a "community synagogue without walls". All fees are based on a sliding scale and are negotiable; no fee for initial contacts. If you are interested in the idea of Kehilla or any of its services call or write.

Jewish Conciliation Board of America
33 W. 60th St. • New York, N.Y. 10023

The aim of the Jewish Conciliation Board of America is to carry out the Jewish ideal of justice without the encumbrances of complicated official legal proceedings. It functions as a "court of first resort" settling disputes that arise in the Jewish community of the New York metropolitan area. Its services are provided without cost to individuals with family problems, or people in conflict with societies, lodges, synagogues, unions, and other communal organizations. It is particularly helpful to the *Landsmannshaften,* who need counsel on their problems and help resolving inter-society disputes, and to traditional Jews. The procedure is first for a complaint to be registered at the Board's office; it is then arranged for both parties to appear at one of the twice-monthly sessions of the Board. If the case involves property, both parties sign an agreement to abide by the Board's decision; this makes the outcome legally binding as if it were brought to a Civil Court. The Board was founded in 1920 and processes about six hundred cases a year. It serves a similar function to the traditional Bet Din or religious court, solving many problems that were once brought before rabbis, fraternal orders, or burial societies. The Board is staffed by volunteers—a rabbi, a lawyer, and a businessman; a psychiatrist functions in an advisory position. Even though many of the readers of this book will not, because of geographic reasons, be able to use the services of the Conciliation Board in unfortunate times of strife, I describe it here because it seems a very worthwhile organization to emulate. Many of the new havurot (communities) might consider setting up similar institutions to serve the changing needs of America's Jews in outlying areas, just as the Board came into being in response to the Americanization of the immigrant generation.

Jewish Family Service
33 W. 60th St. • New York, N.Y. 10023

Staffed by qualified psychologists, social workers, and psychiatrists, the Jewish Family Service is a counseling agency for families and individuals. However, the emphasis is on family therapy. J.F.S. has offices all over the city and annually helps more than 15,000 families.

Steven A. Moss
B'nai Israel Reform Temple
Idle Hour Blvd., Box 158
Oakdale, N.Y. 11769

Steven Moss is a rabbi/chaplain who has cared for cancer and terminally ill patients at a number of hospitals in the metropolitan New York area. He has also helped to coordinate groups of lay people to visit community members in hospitals and nursing homes. He offers his expertise to cancer patients and their families and to communities beginning a hospice. Rabbi Moss will be glad to advise rabbis in the care of cancer patients, the terminally ill, and the bereaved. He can also help organize *bikkur holim* (visiting the sick) groups in your community.

National Association of Jewish Homes for the Aged
2525 Centerville Rd.
Dallas, Tex. 75228

The National Association of Jewish Homes for the Aged has a directory of facilities for the elderly available all over the country.

New York Board of Rabbis
10 E. 73rd St. • New York, N.Y. 10021
(212) TR 9–8415

In recent years, a number of social-service agencies have established "hot lines," numbers to call when one is in trouble, or has problems. To my surprise I found that the New York Board of Rabbis has been offering this type of spontaneous counseling since 1881. Initially, of course, it functioned without telephones, but the concept is the same. One thousand rabbis (Orthodox, Conservative, and Reform) serve on a volunteer basis helping with personal problems and replying to questions on Jewish life and religion. If the problem warrants it they refer the caller to other services—medical, psychiatric, financial, etc. They will answer any question by mail. The walk-in and telephone counseling are available Monday–Thursday from 10 A.M.–3 P.M. Similar, though not identical, services exist in other major cities. Some of the most significant ones are listed below.

Rabbinical Association of Greater Miami
2443 Meridian Ave. • Miami, Fla. 33140
(305) 531–4631

Board of Rabbis of Greater Philadelphia
117 S. Seventeenth St. • Philadelphia, Pa. 19103
(215) LO 3-1463

Chicago Board of Rabbis
72 E. 11th St. • Chicago, Ill. 60605
(312) HA 7–5863

Rabbinical Court of Justice (Bet Din)
177 Tremont St. • Boston, Mass. 02111

The Rabbinical Court sits in judgment on religious matters.

Charles Tucker
111a Nether St.
Finchley, London, N.12, England

Charles Tucker will do genealogical research throughout the United Kingdom for those whose forebears resided in the U.K. and are eager to have their pedigrees traced. He will also help you find relatives there with whom you might have lost contact in the passage of time. ("*Not*," says Mr. Tucker, "runaway daughters, absconding husbands, et al.") He will also be helpful in finding next of kin of intestates, who will, if found, share in the deceased's estate. Current charge for all research is $7 an hour, plus expenses. Estimates of likely overall costs of a project are always provided in advance, following receipt of an outline of the client's wants. Deposit required in advance of start of research. SASE or international reply coupon appreciated from enquirers.

DEATH AND BURIAL

(photo: © Laurence Salzmann; see *Creating: Pictures*)

My father left me a wonderful legacy. When he died rather suddenly my mother was able to tell my sister and me that the *Landsmannschaft* (fraternal order) to which my father had belonged had voted only the week before that its members were to be buried in the traditional shroud and plain wooden coffin. So, just hours after we had last seen our beloved Daddy in his hospital bed, when the funeral director led us around a showroom full of kosher-cadillac-coffins, we were able to point securely to the austere pine box which looked so raw compared with the illusory "comfort" of coffins cushioned in satin and obscenely more elaborate than many Torah arks, and say, ''That's what our father wanted.'' The funeral director was annoyed, and showed it, but we fortunately were too numb to really notice, as we told him to remove the curls of wood shavings which replaced the pillows of the fancier models and to put in their stead a small cushion we had made as a Passover present a few months before. When our mother died suddenly a little more than a year after our father, my sister and I felt that we had it all down pat, thanks to the foresight and thoughtfulness of our parents. We only had to mourn; they had provided us with complete instructions for their funerals, burial sites, tombstone, and even who to call to arrange for food to be prepared for those coming back to the house where the mourning period was observed after the funeral. Everyone in the family learned a lot and came to the conclusion that we too would prepare in advance for the inevitability of death and spare the remaining family additional grief.

There are unfortunately very few traditional burial societies in the U.S. These societies of volunteers who cleanse the body and look after it throughout the funeral and burial have been replaced by commercial undertaking establishments. When there is a death in the family most people call the rabbi. If one can't find a rabbi on one's own, then the local undertaking establishment should be called. Even a non-Jewish one should be able to contact a rabbi to help arrange a funeral and burial in the Jewish tradition. (In large metropolitan centers there are usually Jewish funeral homes that can be found easily in the telephone book.) Synagogues quite often own land in the closest Jewish cemetery and can arrange for the sale of plots to congregation members (many synagogues will sell plots to non-members as well). It is a good idea to look into your local situation before the need arises and if it does not meet with your sensibilities, the next step is to work within your community towards creating a burial society which meets your needs.

ABC Media Concepts
att: Noel Bechtold
1330 Avenue of the Americas
New York, N.Y. 10019

''A Plain Pine Box'' is a moving documentary, filmed in Minneapolis, which describes the Adath Jeshurun Congregation's funeral society, the Chevra Kevod Hamet. The 30-minute color film powerfully states the purpose of the Chevra which is ''to honor the deceased and to strengthen the living''. 16mm film or ¾inch videotape available for $100 to synagogues and churches and for $325 to other groups and individuals.

Adath Jeshurun Congregation
3400 Dupont Avenue South
Minneapolis, Minn. 56408

Congregational members of Adath Jeshurun in Minneapolis did a lot of research and soul-searching in the formation of their funeral society which offers immediate help to a bereaved family. The services of the Chevra are available to all members of the Aduth Jeshurun Congregation. There is no cost to the family of the bereaved for the *aron* (a dignified, simple coffin), the services of the funeral director, transportation for the *met* (dead person), traditional shroud, chapel and graveside services, or preparation of the body. The congregation has made available a packet of materials outlining the work of organizing their society which includes a page describing the procedure followed by the *shomrim* (those who stay with the body until it is buried), a pamphlet with autopsy guidelines, and much other informative and useful material. The complete packet is available for $4 from the synagogue office. What they have done is very much worth emulating by congregations all over the country. The congregation's rabbi, Arnold M. Goodman, is available for lectures.

(photo: © Richard Sobol).

Alternatives in Religious Education
3945 South Oneida Street
Denver, Colo. 80237

In keeping with their practice of taking on all the hard issues, A.R.E. has produced an excellent mini-course on "Death, Burial and Mourning in the Jewish Tradition", as part of its series of life cycle courses. See other entries in this book about their various offerings and write for complete catalog.

Hebrew Free Burial Association, Inc.
Hesed Shel Emet
1170 Broadway • New York, N.Y. 10001
(212) MU 6-2433

This traditional burial society offers advice twenty-four hours a day to anyone who needs help in arranging a burial.

(photo: © Laurence Salzmann; see *Creating: Pictures*)

Mitzvot

"To love God truly, you must first love people.
If anyone tells you that he loves God and does not
love his fellow man, he is lying."

Hasidic saying

(photo: © Bill Aron; see *Creating: Pictures*)

The word mitzvah, which we usually use to mean "good deed", is derived from the Hebrew root meaning "to command" or "ordain". While we ordinarily think there are 10 commandments, there are in reality 613 mitzvot—"ordained good deeds"—in the Torah. Women are responsible for the mitzvot from the age of twelve years plus one day and men from the age of thirteen years plus one day. The 365 negative commandments, or prohibitions, are equally binding for men and women, as are the mitzvot of Shabbat, Passover, Purim, and Hanukkah. Women, however, are traditionally not required to perform the other affirmative mitzvot which are linked to a particular time or season. Certain mitzvot, such as the wearing of a tallit or tefillin, which are not prohibited to women in the Torah, have become sex-linked through custom. In recent years many women have been assuming responsibility for mitzvot which previously were associated only with men, and in some egalitarian communities and families it is not unheard of for men to bless the Shabbat candles. Throughout the book you will find objects and materials to help you in understanding and observing the 613 mitzvot. This section contains information related to several specific mitzvot such as wearing a tallit and tefillin and lighting candles.

(photo: © Bill Aron)

Gladys Hoisington
1227 S.E. 12th Terr.
Deerfield Beach, Fla. 33441

Gladys Hoisington weaves a tallit with bands of the intense colors used in the ancient desert tent of worship—purple, red, royal blue, black, orange, yellow, green, and wine. It is called the B'nai Or (Children of Light) tallit. She also weaves a blue-and-white tallit with seven stripes of three shades of blue. The tallitot are available in three different sizes, with or without matching tallit bags. Since each tallit is woven to order and they are very popular, expect to wait four to six months after receipt of your order for delivery. For more about Glady's work see *Creating: Textiles*.

Jewish Community Center
60 S. River St. • Wilkes-Barre, Pa. 18701

I have long felt that our Jewish centers and synagogues should not only be places we go to listen, watch, and consume, but should also be places where ideas and things for Jewish life come into being—genuine centers of creativity. There are some centers that have artist- or writer-in-

GLADYS HOISINGTON, multi-colored B'nai Or tallit, 20" × 60", handwoven in natural wool. (photo: Richard Speedy)

residence programs, and these are to be commended and emulated. Under the creative leadership of Sy Hefter, the Wilkes-Barre Jewish Center produces and sells limited quantities of hand-made wooden dreidels and graggers, natural hand-made horn shofars, tallitot, mezuzot, Haggadahs for Tu Bi-Shevat, and steel Magen David and Chai hangings. It also does hand-written mezuzah parchments and recovers old tefillin containers. Write for buying information.

Phyllis Kantor
250 E. 38th St. • Eugene, Oreg. 97405

Along with her other textile work, Phyllis Kantor weaves very fine tallitot. See *Creating: Textiles*.

PHYLLIS KANTOR, linen tallit, hand woven on a 16-harness loom.

Na'ahseh V'Nishma
38 W. 69th Street
New York, N.Y. 10023

This firm has two kits available for making your own tallit. One kit, offered in either cream or blue, consists of a length of wool challis with a design for a needlework atarah and wool tzitzit ($40). The second is for a knitted version of the conventional tallit pattern of blue stripes edging a long white scarf, wool tzitzit included, finished size 25" × 60"; also available with purple stripes ($30). Na'ahseh V'Nishma also has kits for making kippot, a mizrah, a baby blanket, and instructions and patterns for making a kittle. Custom work is also possible. Write for the brochure detailing these items and others, and if you are interested in personalized items (such as coordinated items for an entire bar mitzvah or wedding) ask for an estimate.

Rabbi Piotrkowski's Judaica Center
289 Montgomery Ave.
Bala Cynwyd, Pa. 19004

A Piotrkowski sister lives in Israel where she oversees the creation of several types of hand-woven tallitot available exclusively through Piotrkowski's Judaica Center. The three tallit styles are all woven in off-white polyester. The most elaborate is embroidered with motifs representing the twelve tribes. Matching hand-woven tallit bags and kippot are also available. Write for an illustrated brochure and complete price list.

Elsa Wachs
2 S. Providence Rd.
Wallingford, Pa. 19086

Elsa Wachs treats the tallit as a personal art form, custom-designed and hand-woven for each individual. Her tallitot are made of 100 percent wool or 100 percent silk. Colors are selected to suit the wearer; sample threads and a design sketch are sent for approval before the work begins. Hebrew names or blessings may be embroidered on the atarah (collar), and a tallit bag can be woven to match if desired. The tzitzit are attached and tied in the prescribed manner or are sent along with the tallit if the purchaser prefers to tie his own. Any width up to 45" is available; suggested lengths are 72", 78", or 84". The shoulders may be pleated so that the tallit will always remain in place while being worn. Prices depend on size and yarn desired. Write, being as specific as possible about what you would like.

Ziontalis Mfg. Co. Inc.
48 Eldridge St.
New York, N.Y. 10002

Ziontalis is the largest manufacturer of tallitot in the United States and Israel. They are also distributors to the trade and synagogues of all religious articles for synagogue and home use.

Other weavers who specialize in handwoven tallitot are:

ROSE S. BANK
3 Roselawn Terr. • Pittsburgh, Pa. 15213

DORETTE BOEHM
411 N. Sterling Rd. • Elkins Park, Pa. 19117

IRENE TABATSKY
231 Parker St. • Manchester, Conn. 06040

JUDY TSUKROFF
Sun Porch Weaving Studio • Norfolk, Conn. 06058

KIPPOT

Crocheted kippot are being worn all over the country. Many people make their own, but others would like the homey look and either don't have the skills or the time for it. The following craftspeople will crochet a kippah for you in a

Kippah design by "Netzach"; see *Buying: Needlework* for more information.

variety of styles and yarns. Prices vary depending on size or complexity of the design. Write for particulars.

Anita Freimark
7054 Roundelay Rd. North
Reynoldsburg, Ohio 43068

Anita also makes some interesting toys; see *Playing: Toys and Games*.

Rosa Fischer Misrach
1709 Shattuck Ave. • Berkeley, Calif. 94709

Kippot crocheted in natural burlap. Ms. Misrach writes that she is "still going strong at 75 plus".

Deborah Pessa Oles
3649 Jasmine Ave.
Los Angeles, Calif. 90034

As well as kippot, Ms. Oles will also crochet mezuzot, hallah covers, tallitot, puppets, and baby blankets with Hebrew names or phrases.

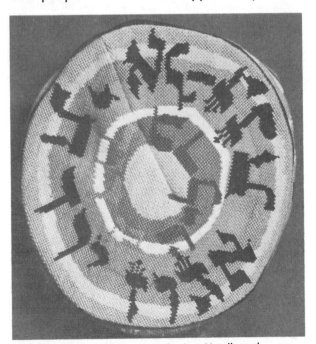

Kippah by Alice Nussbaum; see *Buying: Needlework*.

OTHER MITZVOT

Putting on tefillin is an ancient mitzvah that has been observed for thousands of years. It has its origin in the Torah precept which says "And thou shalt bind them upon thine hand, and they shall be

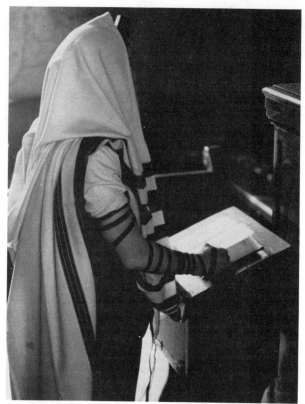

Still photo from the film "Prayer"; see *Learning: Media*.
(photo: Michoel Behrman, courtesy Taryag Media Inc.)

for frontlets between thine eyes." (Deut. 6:8) The tefillin are two small leather boxes containing the Shema and Vehayah (Deut. 6:4–9; Deut. 11:13–21; Ex. 13:1–10; Ex. 13:11–16) inscribed on parchment. Tefillin are customarily put on before the morning prayer on weekdays only. A boy is usually taught how to put on tefillin a few weeks before he is called to the Torah as a bar mitzvah. Detailed information about the miztvah and how to observe can be had by writing to the Mitzvah Campaign at Lubavitch Headquarters (address below). Tefillin are obtainable from many of the scribes listed in the *Creating: Calligraphy* section and from the bookstores in the *Observing: Holidays and Ceremonies* section.

Mitzvah Campaign
770 Eastern Pkwy. • Brooklyn, N.Y. 11213

The Lubavitch Youth Organization actively seeks to help Jews observe as many mitzvot as possible. Its "Mitzvah Mobiles" or "tanks," as they are often called, have become an almost familiar sight in the New York area. In addition, the Lubavitchers are very helpful through the mails. If you have trouble finding tefillin or mezuzot, or want a charity box, write to them. They have folders explaining the mitzvot and giving the proper blessings. A particularly handsome brochure has a mother and daughter lighting the Shabbat candles together. Girls from the age of three are encouraged to light one candle for Shabbat and holidays. The brochure has the blessings and a schedule for the year's candlelighting times. The Lubavitchers also distribute a button which says "I light Shabbos Candles, Do You?" The Lubavitch goal is frankly to encourage more and more Jews to live complete Halakhic lives. Nevertheless, they accept everyone whatever their level of observance and are genuinely helpful and friendly.

"Tefillin", drawing by Mark Podwal; see: *Creating: Pictures*.

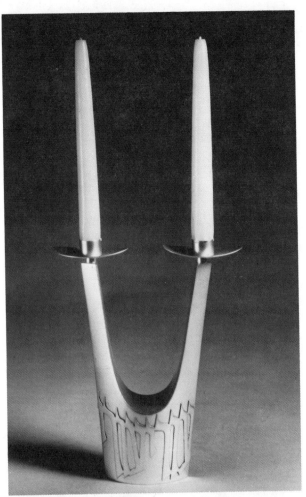

Harold Rabinowitz, handmade silver Sabbath candlesticks. See *Creating: Metal* for information about Mr. Rabinowitz' work and for other handmade ritual items to enhance your personal observance. (photo: Otto E. Nelson)

Shatnes Laboratory of Torah and Mitzvoth
Josef Rosenberg, founder
204 Hooper St.
Brooklyn, N.Y. 11211

The law of sha'atnez ("mingling of the fibers") is stated in the Torah (Leviticus 19:19; Deuteronomy 22:11); it prohibits the mixture of linen and wool in fabrics which are used for clothes, upholstery, and other articles of warmth. A parokhet should also conform to this law, since it is conceivable that in times of great need one could use an ark curtain as a blanket. None of the explanations offered for this rule are completely satisfying. Nevertheless, since the sha'atnez prohibition is explicitly stated in the Bible, Orthodox Jews interpret it as a divine decree whose full meaning may be outside the realm of human understanding but which is meant to be accepted on faith alone. The Shatnes Laboratory will test your clothing or other articles to see if they are kosher. By writing to the main laboratory you can obtain the addresses of more than fifty branches in New York and other states. Or you can mail your clothing to the Brooklyn laboratory, where it will be tested and mailed back to you. In addition to the laboratory fee and postage there is a handling fee for "packing it, bringing it thirteen blocks to the post office, and standing there in line". Send an SASE for information on learning how to test for sha'atnez yourself and for a folder describing the mitzvah called "Science in the Service of Truth" by Rabbi Joseph Hager.

Vaad Mishmeres Stam
4902 16th Ave. • Brooklyn, N.Y. 11204

Vaad Mishmeres Stam is a nonprofit organization which is dedicated to sensitizing the public to the fact that a good many mezuzot which have been innocently affixed to doorposts of Jewish homes are halakhically invalid. The Vaad is working towards training a new generation of skilled scribes, setting up a free loan fund to assist in the purchase of tefillin and mezuzot, and publishing a halahkic encyclopedia of the Hebrew alphabet. As much as membership ($10 annually), the organization badly needs volunteer help. If you are interested in this important work write for more information.

Los Angeles, California (photo: Richard Sobol).

INDEX

(photo: © Bill Aron)